Antibody Engineering

A Practical Guide

Breakthroughs in Molecular Biology

Antibody Engineering is the third volume to appear in this exciting new series of high quality, affordable books in the fields of molecular biology and immunology. This series is dedicated to the rapid publication of the latest breakthroughs and cutting edge technologies as well as synthesis of major advances within molecular biology.

Other volumes in the series include:

PCR Technology: Principles and Applications for DNA Amplification
edited by H. Erlich

Lymphokines: The Molecular Biology of Regulators of Immune and Inflammatory Responses
by K.-I. Arai and J. de Vries

Gene Targeting
by J. Sedivy and A. Joyner

YAC Libraries: Construction and Use
edited by B. Brownstein and D. Nelson

DNA Fingerprinting: An Introduction
by L. T. Kirby

Adhesion: Its Role in Inflammatory Disease
edited by J. Harlan and D. Liu

Antibody Engineering

A Practical Guide

Carl A. K. Borrebaeck

Editor

W. H. Freeman and Company

New York

Library of Congress Cataloging-in-Publication Data

Antibody Engineering: A Practical Guide / edited by Carl Borrebaeck.
        p. cm.
    Includes bibliographical references and index.
    ISBN 7167-7008-3 (soft cover)
    1. Immunoglobulins—Biotechnology. 2. Protein engineering.
I. Borrebaeck, Carl A. K., 1948-
TP248.65.I49A57 1991
616.07'93—dc20

91-4444
CIP

Printed in the United States of America

1 2 3 4 5 6 7 8 9 0   V B   9 9 8 7 6 5 4 3 2 1

Contributors

Carl A. K. Borrebaeck
Department of Immunotechnology
University of Lund
Lund, Sweden

Janet C. Cheetham
Protein Structure and Modelling Group
AMGEN
Thousand Oaks, California

Lena Danielsson
Department of Immunotechnology
Lund University
Lund, Sweden

Stephen D. Gillies
Abbott Biotech, Inc.
Needham Heights, Massachusetts

Andrew Hiatt
Department of Molecular Biology
Scripps Research Institute
La Jolla, California

William Huse
Ixsys, Inc.
San Diego, California

Arthur M. Lesk
Department of Haematology
University of Cambridge
Cambridge, United Kingdom

Terje E. Michaelsen
Department of Immunology
National Institute of Public Health
Oslo, Norway

Ruth Pinney
Department of Medicine
University of California at San Diego
San Diego, California

Inger Sandlie
Department of Biology
Oslo University
Oslo, Norway

Anna Tramontano
Instituto di Ricerche di Biologia Moleculare
Rome, Italy

E. Sally Ward
Southwestern Medical Center
University of Texas
Dallas, Texas

Contents

Preface

Antibody engineering, that is, construction of designer antibodies, is one of the fastest growing fields in molecular biology. The first generation of recombinant antibody studies, published in the early 1980s, described the joining of DNA-encoding mouse variable regions with gene segments encoding the human Ig constant regions, giving rise to so-called chimeric antibodies. This was followed by the second generation of recombinant antibodies, which consists of CDR engrafted or "humanized" antibodies, where only the DNA encoding the complementarity-determining regions of a mouse antibody is joined with genes encoding the human framework and constant regions. The third generation of designer antibodies is only one or two years old and comprises the recombinatorial cDNA libraries of heavy and light chains and the expression of antibody fragments on the surface of filamentous bacteriophages such as M13 or fd. The latter approach may solve the analytical problems that arise when libraries of 10^8–10^{10} members are to be screened.

The advances briefly outlined above have been greatly facilitated by the introduction of techniques such as the polymerase chain reaction and the use of degenerate primers for easy cloning of DNA-encoding Ig variable regions. Recently, understanding of bacterial expression and design of better prokaryote vectors have also facilitated the selection of clones expressing desired antibody specificities. These antibody encoding gene segments can further be cloned into a eukaryote expression vector and expressed in a mammalian host to give a functionally optimal antibody molecule. Most of these techniques for gene shuffling/expression have been available to only a few specialized laboratories, and the aim of this first volume on antibody engineering is to explain all the steps necessary for construction of designer antibodies in any laboratory. With widespread use of antibody engineering, antibodies as drugs may finally be the pharmaceutical triumph that has been proposed for these molecules since the introduction of monoclonal antibodies.

Carl A. K. Borrebaeck, D.Sc.
Lund, Sweden
May 1991

CHAPTER 1

Antibody Structure and Structural Predictions Useful in Guiding Antibody Engineering

Arthur M. Lesk, Anna Tramontano

Structural analysis of antibodies, based on the few known structures and the many known sequences, should provide answers to several important questions about the functional properties of antibodies and guide attempts to engineer changes in them. The questions include

- What are the common features of antibody structures that form the basis of the properties shared by different immunoglobulins?
- Where in the structure does the antigen-binding site reside? As is well known, Kabat and his coworkers recognized certain regions of the sequences as hypervariable and suggested—correctly and presciently—their involvement in antigen binding,[1, 2] a conclusion that was later confirmed by analysis of crystal structures of antibodies.
- What is the nature of the antigen-antibody interaction?
- How is the diversity in antigen-binding specificity achieved, in terms of changes in three-dimensional structure?
- How, during the maturation of the antibody response, are antigen-binding sites progressively "tuned" in affinity?

1

- To what extent do the elements of antigen-binding sites have an independent structure that would permit us to modify them or "transplant" them from one immunoglobulin to another?
- Are there systematic differences between antibodies of different subgroups, or different species, that might hinder or even preclude the construction of hybrid molecules containing some parts of one type of molecule and some parts of another? This is important in attempting to create antibodies for therapy containing the antigen-binding site from a nonhuman source grafted onto a human antibody (in order to reduce allergic reaction from a human patient).

Investigations that bear on these questions will be reviewed. This chapter addresses the first three in detail.

An understanding of the general principles of protein structure and their particular application to immunoglobulins has made it possible to attempt to predict the conformations of antigen-binding sites of immunoglobulins.

The basic theoretical principle underlying this discussion is that *amino acid sequence determines protein conformation.* If our understanding of Nature's "algorithm" were complete, we could predict protein structure from amino acid sequence *a priori,* without reference to any known structure. As this is not yet possible, we attempt to understand the determinants of conformation of immunoglobulins from a detailed comparison of known sequences and structures. It follows from the basic principle that the common structural features of a family of proteins must be reflected in common patterns in the amino acid sequences. Conversely, structural variations must be reflected in variations in patterns in the sequences. It is because these patterns and their variations are often very subtle that it is a challenge to discover them in the available data.

Although it is not now possible to predict the overall fold of a protein from the sequence alone, there has been some success in predicting (1) the degree of structural similarity among the major portions of homologous proteins, and (2) the conformations of constrained short regions, in the context of a given structure. The basic folding pattern of the immunoglobulin domain is fairly well conserved among antibodies, affording an approach to the prediction of the conformation of the framework region of an antibody of unknown structure. The methods for predicting conformations of short regions, which are useful in predicting the conformations of antigen-binding loops, comprise three main approaches:

1. *A priori* methods based on evaluation of alternative structures by conformational energy calculations, the alternatives generated either by exhaustive search in conformation space or by molecular dynamics
2. Methods based on searching the database of known protein structures for loops than can be brought in

3. Methods based on understanding the structural determinants of individual loops of different conformation and recognizing them in the sequences of immunoglobulins of unknown structure

GENERAL CHARACTERISTICS OF IMMUNOGLOBULINS

Common features of immunoglobulins were first recognized physiochemically and serologically, then described in terms of the amino acid sequences, and only much later revealed in atomic detail by x-ray crystallography.

Attempts to fractionate serum proteins produced a γ globulin fraction containing a population of molecules with similar though not identical physiochemical properties, which shared certain antigenic determinants. Very large amounts of a single species occurred in the serum—and frequently in the urine—of patients with multiple myeloma. This disease arises from neoplastic plasma cell growth in the bone marrow, producing a great excess of what are in effect monoclonal antibodies. (Some myeloma proteins are intact, complete antibodies. Others, called *Bence Jones proteins*, are assemblies of incomplete antibodies.) Until monoclonal antibodies from hybridomas were available, myeloma proteins provided the source of unique antibodies for detailed characterization.

Limited proteolytic digestion and cleavage of disulfide bonds revealed that antibodies contain multiple polypeptide chains.[3, 4] The chains can be distinguished according to size into light (L) and heavy (H) chains. (The Bence Jones proteins contain light chains only.) Systematic internal homologies in the amino acid sequences suggested that immunoglobulins were composed of multiple variants of related domains, with the basic folding unit containing approximately 100 amino acids.[5] Light and heavy chains contain different numbers of domains. The similarities in the amino acid sequences indicated that each of these basic units forms an individual, quasi-independent, three-dimensional structure, with a generally similar folding pattern common to all.

It is possible to distinguish within the sequences two types of domains: variable (V) domains and constant (C) domains; the variability in sequence is much lower in constant domains than in variable domains. The variable domains contain regions of still higher variability—the hypervariable regions—that correspond to the antigen-binding site.

Immunoglobulins of different classes—IgG, IgA, IgM, IgD, and IgE—contain different assemblies of domains. In all cases, the V domains are at the N-terminus of each polypeptide chain and contain the antigen-binding site.[1, 2]

Figure 1-1A shows the domain structure of an IgG. The molecule contains four polypeptide chains: two identical light chains each containing one

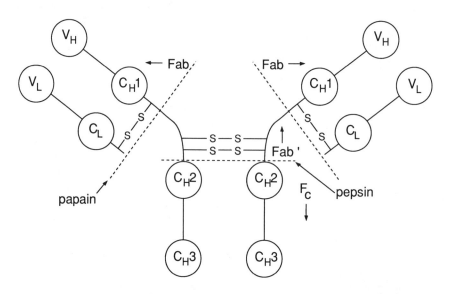

Figure 1-1. (A) A schematic diagram of the structure of an IgG, showing the distribution of domains in the heavy and light chains, and the interchain domain bridges.

variable and one constant domain, denoted V_L and C_L; and two identical heavy chains each containing one variable and three constant domains, denoted V_H, C_H1, C_H2, and C_H3. Figure 1-1A also shows the disulfide bridges linking the chains together. In addition, immunoglobulins contain carbohydrate moieties that are not indicated in this figure.

Limited proteolytic cleavage with enzymes (or cyanogen bromide) produces well-defined fragments of the molecule, containing different combinations of domains. Figure 1-1B defines these fragments.

CRYSTAL STRUCTURE DETERMINATIONS

X-ray crystal structure analyses of immunoglobulins have been carried out on intact antibodies, Bence Jones proteins consisting of light chain dimers, Fc fragments, and (most commonly) Fab or Fab' fragments (Table 1-1). Crystal structures of Fab fragments include some unligated molecules and others that contain bound antigens. In some cases, the structure of an antibody fragment is known in both the unligated state and with antigen bound; these cases are important because they reveal the conformational changes that occur upon ligation of antigen, a subject of considerable interest.

Table 1-1 lists the crystal structures deposited in the protein data bank.[6-19] The early work was done on myeloma proteins. The availability of monoclo-

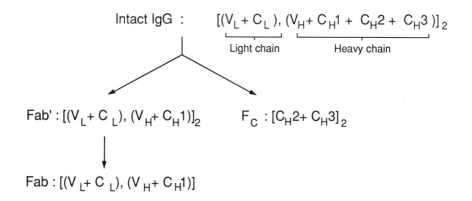

Figure 1-1. (B) Definitions of fragments produced by limited proteolytic digestion. This pattern shows the fragments produced from a human IgG1 by pepsin and papain.

Table 1-1. Crystal Structures of Immunoglobulins, or Fragments, Deposited in the Protein Data Bank (P.D.B.)[6]

Molecule	Fragment	State of Ligation	Resolution Angstroms	P.D.B. Mnemonic	Reference
Bence Jones Protein MCG	V_κ	free	2.3	1MCG	7
Bence Jones Protein REI	V_κ	free	2.0	1REI	8
Bence Jones Protein RHE	V_λ	free	1.6	2RHE	9
IgG J539	Fab	free	2.6	1FBJ	10
IgA McPC603	Fab	free	2.7	1MCP	11
IgA McPC603	Fab	phosphoryl-choline	3.1	2MCP	12
IgG1 KOL	Fab	free	1.9	2FB4	13
IgG NEWM	Fab'	free	2.0	3FAB	14
IgG2 R19.9	Fab	free	2.8	1F19	15
Pooled human Fc	Fc	free	2.9	1FC1	16
IgA HyHEL-5	Fab	lysozyme	2.54	2HFL	17
IgA HyHEL-10	Fab	lysozyme	3.0	3HFM	18
IgG1 KOL	full IgG	free	3.0	2IG2	13
IgG2A 4-4-20	Fab	fluorescein	2.7	4FAB	19

nal antibodies, together with a general growth in interest in immunoglobulin structure, has led to a large number of crystallographic projects in the antibody field. It should be emphasized that the importance of monoclonal antibodies lies not only in the availability of large quantities of pure material, but in the ability to specify the antigen.

What have crystal structures revealed about immunoglobulin structure and antigen binding?

Individual Domains

Figure 1-2 shows the structures of a typical V domain and a typical C domain. Each has the form of a double β-sheet "sandwich." A β-sheet is one of the two basic types of secondary structures in proteins; it is formed by lateral hydrogen bonding between two sections of strand in an extended conformation (Figure 1-3). In immunoglobulin domains and related molecules, the two sheets are oriented with their strands approximately parallel, and the two sheets are pinned together by a disulfide bridge between cysteine residues at conserved positions in the sequence. The other major type of secondary structure in proteins, the α-helix, occurs to only a minor extent in immunoglobulins.

The strands of the β-sheets in immunoglobulin domains and other double β-sheet proteins are connected by loops. In many cases, two adjacent antiparallel strands are connected by a loop; this is called a *hairpin* (see Figure 1-3). But a strand need not be connected to its neighbor; it may be linked by a loop to a strand on the opposite sheet or to a distant strand on the same sheet. The connectivity of the strands—that is, which pairs of strands are connected by loops—defines the topology of the structure. The topology of the connections is the same in all known immunoglobulin domains.

Six loops—three from the V_L domain and three from the V_H domain—form the antigen-binding site. The three loops from the V_L domain are called L1, L2, and L3, in order of their appearance in the amino acid sequence. Alternatively, they are called CDR1, CDR2, and CDR3, where CDR stands for complementarity-determining region (Figures 1-4A and 1-5). The V_H domains contain three corresponding loops—H1, H2, and H3.

Figure 1-4 shows the hydrogen bonding patterns of V_L, V_H, and C domains. In these diagrams, the double β-sheet structure is opened out like a book by rotation of one of the sheets around an axis perpendicular to the strand direction. Connections drawn as sawtooth patterns in the V domains indicate antigen-binding loops. Note that L2, L3, H2, and H3 are hairpins, but that L1 and H1 are not; instead they connect the two different sheets of the domain. The V domains differ systematically from the C domains by the presence of an extra hairpin loop in one of the sheets, containing the loop labeled L2 in Figures 1-4 and 1-5. (After studying the diagrams in Figure 1-5,

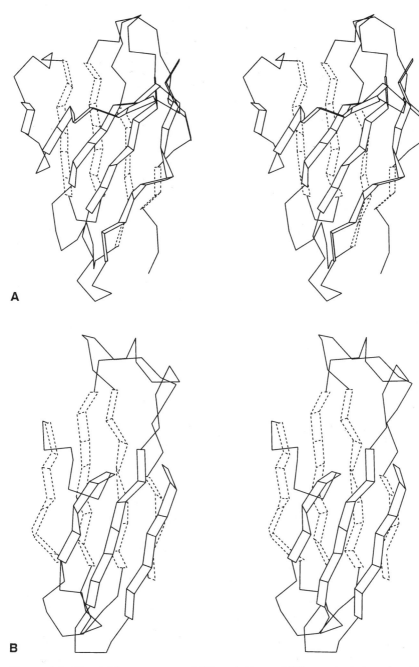

Figure 1-2. The folding patterns of (A) variable and (B) constant domains. The domains shown here are the V_L and C_H1 domains of Fab KOL.

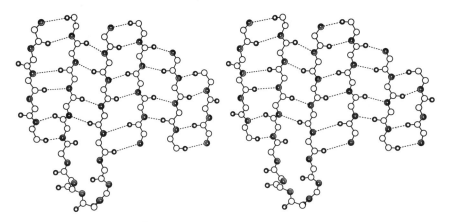

Figure 1-3. The hydrogen-bonding pattern in an antiparallel β-sheet. The region linking the second and third strands from the right is called a *hairpin* loop: A bridge between two successive antiparallel strands of β-sheet. This sheet, taken from concanavalin A, is unusually flat; the sheets in immunoglobulin domains, shown in Figure 1-1, are twisted.

the reader can then return to the structural pictures in Figure 1-2 and make the connection to them.)

Assembly of Domains: Quaternary Structure

Immunoglobulin domains are held together in an intact antibody by disulfide bridges and Van der Waals packing.[20] It is characteristic of native protein structures that interior interfaces are formed by the packing of complementary surfaces. This complementarity of fit fixes the relative spatial disposition of the pieces that interact. In the case of the V_L-V_H interaction, the packing has two important consequences:

1. The conservation of surface topography among V_L domains and among V_H domains explains why different V_L and V_H domains can combine fairly freely and interchangeably.
2. The fixing of the relative geometry of V_L and V_H domains by the packing at the interface is the basis of the statement, which is true to a reasonable first approximation, that the double β-sheet frameworks of V_L and V_H domains together form a scaffolding of nearly constant structure on which the antigen-binding site is erected.

Figure 1-6 shows the structure of the Fab fragment: $(V_L+C_L; V_H+C_H1) \times 2$ of IgG KOL. The variable domains are at the top of the figure.

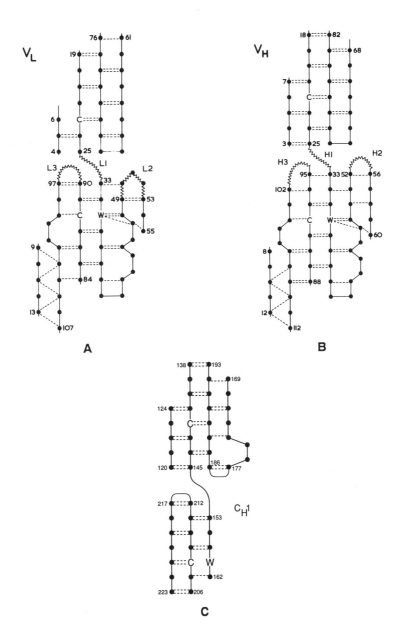

Figure 1-4. Schematic representations of typical hydrogen-bonding patterns of (A) V_L, (B) V_H, and (C) C domains. The two sheets have been opened like a book. Strands in the upper sheets in Figure 1-4A and 1-4C are shown by ribbons drawn with broken lines in Figures 1-2A and 1-2B, respectively; strands in the lower sheets in Figures 1-4A and 1-4C correspond to strands drawn with solid lines in Figures 1-2A and 1-2B, respectively.

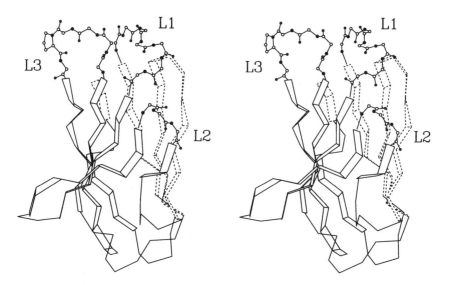

Figure 1-5. The V_L domain V_κ REI, showing the antigen-binding loops L1, L2, and L3.

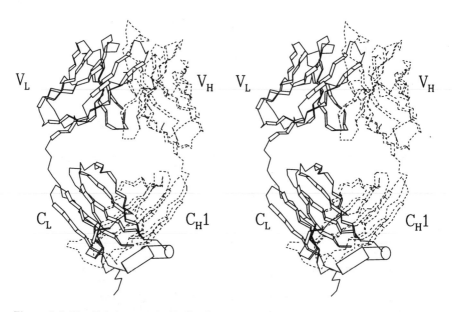

Figure 1-6. The Fab fragment of IgG KOL, showing the spatial relationships between V_L, C_L, V_H, and C_H1 domains. Solid lines: V_L and C_L domains; broken lines: V_H and C_H1 domains.

LOOPS

The term *loops* refers to sections of the polypeptide chain that connect regions of secondary structure. Frequently, helices and strands of sheet run across a protein or domain from one surface to another, and loops are characterized by (1) appearing on the surfaces of proteins and (2) reversing the direction of the chain. A typical globular protein contains one third of its residues in loops.

An understanding of loop conformation is of special importance in the case of immunoglobulins, because their antigen-binding sites are created by six loops. Indeed, antibodies present the general problem of prediction of loop conformation in its most pressing form.

Hairpin loops (those that connect successive strands of antiparallel β-sheet) have been studied extensively in order to classify them and to elucidate the determinants of their conformations.[21–30] Most residues of proteins have their main chains in one of two sterically-favorable conformations (these correspond to the conformations of α-helices and β-sheets). However, in order for a short region of polypeptide chain 3–4 residues in length to reverse direction and fold back on itself to form a loop, a residue that takes up a conformation outside these usual states is generally required. The conformations of short loops therefore depend primarily on the position within the loop of special residues—usually Gly, Asn, or Pro—that allow the chain to take up an unusual conformation. As pointed out by Sibanda and Thornton,[22] the conformation of a short hairpin can often be deduced from the position in the sequence of such special residues.

These general rules are, however, of limited utility for the prediction of the conformations of antigen-binding loops in immunoglobulins. Most of the loops are not short, or not hairpins, or neither; and the determinants of their conformations are not entirely intrinsic to the amino acid sequence of the loop itself, but involve tertiary interactions: hydrogen bonding and packing. Indeed, even for some short hairpins, tertiary interactions can override the predisposition of the sequence, to determine a conformation of the loop that does not follow these sequence-structure correlations.[30] An example important in immunoglobulin structure is the second hypervariable region of the V_H domain (H2). The size of the residue at site 71, a site in the conserved β-sheet of the V_H domain, is a major determinant of the conformation and position of this loop.[30]

This instance of the influence of a specific framework residue on the structure of the antigen-binding site of immunoglobulins has implications for antibody engineering. For constructions in which loops are transferred from one framework to another, keeping framework residue 71 unchanged would be important for maintaining the conformation of H2.[31, 32]

DISTINCTION BETWEEN FRAMEWORK AND HYPERVARIABLE REGIONS OF V_L AND V_H DOMAINS

Kabat and his coworkers[1, 2] analyzed the patterns of variability in immunoglobulin sequences and were thereby able to identify the regions involved in antigen-binding. It is possible to adopt the same approach using the available three-dimensional structures. The basic questions are the same in both investigations: Which regions have conformations common to all known immunoglobulin structures? Which regions are variable? The answers to these questions based on the structures are similar but not identical to those based on sequences. However, the methods of addressing the questions are quite different, and in the next section we describe the technique of least-squares superposition that is the basic tool of investigations of structural similarity.

COMPARISON OF STRUCTURES: LEAST-SQUARES SUPERPOSITION AND ROOT-MEAN-SQUARE DEVIATION

A very common problem in the analysis of proteins is the determination of how similar two or more structures, or portions of structures, are.

A useful mathematical technique is to determine the optimal least-squares superposition of a pair of structures: Fix the position and orientation of one of the structures, and vary the position and orientation of the other to find the minimum value of the sum of the squares of the distances between the corresponding atoms. The square root of the average value of the squared distances between corresponding atoms is the root-mean-square (RMS) deviation. If the two objects were precisely congruent, it would be possible to superimpose them exactly, and the RMS deviation would be zero. In real cases, the "fit" of two nonidentical structures is never exact, and the minimal RMS deviation is a quantitative measure of the structural difference.

If sets of related proteins are examined by such methods, it is clear that the general folding pattern is preserved, but that there are distortions which increase in magnitude as the amino acid sequences diverge.[33] A closer look reveals that the distortion is not uniformly distributed, but that, in any family, there is a core of the structure that retains the same qualitative fold, and other parts of the structure that change conformation. (An analogy: if one were to compare the capital letters R and B, the common core would correspond to those portions of the letters represented by the letter P. Outside this common core, R has a diagonal stroke and B has a loop. Comparison of a roman R and an italic *B* would illustrate a common core that was distorted between the two structures.) In most families of proteins, the common core generally contains the major elements of secondary structure and peptides flanking them, including active site peptides. In the immunoglobulin domains, the core corresponds approximately to the double β-sheet framework.

Figure 1-7 shows the relationship between divergence of sequence and structure for 32 pairs of proteins or domains from 8 different families, including immunoglobulin domains. The divergence of the structure is measured by the RMS deviation of the main chain atoms of the core. The results show that as the sequence diverges, the structure diverges, with a nonlinear dependence. For sequences more closely related than 50% residue identity, the core is observed to contain at least 95% of the residues, and the RMS deviation of the main chain atoms of the core is ≤1.0 Å. In modelling of

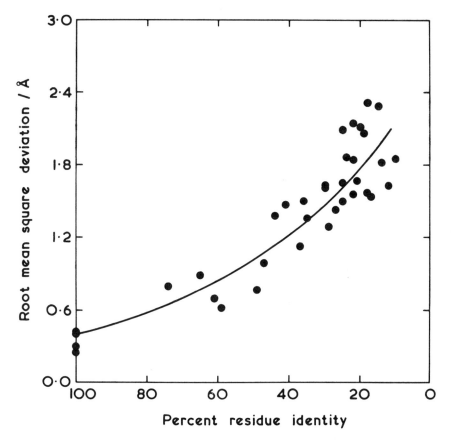

Figure 1-7. The general relationship between the divergence of amino acid sequence and the divergence of protein conformation in families of related proteins. The abscissa shows the percent identical amino acids in the sequences, and the ordinate shows the RMS deviation of the main chain atoms of the core of each pair of structures. (The core is the central region of the structures that retains the same general folding pattern.) (From Chothia, C. and Lesk, A.M. 1986. Relationship between the divergence of sequence and structure in proteins. *EMBO J.* 5:823.)

immunoglobulins, parent structures of a relationship at least this close are usually available. Therefore, the accurate modelling of the main chain atoms of the framework is usually feasible.

CALIBRATION OF THE SIGNIFICANCE OF RMS DEVIATIONS OF LOOPS

To illustrate the relationship between the value of the RMS deviation of the main chain atoms and the extent of structural similarity, three superpositions are shown in Figure 1-8. Figure 1-8A shows the L1 loops of J539 and

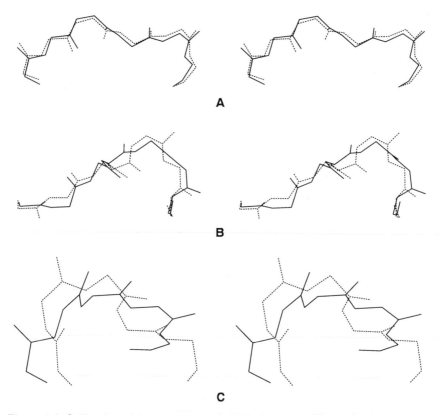

Figure 1-8. Calibration of the measure of similarity between different loop structures. Each pair of structures is superposed by minimizing the RMS deviation between corresponding main chain atoms (N, Cα, C, O). The figure shows superpositions of (A) the L1 loops of J539 (solid lines) and HyHEL-5 (broken lines) (RMS deviation 0.50 Å), (B) the H1 loops of NEWM (solid lines) and McPC603 (broken lines) (RMS deviation 1.02 Å) and (C) the H2 loops of KOL (solid lines) and HyHEL-5 (broken lines) (RMS deviation 1.80 Å).

HyHEL-5. The RMS deviation is around 0.5 Å. It can be seen that the structures are essentially the same. An example of loops with RMS deviation of about 1.0 Å is shown in Figure 1-8B, a superposition of backbone atoms of the H1 loops of NEWM and McPC603. In this case, some of the peptide groups have a different orientation, but the overall course of the chain is the same. These differences arise both from changes in the amino acid sequence and from experimental error. It is a fact of crystallographic life that peptide oxygen atoms are not always securely positioned in medium-resolution structures. It is noteworthy that when comparisons are limited to loops of similar conformation in structures determined at the highest resolution, the RMS deviations tend to be smaller.

An RMS deviation of more than 1.5 Å is indicative of extensive differences in the main chain conformations of the loops. Indeed, the H2 loops of KOL and HyHEL-5 (RMS deviation 1.8 Å) shown in Figure 1-8C can not be described as similar in conformation at all.

RELATION BETWEEN SEQUENCE AND STRUCTURE IN ANTIGEN-BINDING LOOPS: THE CANONICAL STRUCTURE MODEL

Analysis of the antigen-binding loops in known structures has shown that the main chain conformations are determined by a few particular residues and that only these residues, and the overall length of the loop, need to be conserved to maintain the conformation of the loop.[28, 34] The conserved residues may be those that can adopt special main chain conformations—Gly, Asn, or Pro—or those that form special hydrogen-bonding or packing interactions. Other residues in the sequences of the loops are thus left free to vary, to modulate the surface topography and charge distribution of the antigen-binding site.

The ability to isolate the determinants of loop conformation in a few particular residues in the sequence makes it possible to analyze the distribution of loop conformations in the many known immunoglobulin sequences. It appears that at least five out of the hypervariable regions of antibodies have only a few main chain conformations or "canonical structures." Most sequence variations only modify the surface by altering the side chains on the same canonical main chain structure. Sequence changes at a few specific sets of positions switch the main chain to a different canonical conformation.

As an example Figure 1-9 shows the L3 loops from V_κ REI and V_κ McPC603. These loops have the same length, and in each case there is a proline at position 95 in the loop, in a *cis* conformation. Hydrogen bonds from the side chain of the residue at position 90, just N-terminal to the loop, to the main chain atoms of residues in the loop, stabilize the conformation. The side chain is a Gln in REI and an Asn in McPC603; it can also be a His in some

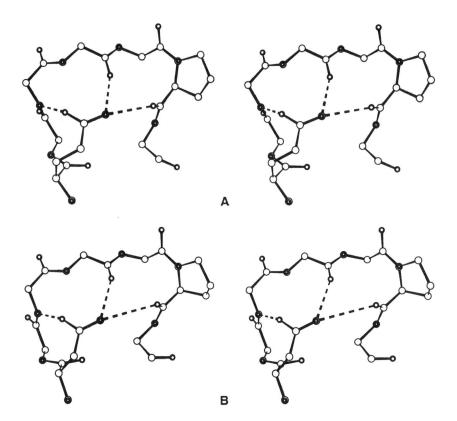

Figure 1-9. The similarity of loops of the same canonical structure from different antibodies. The figure shows the L3 loops from (A) V_κ REI and (B) V_κ McPC603.

V_κ chains. The combination of the polar side chain at position 90 and the proline at position 95 constitutes the "signature" of this conformation in this loop, from which it can be recognized in a sequence of an unknown immunoglobulin.

General support for this model has come from analysis of known sequences[1] and structures[28, 34-36] of immunoglobulins. In studies of sequences, Kabat and coworkers[1] found conserved residues at sites within certain sets of hypervariable regions. The evidence from crystal structures indicates that the canonical structure model describes the relation between amino acid sequence and structure for at least five of the six hypervariable regions. Padlan and Davies,[35] and more recently de la Paz and coworkers,[36] showed that some of the hypervariable regions in the immunoglobulins of known structure have the same main chain conformation in spite of several differences in sequence. Chothia and Lesk[28] identified the residues that through packing, hydrogen bonding, or the ability to assume unusual conformational states are primarily responsible for the main chain conformations of the hypervariable regions in the Fabs NEWM, McPC603, KOL and J539, and the V_L domains REI and RHE.

The conclusion is that the observed conformations are determined by the interactions of a few residues at specific sites in the hypervariable regions and, for certain loops, in the framework regions. Hypervariable regions that have the same conformations in different immunoglobulins have the same or very similar residues at these sites. On the basis of the canonical structure model, we can create a detailed roster of the canonical conformations of each loop —with the possible exception of H3, which is more complicated and still uncertain—and the sets of "signature" residues that permit us to discriminate among them.[34]

Table 1-2 (see next page) shows the current catalog of canonical structures for V_κ light chains and heavy chains, and their signature patterns. Figure 1-10 (page 21) shows the corresponding loop conformations.

HOW SIMILAR ARE LOOPS WITH THE SAME CANONICAL STRUCTURE IN DIFFERENT IMMUNOGLOBULINS?

Four canonical structures have been identified for the L1 loop, one of which is represented in more than one known structure. The RMS deviation of the backbone between L1 loops with the same canonical structure is in all cases lower than 0.6 Å. Only one canonical structure for the L2 loop is known. The RMS deviation between L2 loops of known structures is between 0.2 Å and 1.0 Å, in which the larger values arise from changes in orientation of isolated peptide groups. L3 has four canonical structures. The first and by far the most common one is that shown in Figure 1-9. It is identified by a proline in position 95 and an asparagine or a glutamine in position 90. The RMS deviation of the backbone is typically 1.0 Å.

H1 has one known canonical structure, with RMS deviations of pairs of H1 loops from different antibodies of known structure in the range 0.2-1.0 Å. Within the two sets of structures with the same canonical structure for H2, the RMS deviation is always lower than 1.0 Å.

Because of the effects of experimental error, these ranges are likely to be overestimates of the differences in conformation. In comparisons of homologous loops with the same canonical structure, the best determined structures give low values of the RMS deviations.

To determine whether the loop conformations observed in the relatively few known immunoglobulin structures do indeed account for the loops in a large proportion of all immunoglobulins, the large compilation of sequences tabulated by Kabat and coworkers[37] has been analyzed.[34] Approximately 90% of the hypervariable regions in V_κ domains have the same length and contain the "signature" residues of a known canonical structure, and are

Table 1-2. Canonical Structures for Antigen-binding Loops L1, L2, and L3 of V_κ Domains and H1 and H2 of V_H Domains

L1 Regions

Canonical Structure	Protein	26	27	28	29	30	31	a	b	c	d	e	f	32	2	25	33	71
						*									*	*	*	*
1	J539	S	S	S	V	S	—	—	—	—	—	—	—	S	I	A	L	Y
	HyHEL-5	S	S	S	V	N	—	—	—	—	—	—	—	Y	I	A	M	Y
	NQ10	S	S	S	V	R	—	—	—	—	—	—	—	Y	I	A	M	Y
2	REI	S	Q	D	I	I	K	—	—	—	—	—	—	V	I	A	L	Y
	D1.3	S	G	N	I	H	N	—	—	—	—	—	—	Y	I	A	L	Y
	HyHEL-10	S	Q	S	I	G	N	—	—	—	—	—	—	N	I	A	L	F
	NC41	S	Q	D	V	S	T	—	—	—	—	—	—	A	I	A	L	Y
3	McPC603	S	E	S	L	L	N	S	G	N	E	K	N	F	I	S	L	F
4	4-4-20	S	Q	S	L	V	H	S	—	N	G	N	T	Y	V	S	L	F

Total no. of sequences known for L1 regions: human, 95; mouse, 299.

Canonical structure	1	2	3	4
Human sequences that fit (%)	—	60	5	5
Mouse sequences that fit (%)	15	25	20	10

L2 Regions

Canonical Structure	Protein	50	51	52	48	64
				*	*	
1	REI	E	A	S	I	G
	McPC603	G	A	S	I	G
	J539	E	I	S	I	G
	D1.3	Y	T	T	I	G
	HyHEL-5	D	T	S	I	G
	HyHEL-10	Y	A	S	I	G
	NC41	W	A	S	I	G
	NQ10	D	T	S	I	G
	4-4-20	K	V	S	I	G

Total no. of sequences known for L2 regions: human, 69; mouse, 183.

Canonical structure	1
Human sequences that fit (%)	95
Mouse sequences that fit (%)	95

Table 1-2. *(continued)*

L3 Regions

Canonical Structure	Protein	91	92	93	94	95	96	90
						*		*
1	REI	Y	Q	S	L	P	Y	Q
	McPC603	D	H	S	Y	P	L	N
	D1.3	F	W	S	T	P	R	H
	HyHEL-10	S	N	S	W	P	Y	Q
	NC41	H	Y	S	P	P	W	Q
	4-4-20	S	T	H	V	P	W	Q
	NQ10	W	S	S	N	P	L	Q
2	J539	W	T	Y	P	L	I	Q
3	HyHEL-5	W	G	R	N	P	—	Q

Total no. of sequences known for L3 regions: human, 52; mouse, 152.

Canonical structure		1	2	3
Human sequences that fit (%)		90	—	2
Mouse sequences that fit (%)		80	10	1

H1 Regions

Canonical Structure	Protein	26	27	28	29	30	31	32	34	94
		*	*		*				*	*
1	McPC603	G	F	T	F	S	D	F	M	R
	KOL	G	F	I	F	S	S	Y	M	R
	J539	G	F	D	F	S	K	Y	M	R
	D1.3	G	F	S	L	T	G	Y	V	R
	HyHEL-5	G	Y	T	F	S	D	Y	I	R
	NC41	G	Y	T	F	T	N	Y	M	R
	NQ10	G	F	T	F	S	S	F	M	R
	4-4-20	G	F	T	F	S	D	Y	M	G
1'	NEW	G	S	T	F	S	N	D	Y	R
	HyHEL-10	G	D	S	I	T	D	D	W	N

Total no. of sequences known for H1 regions: human, 50; mouse, 321.

Canonical structure	1
Human sequences that fit (%)	50
Mouse sequences that fit (%)	80

Table 1-2. Canonical Structures for Antigen-binding-loops L1, L2, and L3 of V_κ Domains and H1 and H2 of V_H Domains *(continued)*

H2 Regions

Canonical Structure	Protein	52a	b	c	53	54	55	71
							*	
1	NEW	—	—	—	Y	H	G	
	D1.3				G	D	G	
	HyHEL-10	—	—	—	Y	S	G	
		*					(*)	*
2	HyHEL-5	P	—	—	G	S	G	A
	NC41	T	—	—	N	T	G	L
						(*)		*
3	KOL	D	—	—	D	G	S	R
	J539	P	—	—	D	S	G	R
	NQ10	S	—	—	G	S	S	R
						(*)	*	*
4	McPC603	N	K	G	N	K	Y	R
	4-4-20	N	K	P	Y	N	Y	R

Total no. of sequences known for H2 regions: human, 54; mouse, 248.

Canonical structure	1	2	3	4
Human sequences that fit (%)	15	1	40	15
Mouse sequences that fit (%)	15	40	5	20

Residues shown are those in the antigen-binding loops themselves, and others in the framework regions that are important for determining the conformations of the antigen-binding loops. Residues important in determining loop conformations are indicated by an asterisk. Residue numbers correspond to the convention of Kabat and colleagues.[37] Although this classification of the conformations of antigen-binding loops is derived from only a few structures, inspection of the very many known sequences shows that most loops in immunoglobulins of known sequence should be similar in conformation to the corresponding loop in one of those of known structure.[34] Structures referred to that are not contained in Table 1-1 are the Fab-lysozyme complex D1.3,[47] the Fab-neuraminidase complex NC41, and the Fab-2-phenyloxazolone complex NQ10/12.5.[49]

Source: Reprinted by permission from *Nature,* Vol. 342, pp. 877-883. Copyright © 1989 Macmillan Magazines Ltd.

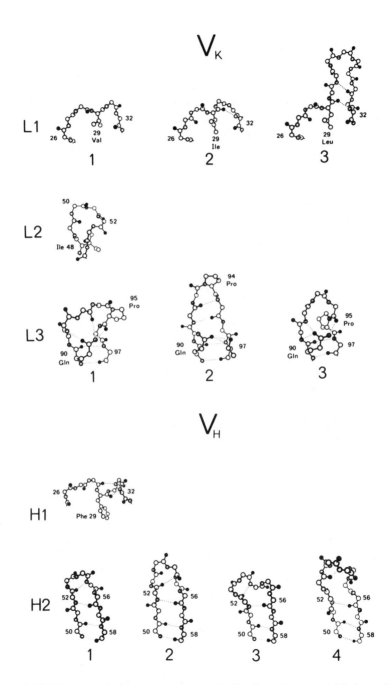

Figure 1-10. The canonical structures known for the three hypervariable loops in V_κ chains and the first two hypervariable regions in V_H chains. (Reprinted by permission from *Nature*, vol. 342, pp. 877–883. Copyright © 1989 Macmillan Magazines Ltd.)

therefore expected to have conformations close to those found in the currently known immunoglobulin structures. Indeed, this estimate is conservative in that it includes only hypervariable regions that match the sequence requirements exactly.

These observations suggest that the main chain conformations of at least five of the hypervariable regions are described by a small repertoire of canonical structures, most of which are present among the immunoglobulin structures already known, and that the conformation present in an immunoglobulin of unknown structure can very often be recognized in the sequence from the presence of specific residues.

The accuracy and completeness of this roster—measured by its effectiveness in prediction of unknown antigen-binding sites from amino acid sequences—depends on (1) correct determination of the sets of residues responsible for the observed conformations and (2) the assumption that changes in the identities of residues at other sites will not significantly affect the conformation of the loop. The model can be tested, refined, and extended by using it to predict the atomic structure of binding sites in new immunoglobulin structures before they have been determined by x-ray crystallography.

DIFFERENT METHODS OF PREDICTION OF THE STRUCTURES OF ANTIGEN-BINDING SITES

The possibility of predicting with good accuracy the three-dimensional structures of immunoglobulins at the atomic level is of central importance for the engineering of antibodies with a prescribed specificity. Moreover, the comparison of the predicted and experimental structures of immunoglobulins has proven to be useful in widening our understanding of sequence-structure relationships in this class of proteins.

Several methods that have been used to predict structures of antigen-binding sites of immunoglobulins will be discussed here, and the tests to which they have been subjected will be described. Some methods are based on applications of information from known structures;[34, 38-40] others are based on *a priori* methods using conformational energy estimates and either exhaustive conformational searches or molecular dynamics.[41-45]

Prediction of the Structures of Antigen-binding Domains by the Canonical Structures Method

A procedure to predict the structures of the variable domains of immunoglobulins has been formulated based on the structures of solved immunoglobulins and the canonical structure model of the conformations of the hypervariable loops.[20,28,33-34,38-40] The V_κ domain of REI and V_H domain of KOL provided the parent structures for V_L and the V_H domains of D1.3. Examination of the amino acid sequences of the variable domains of D1.3 showed that its hypervariable regions were the same size as those in structures then known, and contained the same or similar residues at the sites responsible for the known conformations. On this basis the atomic structure of the V_L-V_H dimer of D1.3 was predicted prior to its experimental determination.[38] Comparison of this prediction with the best available crystal structure of D1.3 has shown that all six hypervariable regions had the predicted main chain conformations.[34]

Several other predictions based on the canonical structure method, and their tests, are discussed in an article by Chothia and colleagues.[34]

DETAILED STATEMENT OF MODELLING PROCEDURE

The modelling procedure based on the canonical structure approach uses the following data derived from known sequences and structures:

- The amino acid sequence of the immunoglobulin molecule to be modelled and its alignment with the sequences of immunoglobulins of known structure.
- Definitions of the regions in the aligned sequences that demarcate the framework and the hypervariable loops. (It should be noted that the definitions of the loop boundaries are based on analysis of the structures and differ in some respects from those of Kabat and colleagues on the basis of analysis of sequences; Table 1-3.)
- Identification of the residues that form the conserved structure of V_L-V_H interface, derived from the sequence alignment
- A tabulation of the positions and identities of the residues distinguishing the canonical structures
- The resolution of the x-ray structure determinations

The model-building procedure comprises the following steps:

1. Align the sequences of V_L and V_H chains of the target immunoglobulin with the sequences of the corresponding domains in the known immunoglobulin structures.

2. For each domain (V_L and V_H), select a parent domain from among the corresponding domains of known structure. This is usually the domain with the highest sequence identity with the target domain, because, in general, the higher the residue identity in the core or framework of a pair of proteins, the more similar the conformation, and hence the higher the quality of the model. However, there may exist another

Table 1-3. Alternative Definitions of Complementarity-Determining Regions (CDR) or Structures

CDR Loop	*Residue Limits Based on Sequence Variability (Kabat)*	*Residue Limits Based on Structural Variability (Chothia and Lesk)*
L1	24–34	26–32
L2	50–56	50–52
L3	89–97	91–96
H1	31–35b	26–32
H2	50–65	52a–55
H3	95–102	96–101

All residue numbers are given according to the convention of Kabat and colleagues.[37]

Source: From Kabat, E.A., Wu, T.T., Reid-Miller, M., Perry, H.M., And Gottesman, K.S. 1987. *Sequences of Proteins of Immunological Interest*, 4th ed. Washington, D.C.: Public Health Service, N.I.H., and Chothia, C. and Lesk, A.M. 1987. Canonical structures for the hypervariable regions of immunoglobulins. J. Mol. Biol. 196:901.

known structure that has been solved to significantly higher resolution, and that has only slightly lower sequence identity. If the difference in sequence identity is no greater than 5%, select the higher-resolution structure to provide the parent domain. The percent residue identity in the framework between the target domain and the parent structure is usually between 45% and 85%.

3. If the selected parent structures for V_L and V_H domains come from different immunoglobulins, pack them together by a least-squares fit of the main chain atoms of residues conserved in the V_L-V_H interface.[20] The RMS deviation between the atoms in these sets of residues, for different structures, is usually below 1.0 Å and often below 0.6 Å. If the RMS deviation is higher than 1.0 Å, delete from the superposition calculation the atoms that are farthest apart, recalculate the RMS deviation, and resuperpose the interface, repeating the procedure if necessary until the RMS deviation is below 1.0 Å.

4. Examine the sequence of each of the hypervariable loops to determine whether a canonical structure can be identified for it. Identify the canonical structures of the loops by checking the sequence for the particular sets of residues that form the signature of each canonical structure. H3 is a special case. This loop is the most variable in length, sequence, and structure. Its variability in conformation has not yet been circumscribed by a suitable "catalog raisonée" of canonical

structures. It is still not understood whether the canonical structure approach is appropriate for this loop, or whether canonical structures exist in a much larger number than for other loops, so that a larger data base of known structures will be needed to identify them. This is currently an incompleteness of the canonical structure model.

5. If the canonical structure identified for a loop is different from that in the parent structure, then select a loop from some other known immunoglobulin structure having that canonical structure. Superpose the residues adjacent to the loop in the model and in the selected structure by a weighted least-squares fit[48] and then graft the loop into the model. It is appropriate to use the four residues before the N-terminus of the loop and the four residues after its C-terminus to superpose the structures; the residue immediately preceding the loop and the residue immediately after it are given weight 1.0, and the weight of each successive residue is multiplied by 0.8. The value of the weighted RMS deviation so calculated is usually below 1.0 Å.

6. If a canonical structure can not be identified, temporarily retain the loop from the parent structure. Delete it at the end of the procedure, and make no prediction for this loop.

7. The conformations of the side chains are then to be modelled. At sites where the parent structure and the model have the same residue, retain the conformation of the parent structure. If the side chain is different, take its side chain conformation, if possible, from an immunoglobulin having the same residue in the corresponding position. If the residue is part of a hypervariable loop, take the side chain conformation only from a loop with the same canonical structure. In other cases, retain the conformation of the side chains in the parent structure as far as the relative length of the side chains will permit.

8. Subject the model to 100 cycles of energy refinement. (It should be emphasized that this step is purely cosmetic, to tidy up the stereochemistry, and that one is not depending on energy calculations to devise or even to significantly refine the model. The RMS difference between the backbone atoms of the initial and final structures is typically 0.1–0.2 Å.

9. Remove any temporary loops from the final coordinate set.

The Expected Quality of the Model

Given the hypothesis that for the three loops of the light chain and for the first two of the heavy chain a canonical structure present in the data base can be identified, how good a model can be expected from this procedure?

Differences between predicted and experimental structures can arise from errors in the prediction of the conformation of each loop, errors in the positioning of the loop with respect to the framework, and errors in the relative position of the V_L and V_H domains, in addition to any inaccuracies inherited from the parent structures themselves. If the structures used as parent structures for the two domains and the loops are high-resolution, well-refined structures, one can expect the backbone of the framework to be correct within 1.0 Å RMS deviation and the backbone of the predicted loops, not including the special case of H3, to differ by about 0.7 Å RMS deviation on average, and by no more than 1.0–1.2 Å in all cases.

The differences in the positions of the hypervariable loops result from sequence differences within the loops, but also from sequence differences in residues in the framework. One can expect the positions of Cα atoms of residues in the loops to shift, relative to the frameworks of V_L and V_H domains, by 1.0–2.0 Å typically and by up to 3 Å in the worst cases.

Automatic Procedure

A computer procedure has been implemented that provides an atomic model of an immunoglobulin V_L+V_H fragment containing the antigen-binding site, reproducing the prediction protocol of the previous section in an automatic and objective way.

The main goal in writing an automatic objective procedure to build an atomic model of immunoglobulin variable domains is to offer the possibility of repeating predictions objectively with the same sets of rules using different data, or with different rules on the same data. The first facility is useful to repeat a prediction when new data are available; the second is useful to test whether a change in the procedure suggested by further analysis of known immunoglobulin structures can improve the quality of the predictions. By specifying the procedure, one can retain the important controls of a "blind test," even after the target structure is published.

An Example: NQ10/12.5

This section describes the application of the canonical structures procedure to the prediction of the variable domains of immunoglobulin NQ10/12.5.[49] The results of the comparison with the experimentally determined structure have been recently published.[34] The amino acid sequence of the hypervariable regions and associated framework sites of NQ10/12.5 are given in Table 1-2. For five of the hypervariable regions, the size and the residue conservation at the relevant sites clearly identify particular canonical structures.

We selected HyHEL-5 and KOL as parent structures for the V_L and the V_H domains, respectively. The fit of the conserved framework residues shows that the RMS deviation is lower than 1.0 Å, so all the residues are used in the superposition.

The next step is the substitution of the mutated side chains. First, noncon-served side chains are substituted, with the side chain initially left in a conformation similar to that of the parent structure. Then, the alignment table is searched to find an immunoglobulin having the substituted residue in the corresponding position, and its side chain conformation is transferred.

Five of the six NQ10/12.5 hypervariable loops correspond to a canonical structure; for H3 no prediction was made. The H3 loop from KOL (the parent structure for the V_H domain) was temporarily retained and was subsequently deleted after the energy refinement steps. Four of the hypervariable loops of NQ10/12.5 have the same canonical structure as the corresponding loops in the parent structures for the framework. The L3 loop canonical structure of the V_L domain parent, HyHEL-5, is different from that of L3 in NQ10/12.5, but it is the same as in 1REI. The L3 loop of 1REI was therefore grafted into the model.

Finally, the model was subjected to 100 cycles of energy minimization and the H3 loop was deleted.

Recently a crystal structure has been determined for NQ10/12.5 at a resolution of 2.8 Å.[49] Figure 1-11 shows the predicted and observed structures of each of the hypervariable regions, superposed by a least-squares fit of their main chain atoms. Figure 1-12 shows the relative positions of the predicted and observed hypervariable regions after superposition of the V_L and V_H frameworks. Table 1-4 gives the RMS differences in position of the main

Table 1-4. Results of Prediction of the V_L–V_H Domains of NQ10/12.5 by the Canonical Structures Method

Fragment	*RMS Deviation of Main Chain Atoms (Å)*
V_L framework	0.5
V_H framework	0.7
$V_L + V_H$ frameworks	0.8
L1	0.4
L2	0.9
L3	0.7
H1	0.3
H2	0.3

Shifts in Cα atoms of loop residues (Å) after superposition of V_L and V_H frameworks:

L1	0.4–2.7
L2	0.5–1.4
L3	0.6–1.5
H1	0.6–1.2
H2	0.6–0.9

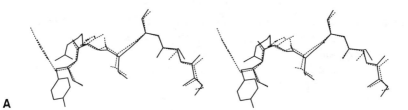

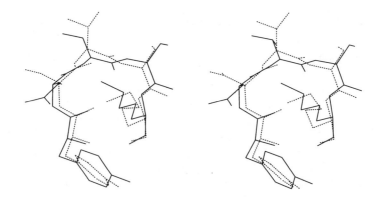

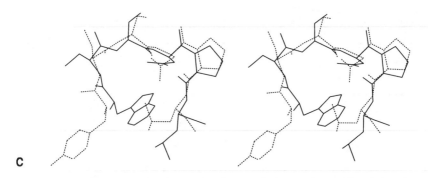

Figure 1-11. Individual superpositions of experimental (solid lines) and predicted structures (broken lines) of the antigen-binding loops of the antioxazolone antibody NQ10/12.5. (A) L1, (B) L2, (C) L3, (D) H1, (E) H2.

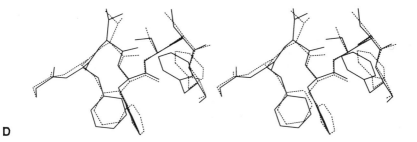

D

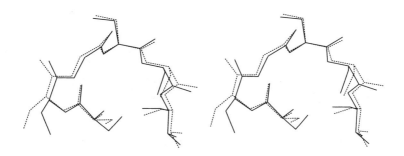

E

Figure 1-11. *(continued)*

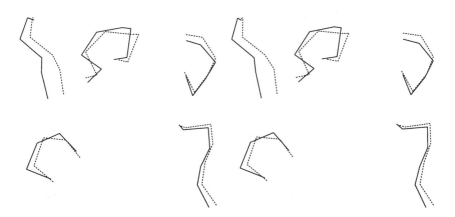

Figure 1-12. The shifts in position between experimental (solid lines) and predicted structures (broken lines) of the antigen-binding loops of the antioxazolone antibody NQ10/12.5. The predicted and experimental structures were superimposed on the frameworks of V_L and V_H domains.

chain atoms, and the shifts of the $C\alpha$ atoms of the loops after superposition of the V_L and V_H frameworks.

There is close agreement between the predicted and observed main chain conformations of the hypervariable regions: the RMS differences in atomic position are between 0.3 and 0.9 Å (see Table 1-4). There is also close agreement in the relative positions of the hypervariable regions. The $C\alpha$ atoms of all residues differ in position by no more than 2.6 Å, and all but two are correctly placed to within 1.7 Å.

PREDICTION OF ANTIGEN-BINDING LOOP CONFORMATION BY ENERGY CALCULATIONS

The main chain conformation of an antigen-binding loop attached to a given framework must obey the constraint that the chain must connect two fixed endpoints with a specified number of residues. For loops of fewer than about six residues, it is possible to enumerate a fairly complete set of main chain and side chain conformations that bridge the given endpoints and do not make steric collisions within the loop or between the loop and the rest of the molecule. The search procedure can be fine enough to produce a loop close to the correct one. By choosing this order, each loop is built into a structure that already contains as many of its important interactions as possible.

However, there are in general many possible loops of different internal conformations that bridge a given pair of endpoints. To choose one of them as the predicted conformation, it is possible to estimate conformational energies and evaluate the accessible surface areas of each loop—in the context of the remainder of the protein—and set criteria for selecting the one that appears the most favorable. Typical conformational energy calculations include terms representing hydrogen bonding, Van der Waals, and electrostatic interactions. Accessible surface area calculations give estimates of the interaction between the protein and the solvent.

Procedures for conformation generation and evaluation have been implemented in a number of computer programs.[43-46] An application to predicting all six antigen-binding loops of McPC603 and HyHEL-5, based on the program CONGEN,[44] has been described by Bruccoleri and coworkers.[46]

The CONGEN procedure generates conformations for a single loop and calculates energies of that loop in the context of the fixed portion of the structure. To apply this procedure to the prediction of all six loops of an antigen-binding site, Bruccoleri and coworkers had to develop a protocol involving the sequential prediction of the loops, one by one. Because the first loop is predicted in the absence of the other five, the interactions of the first loop predicted with the other five are missing from the energy estimates; only the sixth loop has its complete context. In order to minimize the errors arising from these missing interactions, Bruccoleri and coworkers predicted the loops in the following order: L2, H1, L3, H2, H3, L1.

Using a criterion based on protein conformational energies and accessible surface area, the predictions of the individual antigen-binding loops of McPC603 and HyHEL-5 had RMS deviations in the range 0.3–2.6 Å (backbone) and 1.4–4.1 Å (all atoms).

The procedure of Bruccoleri and coworkers and improvements arising from its further development have many attractive features. It is in principle a completely general, automatic, and objective procedure. It need not suffer, for example, from the incompleteness in the current canonical structures model that the structural repertoire of H3 is not yet under control. However, the results presented with this method so far do not include a "blind" test. Not only were the predicted structures already known, but the frameworks were taken without change from the crystal structures, rather than from the approximations to them that would be available if a loop prediction were attempted using a model of the framework of an immunoglobulin of unknown structure.

PREDICTION OF ANTIGEN-BINDING LOOP CONFORMATION BY DATA BASE SCREENING

Jones and Thirup[41] have developed a different method of building loops, based on selecting loops from proteins in the data base of known structures that span the given loop endpoints and overlap with peptides at the loop termini. For this procedure to be useful, several things must be established:

1. That the loops in immunoglobulin antigen-binding sites are to be found in proteins in the data base
2. That the geometrical relationship between the loop and the peptides that flank it are the same in immunoglobulin antigen-binding sites and proteins in the data base containing loops of the same conformation
3. If several loops are found in the data base that correctly join the peptides flanking and antigen-binding loop, that it is possible to select the correct one

Tramontano and colleagues[48, 50] studied these questions and reached the following conclusions:

1. The main chain conformations of most antigen-binding loops recur both in other antibody structures (this is of course one of the elements of the canonical structure model) and also in unrelated proteins. The exceptions are unusually long loops such as the L1 of McPC603 or H3 of KOL.

2. The geometric relationship between the loop and its flanking peptides is usually different when comparing an antigen-binding loop with a loop of similar conformation in an unrelated protein (except for short hairpins of standard conformation). In these cases it would not be possible to identify nonhomologous loops of proper conformation in building a model of an unknown immunoglobulin.

   As the number of known immunoglobulin structures increases, searching proteins other than immunoglobulins becomes less necessary or useful for model building. However, comparisons of the structural context and determinants of conformation of loops of similar structure in nonhomologous proteins remain interesting for their implications about general principles of protein structure.[50]

3. If the selection from candidate loops identified from homologous regions of other immunoglobulins by data base searching is based on the signature patterns in the sequences, the procedure reduces in effect to the canonical structure method. The integration of data base search methods with conformational energy calculations is described in the next section.

PREDICTION OF ANTIGEN-BINDING LOOP CONFORMATION BY COMBINED DATA BASE SEARCHING AND CONFORMATIONAL ENERGY CALCULATIONS

Martin and coworkers[51] have described a protocol that combines the approaches of conformation generation and evaluation as in the CONGEN procedure with data base searching. Because the CONGEN procedure involves a combinational search, the time required increases steeply with the number of residues in the loop. Martin and coworkers propose using a CONGEN procedure alone for short loops, and supplementing it with data base search techniques for longer loops.

For loops of length ≤ 5 residues, CONGEN alone is used, with a combination of conformational energy estimates and accessible surface area providing the criterion for selection.

For loops of length 6–7 residues, a data base search procedure provides candidate main chain conformations of the loops, and a CONGEN-like search procedure generates candidate side chain conformations and evaluates the results.

For loops of length ≥ 8 residues, data base searches provide candidate loops, from which the central five residues are removed and are rebuilt with CONGEN.

This method has been tested on the known crystal structures of the antilysozyme antibodies of HyHEL-5 and Gloop2. The results reported have

RMS deviations of individual loops in the range 0.76–1.45 Å (main chain) and 1.01–2.85 Å (all atoms). The definitions of the loop regions are those of Kabat and colleagues [37] (see Table 1-3).

Again, it may be noted that these results do not include any "blind" test.

PREDICTION OF ANTIGEN-BINDING LOOP CONFORMATION AND ANTIGEN-BINDING SITES BY MOLECULAR DYNAMICS

Holm and coworkers have used molecular dynamics in predicting the structures of the antigen-binding sites of two mouse antibodies against 2-phenyloxazolone.[52] The construction of the antibody V domains was based on the use of the crystal structure of Fab J539 as a parent. The loop conformations were identified with reference to the canonical structure model. Thus, in the light chain, L1 and L2 were retained from the parent domain, V_κ J539, but L3 was imported from V_κ McPC603. In the heavy chain, H1 was retained from the parent domain, VH J539. H2 is one residue shorter in the target domain than in the parent, and the hairpin containing the deletion was replaced by a loop found by data base searching. H3 was very short in the target structure and was constructed by deleting residues from the parent domain and closing the loop around the gap.

Holm and coworkers set themselves a more ambitious goal than the other authors whose work we have discussed, in that they attempted also to "dock" the hapten into the model. After constructing the model of the antibody-combining site, they identified plausible approximate positions for the hapten by interactive graphics, which were subsequently refined by molecular dynamics. One may note the appropriate "division of labor" between human and computer in that using interactive graphics, the scientist can see the general features of the system and identify (or at least suggest) the general features of the mode of binding. The computer, more sensitive to the details of the energies of interaction between all the individual pairs of atoms, can determine the optimal position and orientation of the hapten and refine conformational details. In other words, the human is good at identifying approximations to global solutions of problems involving only a few variables (the position and orientation of the hapten), and the computer is good at refining the solutions by examining small variations in very many parameters (precise atomic coordinates of the optimal structure similar in general features to the starting model).

Holm and coworkers examined two related antibody sequences and found two possible modes of binding of the hapten. Although these predictions have not been subjected to a direct experimental test by the solution of the crystal structure of either complex, the authors were able to rationalize the changes in affinity arising from mutations in this series of antibodies on the basis of their models.

PROSPECTS

Each of the methods described will gain power through the inevitable combination of the growth in the data base of known antibody structures, the increase in power of computers and programs, and the refinement of the methods through more extensive testing.

The solutions of many more antibody crystal structures, in different states of ligation, will provide the following:

1. A more complete set of loop conformations to be used in modelling either using the canonical structure method or methods using data base searching. It may be hoped that an understanding of the determinants of H3 conformations will emerge from analysis of the structures.

2. An understanding of the effects of antigen ligation on the structure of antibodies: These effects include changes in quaternary structure—changes in relative geometry of the V_L-V_H domains—and changes in conformations and shifts in loops, and changes in side chain conformations.

3. An understanding of general principles of binding site design—from an analysis of the relationship between the choices of individual loop conformations and the overall shape of the binding site; granting that the detailed surface topography of the binding site depends on the identities of the exposed side chains.

4. Material to test improved procedures for "docking:" the prediction of the interaction of antigen and antibody. At present, it may be conceded that it would be difficult to "dock" the antigen and antibody from a complex of known structures, and the problem is more difficult still if one is working only with models of the antigens and the antibody.

As a result, it is not unrealistic to be confident of improved predictions and to be optimistic about the prospects for "designer" antibodies, that is, the development of procedures to predict sequences of antibodies that will bind prespecified epitopes. However, it will certainly be a long time before theoretical methods can compete with the ability of the immune system to create mature antibodies of finely tuned affinity and specificity.

Acknowledgments: We thank Drs. C. Chothia and E. Gherardi for helpful discussions. A.M.L. thanks the Kay Kendall Foundation for generous support.

REFERENCES

1. Kabat, E.A., Wu, T.T., and Bilofsky, H. 1977. Unusual distribution of amino acids in complementarity-determining (hypervariable) segments of heavy and light chains of immunoglobulins and their possible roles in specificity of antibody-combining sites. *J. Biol. Chem.* 252:6609.
2. Kabat, E.A. 1978. The structural basis of antibody complementarity. *Advan. Protein Chem.* 32:1.
3. Porter, R.R. 1959. The hydrolysis of rabbit γ-globulin and antibodies with crystalline papain. *Biochem. J.* 73-119.
4. Edelman, G.M. and Poulik, M.D. 1961. Studies on structural units of the γ-globulins. *J. Exp. Med.* 113:861.
5. Edelman, G.M. 1970. The covalent structure of a human γG-immunoglobulin. XI. Functional Implications. *Biochemistry* 9:3197.
6. Bernstein, F.C., Koetzle, T.F., Williams, G.J.B., Meyer, E.F., Jr., Brice, M.D., Rodgers, J.R., Kennard, O., Shimanouchi, T., and Tasumi, M. 1977. The protein data bank: A computer-based archival file for macromolecular structure. *J. Mol. Biol.* 112:535
7. Schiffer, M., Girling, R.L., Ely, K.R., and Edmundson, A.B. 1973. Structure of a λ-type Bence-Jones protein at 3.5-angstroms resolution. *Biochem.* 12:4620.
8. Epp, O., Lattman, E.E., Schiffer, M., Huber, R., and Palm, W. 1975. The molecular structure of a dimer composed of the variable portions of the Bence-Jones protein REI refined at 2.0 angstroms resolution. *Biochem.* 14:4943.
9. Furey, W., Jr., Wang, B.C., Yoo, C.S., and Sax, M. 1983. Structure of a novel Bence-Jones protein (Rhe) fragment at 1.6Å resolution. *J. Mol. Biol.* 167:661.
10. Suh, S.W., Bhat, T.N., Navia, M.A., Cohen, G.H., Rao, D.N., Rudikov, S., and Davies, D.R. 1986. The galactan-binding immunoglobulin FabJ539: An X-ray diffraction study at 2.6Å resolution. *Proteins: Structure, Function, Genetics* 1:74.
11. Satow, Y., Cohen, G.H., Padlan, E.A., and Davies, D.R. 1986. Phosphocholine binding to immunoglobulin FabMcPC603. An X-ray diffraction study at 2.7Å. *J. Mol. Biol.* 190:593.
12. Segal, D.M., Padlan, E.A., Cohen, G.H., Rudikoff, S., Potter, M., and Davies, D.R. 1974. The three-dimensional structure of a phosphorylcholine-binding mouse immunoglobulin Fab and the nature of the antigen binding site. *Proc. Natl. Acad. Sci. USA* 71:4298.
13. Marquart, M., Deisenhofer, J., Huber, R., and Palm, W. 1980. Crystallographic refinement and atomic models of the intact immunoglobulin molecule Kol and its antigen-binding fragment at 3.0Å and 1.9Å resolution. *J. Mol. Biol.* 141:369.
14. Saul, F.A., Amzel, L.M., and Poljak, R.J. 1978. Preliminary refinement and structural analysis of the Fab fragment from the human immunoglobulin New at 2.0Å *J. Mol. Biol.* 253:585.
15. Lascombe, M.B., Alzari, P.M., Boulot, G., Saludjian, P., Tougard, P., Berek, C., Haba, S., Rosen, E.M., Nisonoff, A., and Poljak, R.J. 1989. Three-dimensional structure of Fab R19.9, a monoclonal murine antibody specific for the p-azobenenearsonate group. *Proc. Natl. Acad. Sci. USA* 86:607.

16. Deisenhofer, J. 1981. Crystallographic refinement and atomic models of a human Fc fragment and its complex with fragment b of protein a from *Staphylococcus aureus* at 2.9- and 2.8-Å resolution. *Biochem.* 20:2361.

17. Sheriff, S., Silverton, E.W., Padlan, E.A., Cohen, G.H., Smith-Gill, S.J., Finzel, B.C., and Davies, D.R. 1987. Three-dimensional structure of an antibody-antigen complex. *Proc. Natl. Acad. Sci. USA* 84:8075.

18. Padlan, E.A., Silverton, E.W., Sheriff, S., Cohen, G.H., Smith-Gill, S.J., and Davies, D.R. 1989. Structure of an antibody-antigen complex. Crystal structure of the HyHEL-10 Fab-lysozyme complex. *Proc. Natl. Acad. Sci. USA* 86:5938.

19. Herron, J.N., He, X., Mason, M.L., Voss, E.W., Jr., and Edmundson, A.B. 1989. Three-dimensional structure of a fluorescein-Fab complex crystallized in 2-methyl-2,4-pentanediol. *Proteins: Structure, Function, Genetics* 5:271.

20. Chothia, C., Novotny, J., Bruccoleri, R., and Karplus, M. 1985. Domain association in immunoglobulin molecules: The packing of variable domains. *J. Mol. Biol.* 186:651.

21. Venkatachalam, C. 1968. Stereochemical criteria for polypeptides and proteins. V. Conformation of a system of three linked peptide units. *Biopolymers* 6:1425.

22. Sibanda, B.L. and Thornton, J.M. 1985. β-hairpin families in globular proteins. *Nature (London)* 316:170.

23. Wilmot, C.M. and Thornton, J.M. 1988. Analysis and prediction of the different types of β-turns in proteins. *J. Mol. Biol.* 203:221.

24. Sibanda, B.L., Blundell, T.L., and Thornton, J.M. 1989. Conformation of β-hairpins in protein structures. A systematic classification with applications to modelling by homology, electron density fitting and protein engineering. *J. Mol. Biol.* 206:759.

25. Efimov, A.V., 1986. Standard conformations of polypeptide chains in irregular regions of proteins. *Mol. Biol. USSR* 20:208.

26. Rose, G.D., Gierasch, L.M., and Smith, J.A. 1985. Turns in peptides and proteins. *Adv. Protein Chem* 37:1.

27. Leszczynski, J.F. and Rose, G.D. 1986. Loops in globular proteins: A novel category of secondary structure. *Science* 234:849.

28. Chothia, C. and Lesk, A.M. 1987. Canonical structures for the hypervariable regions of immunoglobulins. *J. Mol. Biol.* 196:901.

29. Milner-White, E.J., Ross, B.M., Ismail, R., Belhadj-Mostefa, K., and Poet, R. 1988. One type of gamma-turn, rather than the other, gives rise to chain-reversal in proteins. *J. Mol. Biol.* 204:777.

30. Tramontano, A., Chothia, C., and Lesk, A.M. 1990. Framework residue 71 is a major determinant of the position and conformation of the second hypervariable region in the V_H domains of immunoglobulins. *J. Mol. Biol.* 215:175.

31. Jones, P.T., Dear, P.H., Foote, J., Neuberger, M., and Winter, G. 1986. Replacing the complementarity-determining regions in a human antibody with those from a mouse. *Nature* 321:522.

32. Reichmann, L., Clark, M., Waldmann, H., and Winter, G. 1988. Reshaping human antibodies for therapy. *Nature* 332:323.

33. Chothia, C. and Lesk, A.M. 1986. Relationship between the divergence of sequence and structure in proteins. *EMBO J.* 5:823.

34. Chothia, C., Lesk, A.M., Tramontano, A., Levitt, M., Smith-Gill, S.J., Air, G., Sheriff, S., Padlan, E.A., Davies, D., and Tulip, W.R. 1989. The conformations of immunoglobulin hypervariable regions. *Nature* 342:877.

35. Padlan, E.A. and Davies, D.R. 1975. Variability of three-dimensional structure in immunoglobulins. *Proc. Natl. Acad. Sci. USA* 72:819.

36. de la Paz, P., Sutton, B.J.., Darsley, M.J., and Rees, A.R. 1986. Modelling of the combining sites of three antilysozyme monoclonal antibodies and of the complex between one of the antibodies and its epitope. *EMBO J.* 5:415.

37. Kabat, E.A., Wu, T.T., Reid-Miller, M., Perry, H.M., and Gottesman, K.S. 1987. *Sequences of Proteins of Immunological Interest*, 4th ed. Washington, D.C.: Public Health Service, N.I.H.

38. Chothia, C., Lesk, A.M., Levitt, M., Amit, A.G., Mariuzza, R.A., Phillips, S.E.V., and Poljak, R. 1986. The predicted structure of immunoglobulin D1.3 and its comparison with the crystal structure. *Science* 233:755.

39. Colman, P.M., Laver, W.G., Varghese, J.N., Baker, A.T., Tulloch, P.A., Air, G.M., and Webster, R.G. 1987. Three-dimensional structure of a complex antibody with influenza virus neuraminidase. *Nature* 326:358.

40. Tramontano, A., Chothia, C., and Lesk, A.M. 1990. An objective and automatic procedure to predict the atomic structure of immunoglobulin variable domains. Manuscript in preparation.

41. Jones, T.A. and Thirup, S. 1986. Using known substructures in protein model building and crystallography. *EMBO J.* 5:819.

42. Go, N. and Scheraga, H.A. 1980. Ring closure and local conformational deformation of chain molecules. *Macromolecules* 3:178.

43. Moult, J. and James, M.N.G. 1986. An algorithm for determining the conformation of polypeptide segments in proteins by systematic search. *Proteins: Structure, Function, Genetics* 1:146.

44. Fine, R.M., Wang, H., Shenkin, P.S., Yarmush, D.L., and Levinthal, C. 1986. Predicting antibody hypervariable loop conformations. II. Minimizing and molecular dynamics studies of McPC603 from many randomly generated loop conformations. *Proteins: Structure, Function, Genetics* 1:342.

45. Bruccoleri, R.E., and Karplus, M. 1987. Prediction of the folding of short polypeptide segments by uniform conformational sampling. *Biopolymers* 26:137.

46. Bruccoleri, R.E., Haber, E., and Novotny, J. 1988. Structure of antibody loops reproduced by a conformational search algorithm. *Nature (London)* 335:564.

47. Amit, A.G., Mariuzza, R.A., Phillips, S.E.V., and Poljak, R.J. 1986. Three-dimensional structure of an antigen-antibody complex at 2.8 $\mathring{A}$ resolution. *Science* 233:747.

48. Tramontano, A. and Lesk, A.M. Manuscript in preparation.

49. Alzari, P.M., Boulot, G., Mariuzza, R.A., Spinelli, S., and Poljak, R.J. 1990. The structure of an anti-oxazolone Fab fragment and of its complex with the hapten. *Acta Crystallogr.* A46 (supplement):C-109.

50. Tramontano, A., Chothia, C., and Lesk, A.M. 1989. Structural determinants of the conformations of medium-sized loops in proteins. *Proteins: Structure, Function, Genetics* 6:32.

51. Martin, A.C.R., Cheetham, J., and Rees, A.R. 1989. Modelling antibody hypervariable loops: A combined algorithm. *Proc. Natl. Acad. Sci. USA* 72:819.

52. Holm, L., Laaksonen, L., Kaartinen, M., Teeri, T.T., and Knowles, J.K.C. 1990. Molecular modelling study of antigen binding to oxazolone-specific antibodies: The OX1 idiotypic IgG and its mature variant with increased affinity to 2-phenyloxazolone. *Protein Engineering* 3:403.

CHAPTER 2

Engineering Antibody Affinity

J.C. Cheetham

Antibodies show a vast natural repertoire of binding specificities, coupled with selected modular functions such as complement activation.[1] Because an antibody can be produced against virtually any antigen with precise structural specificity, the possibility exists that these molecules can offer an almost infinite production source of proteins with preselected ligand specificity or novel functional properties. In practical terms the problem of engineering antibody affinity can be approached from two directions. On the one hand, one can rely on the existing *in vivo* mechanisms within the immune system itself. This strategy is by far the most widely used for the generation of prescribed antibody specificities. The recent exciting developments in the use of antibodies as new catalytic enzymes, or abzymes,[2, 3] provide us with a topical example of the success of this method. Antibodies catalyzing a range of chemical transformations have been produced using conventional monoclonal antibody technology and transition state analogues for the individual reaction schemes as immunogens. At the other extreme, with the advent of molecular biology techniques, such as site-directed mutagenesis (SDM), an alternative philosophy has begun; that is, to engineer antibody specificity and affinity *in vitro* through rational design, with existing knowledge of antibody structure providing a route by which to identify and select the molecular template on which to build.

The IgG antibody is a multi-domain protein composed of four polypeptide chains, two light (L) chain and two heavy (H) chain, bridged by interchain disulfide bonds and folded to form globular domains.[4] These interact spatially through predominantly hydrophobic interactions,[5] each individual domain being an autonomous folding unit.[6] The variable region domains (V_H and V_L) are responsible for the formation of the antibody-combining site (ACS), in which the antigen binds. Wu and Kabat demonstrated in the 1970s that, within the V regions, the highest sequence variability is clustered into three distinct locations along each chain, separated by relatively invariant framework segments.[7] Later, structural studies of antibody fragments by x-ray crystallography[8] showed that these areas of hypervariability correspond to six loop regions, projecting from one end of the V_H/V_L domain pair and supported on a conserved β-barrel framework (Figure 2-1). These loops are termed *hypervariable* or *complementarity-determining regions* (CDRs). As well as varying greatly in sequence, the lengths and conformations of these

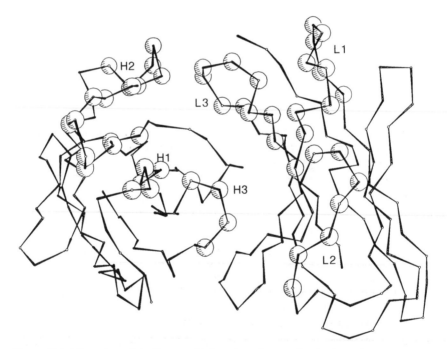

Figure 2-1. View down into the combining site of an antibody, form the direction of an antigen. The Cα positions of residues within the complementarity-determining regions (CDRs) are encircled.

loops also differ widely from one antibody to the next. The antigen-binding properties of a given antibody are thus principally encoded within the primary and tertiary structure of its CSRs.

Because the ACS is involved in both the recognition and binding of an antigen target, attempts to generate antibodies with specified antigen-binding properties have primarily focused on direct manipulation of the architecture of the CDRs. Several quite different approaches have been applied to the problem, and the methods can be grouped under the following categories:

- Transfer of affinity and specificity characteristics between different antibodies by direct substitution of the loops that form the antigen-binding site. This method, pioneered by Winter and associates, is termed *CDR replacement.* [9-11]
- Introduction of novel ligand recognition properties (for example, for a metal ion) by construction of the binding site motif for that ligand, taken from another protein structure, within the ACS. [12, 13]
- Engineering of the antigen-binding properties by site-directed mutagenesis of individual residues in the antibody CDRs. [14, 15]

This chapter will focus on the last approach. For a given antibody, there are essentially two ways in which one can go about making specific mutations within the CDRs to modify the antigen-binding properties. One method is to introduce amino acid substitutions throughout the ACS in a somewhat arbitrary fashion. Thus, each residue in turn could be mutated to an alanine, for example, in order to establish its contribution to the binding of antigen. However, because it is known that for each antibody the antigen-binding properties are etched into the tertiary architecture of the combining site, it is clearly more desirable to use a method that incorporates some rationalization of the choice of mutations at the structural level, that is, an approach in which the antibody structure itself guides the design of the mutagenesis experiments. The protocols described below provide a general outline as to how such a combined strategy can be applied to the engineering of antibody affinity (Figure 2-2).

DEFINING THE PARENT ANTIBODY SYSTEM

When attempting to modify affinity through site-specific mutagenesis, one must begin by first characterizing the parent molecule, which provides a template for the subsequent protein engineering. It is important to establish

- the three-dimensional structure of the ACS
- the mode of antigen binding

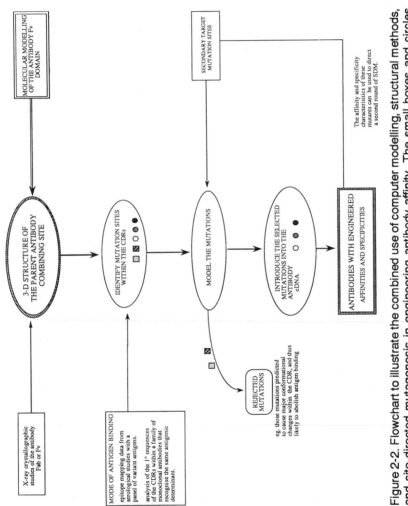

Figure 2-2. Flowchart to illustrate the combined use of computer modelling, structural methods, and site-directed mutagenesis in engineering antibody affinity. The small boxes and circles represent single mutation sites within an antibody CDR.

In an ideal situation, this information would be obtained from an analysis of the crystal structures of the free antibody and the antibody in its complex with antigen. The number of antibodies whose structures have been determined by crystallography is far less than the number for which 1° sequence data is available. If antibody-antigen complexes are examined, then the number is still fewer. Only two examples have been reported where the three-dimensional structures of the antibody both with and without the antigen have been determined: one with a peptide antigen[16] and the other with a protein ligand.[17] Realistically, therefore, one must look at other means of establishing both the structure of the ACS and the mode of antigen binding. The latter issue can be addressed, in part at least, through the use of epitope mapping studies.[18-20] To circumvent the absence of a crystal structure for the antibody of interest, the methods of molecular modelling can be used.

MODELLING THE ENTIRE ANTIBODY-COMBINING SITE

The majority of the structure of the antigen-binding fragment is conserved from one antibody to the next (as already discussed). Predicting the tertiary structure of the ACS, therefore, reduces to a problem of modelling the conformation of the individual CDRs that form it (see Figure 2-1). Molecular modelling of protein structure, in general, is regarded as a rather hit-or-miss procedure. At the end of the day, the outcome of any modelling exercise will be largely determined by the accuracy with which the method is able to reproduce the conformational constraints exerted on the polypeptide chain in the environment of the protein structure where it folds. In this respect, the antibody hypervariable loops represent a comparatively well-defined system. Chothia and Lesk have demonstrated that for at least five of the six antibody hypervariable loops (L1 to L3, H1 and H2), despite the high sequence variability between them, only a small number of main chain conformations are adopted.[21] In addition, the particular conformation adopted by a given CDR is determined by a few key, conserved residues in the loop sequence. The identities of these residues, and the canonical structure sets they delineate, are discussed by Chothia and Lesk[21] in the section entitled The Modelling of Antibody-Combining Sites. The conformational space available to these loops appears significantly less than one might have predicted for structures of this typ located on the surface of a protein molecule. As a consequence, one can be more optimistic about the success of molecular modelling techniques in the prediction of CDR conformations than for loop structures within proteins in general.

Constructing the F_V Framework

Before modelling the antibody CDRs, it is necessary to build the framework onto which they are placed. Because its structure is highly conserved,[22] this is a relatively straightforward exercise. A single high-resolution antibody structure, with high sequence homology to the antibody under study, can be extracted from the Brookhaven Protein Data Bank.[23] Sequence differences can be corrected using the maximum overlap procedure (MOP); this method is described in detail in the next section. Alternatively, the light and heavy chains can be modelled from separate starting structures. The individual V_L and V_H domains are selected from different antibodies, composed of V_L1/V_H1 and V_L2/V_H2, on the basis of sequence homology. A least-squares fit of V_L1 onto V_L2 in the V_L2/V_H2 pair is performed, and the the V_L2 domain is removed to leave a framework corresponding to V_L1/V_H2, with the domain pairing of antibody 2 (Figure 2-3).

In some instances, the framework regions taken from antibody crystal structures deposited in the data base have been found to contain a number of areas where the positions of the residues within it are poorly defined,[24] as indicated by their high temperature factors. These regions should be replaced with consensus conformations taken from other antibodies in the data base.

Modelling the CDRs

For the antibody of interest, one can proceed with the modelling of the six CDRs that constitute the antigen-binding site. Several options can be considered.

Modelling by Homology. This method, termed the *maximum overlap procedure* (MOP),[25, 26] is in some ways analogous to the use of canonical structure groups of the type advocated by Chothia and Lesk[21] (see text following). An outline of the procedure is given in Figure 2-4. First, a data base of possible loop conformations is obtained for each CDR type from the coordinate sets for all the antibody structures deposited in the Brookhaven Protein Data Bank, and for those that may be available from crystallographic laboratories on request. The CDR to be modelled, say L1, is then compared with all the L1 loop structures represented in the data base. A template structure for the backbone conformation of the new CDR is chosen on the basis of both length and sequence homology with existing structures. The selected loop is then fitted onto the model framework, using an interactive molecular graphics program such as FRODO[27] or HYDRA,[28] matching the take-off positions of the loop from the framework, at the N and C termini, with those of the original CDR it has replaced. Side chain substitutions between the template structure and the modelled CDR must then be introduced. This can be readily achieved using the REPLACE and REFI com-

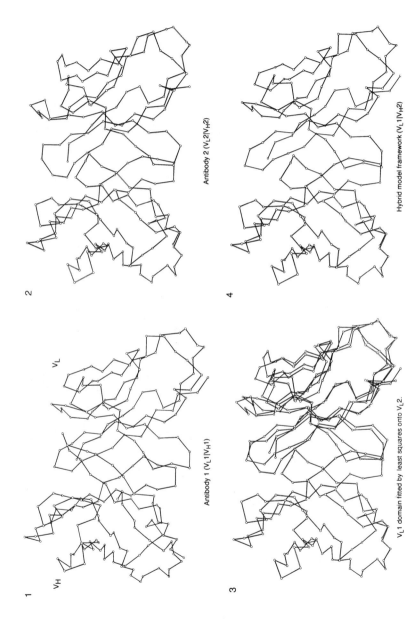

Figure 2-3. Construction of a hybrid modelled F_v framework, using V_H and V_L domains that are not selected from the crystal structure of the same antibody, but from two different Fabs.

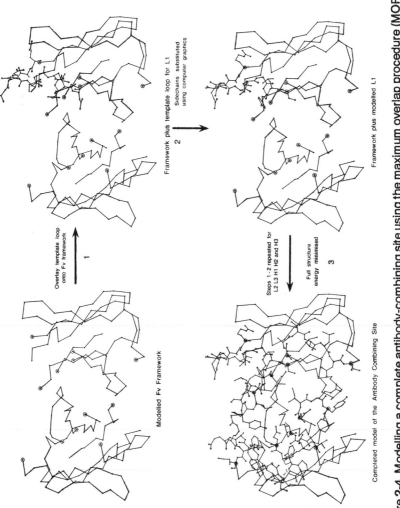

Figure 2-4. Modelling a complete antibody-combining site using the maximum overlap procedure (MOP). The hatched circles indicate the Cα take-off positions of the CDRs from the Fv framework.

mands available within FRODO. The new side chain is positioned onto the parent structure using a template conformation (in REPLACE), and the fit between them is then optimized using REFI.[29] Typically, 50 cycles of optimization are required to give a convergence of <0.01 Å. Atoms in the substituted side chain are thus overlapped, as far as possible, onto those in the parent structure. The procedure is then repeated for the remaining five CDRs, and the final model is subjected to energy minimization, using the CHARMM[30] OR GROMOS[31] potentials, to obtain a final prediction for the F_v structure.

The situation becomes more complex if the CDR to be modelled is of a length not represented in the structural data base being used. In this event, it is necessary to make manual insertions or deletions in the closest template structure for the loop, using the computer graphics, while ensuring that the overall shape of the loop and intraloop hydrogen bonding is maintained. As a consequence, the results of this procedure are highly dependent on user interaction, and the overall success of the method falls off rapidly. The procedure also requires one to make the assumption that any changes resulting from the insertion or deletion of residues within the loop structure are accommodated locally, and not transmitted to other regions of CDR or the framework. For this reason, the method is only really applicable to those cases where the insertions or deletions must be made in the middle section of the template loop.[32] In all other instances, CDRs in this category should be modelled using an alternative procedure, such as the combined algorithm method,[33] that allows the loop greater conformational freedom to respond to any changes made within it.

In summary, the MOP method can be expected to work well if a good template for the modelled loop is already present in the data base. However, if a suitable starting structure for the model loop cannot be found, on either the criterion of residue length or sequence homology, this approach can not be used with any confidence (Table 2-1). This is principally because the method makes no allowance for any changes in the backbone conformation of a loop, which may result from residue substitutions, insertions, or deletions in the model loop sequence and that of the template on which it is based. As a result, the CDR is effectively trapped in a local potential energy minimum, and the method is liable to give an incorrect model.[24, 34]

The Key Residue or Canonical Structure Method. This approach, devised by Chothia and colleagues,[35] also exploits the antibody structural data base. The modelled conformation for a particular loop is chosen on the basis of the presence of critical or key residues at particular positions in the CDR sequence, rather than on the basis of length and sequence homology sampled over the entire loop length, as in the MOP method. As with the latter, this procedure must currently be implemented manually. Details of its application can be found in Chapter 1.

Table 2-1. RMS Differences Between the Modelled and Observed Structures of the CDRs for the Gloop2 Antibody

	MOP method				CAM method			
	Global fit		Local fit		Global fit		Local fit	
CDR	MC	all	MC	all	MC	all	MC	all
L1	0.88	2.36	0.70	1.99	0.93	1.98	0.86	1.95
L2	0.95	1.39	0.44	1.17	0.54	1.29	0.44	1.20
L3	0.55	1.82	0.54	1.74	1.19	1.82	0.72	1.74
H1	0.60	1.47	0.44	1.31	0.69	1.35	0.43	0.62
H2	1.70	2.80	1.42	2.55	0.66	1.46	0.66	1.46
H3	1.76	4.89	1.12	4.28	0.51	2.41	0.48	2.26

Data taken from the 2.8Å x-ray structure of Gloop2, in the P1 crystal form (Jeffrey, P. Personal communication).

For modelling loops that contain the required key residues, which determine the particular structure adopted within the canonical group, the method works very well.[35] Where the lengths of the loop to be modelled and the template structure on which it is based are identical, and the sequence homology between them is also high, the results of the canonical structure and MOP methods will in most instances be comparable. If the CDR to be modelled shows relatively low sequence homologies to all the data base loops, the canonical approach has a distinct advantage over the MOP procedure. This is because in these circumstances the identification of a small number of conserved, structure-determining residues, in a sequence that otherwise shows poor homology with all the loops in the antibody data base, can provide a clearcut choice as to the best structure on which to model the conformation of the unknown CDR. With the MOP method, one would have to resort to a guess.

The Combined Algorithm Method.   When the antibody to be modelled contains CDRs of lengths that are not represented in the database, or which lack the critical key residues, the use of either the MOP or the canonical structure method to predict the conformations of these loops is unsatisfactory. If these methods are used, the results are likely to be poor[36,37] (see Table 2-1). Therefore, an alternative protocol is required to tackle the modelling of these loops. This is available in the form of the combined algorithm method of Martin and coworkers.[33] The method, which is applicable to all CDRs, combines the advantages of the data base methods with those of the *ab initio* conformational searching routine, CONGEN.[38] In the latter, a much wider sampling of the conformational space available to a given loop is achieved than when using a data base method alone (for example, MOP). The model structure is therefore less likely to become trapped in a false, local minimum, but the expense in computing time of such procedures is high. Combining the conformational search algorithm with a data base method allows one to reduce the search time while retaining the wider sampling of possible conformations available to the loop.

The combined algorithm method is implemented using the modelling package CAMAL.* This incorporates the basic algorithm with a range of other facilities that will allow a CDR loop to be processed from its 1° sequence through to a prediction for the tertiary structure. In order to identify protein loops of the same general shape as those seen in antibodies, sets of inter-loop Cα distance constraints were derived from an analysis of known antibody crystal structures.[39] A different set of constraints is used for each CDR type (for example, L1 or L2 or L3).

Full documentation on the modelling of an antibody-combining site by use of the combined algorithm is provided with the program suite, but the overall strategy for using this protocol can be summarized as follows:

1. Construct the model ACS framework.
2. Model CDRs of five residues or shorter, using the conformational search procedure (CONGEN) alone. Go to #8.
3. For loops of six residues or longer, search the Protein Data Bank using the appropriate distance constraint set. Extract the loops that match these constraints at both the N and C termini. This will provide a family of template structures for the backbone conformation of the modelled loop (Figure 2-5).
4. Overlap the data base loops onto the framework. In order to orient the loops correctly, they are overlapped onto the CDRs present on the original framework, which are then deleted from the coordinate set.
5. Correct the sequences and add explicit hydrogens.
6. In the case of loops of six or seven residues, the conformational space available to the backbone of the loop appears to be well-saturated in the current data base of crystal structures. It is therefore only necessary to carry conformational searching of the side chain positions. Go to #8.
7. For loops of eight or more residues, delete the midsection of the loop and reconstruct with CONGEN (Figure 2-6).
8. Reconstruct all the residue side chains of the loop with CONGEN.
9. Calculate the energy for each conformation using a solvent modified potential implemented in GROMSCAN, a modified version of the molecular dynamics program suite from van Gunsteren in Groningen (GROMOS).

---

* The modelling package and comprehensive documentation for its use can be obtained from Oxford Molecular at the University of Oxford, Oxford, England.

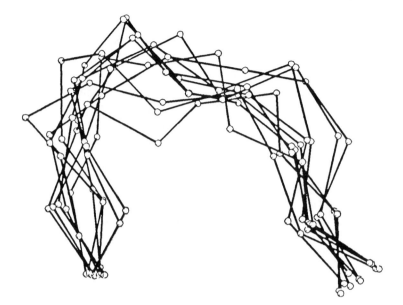

Figure 2-5. Family of data base loops extracted from the protein data bank for CDR-L1 of HyHel 5, using Cα distance constraints derived from an analysis of immunoglobulin structures.[33, 39]

10. Screen the five lowest energy conformations using FILTER, an algorithm that scores each loop conformation according to the similarity of the residues at each position in the CDR to those in the corresponding data base loop from which it was derived. Out of this group, the final model chosen for the CDR is that which shows the highest sequence homology to the data base template used in its construction.

Table 2-1 shows the accuracy with which antibody loop structures can be predicted using the combined algorithm method.

When an entire combining site is built using this method, it is important to define an order for the construction. This is because the individual CDRs are not isolated units on the framework, but interact to differing degrees with one another across the combining site. The packing of a given CDR will therefore be influenced by the environment of its neighbors. An analysis of the inter-loop contacts in antibodies for which crystal structures are available suggests that the following order of construction should be used:

L2 < H3 < H1 < H2 < L1 < L3

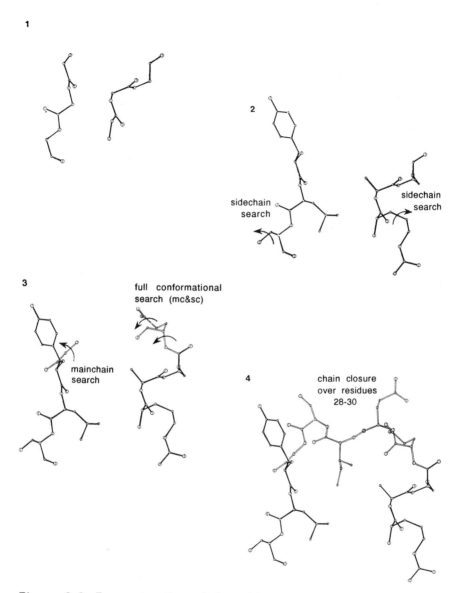

Figure 2-6. Reconstruction of the mid-section of an antibody CDR {RAS[IS(ISG)Y]LS} using CONGEN. (1) The bottom sections of the loop, which join to the F_v framework, are taken from a family of template structures extracted from the protein data bank (see Figure 2-5). (2) A conformational search is carried out for each side chain position in the lower regions of the loop (residues 24, 25, 26, 33, and 34). (3) A full conformational search is then made for both the main chain and side chain of the residues flanking the top (ISG) of the CDR. (4) The top of the loop is reconstructed using the chain closure algorithm of Go and Scheraga.[57] Steps 2–4 are carried out using the conformational searching algorithm within CONGEN.[38]

Optimizing the Construction of a Combining Site

As discussed in the preceding sections, the MOP and key residue methods can work well when the CDR being modelled is represented by a loop of identical length and high sequence homology in the available data base of antibody crystal structures or, alternatively, fits into one of the canonical sets defined by Chothia. Both methods, however, are severely limited by the small size of the current data base of antibody crystal structures from which to model a given loop. This can be overcome, to some extent, by expanding the template set to include loops from all known protein crystal structures. The use of nonhomologous structures in modelling protein loops was proposed by Jones and Thirup,[40] and has been implemented in the program COM-POSER by Sutcliffe and coworkers.[41] In contrast to the purely knowledge-based approaches, the combined algorithm method has been shown to perform extremely well for all CDRs in the five antibody systems on which it has been tried,[24, 33, 36] but the disadvantage of this procedure is that it is very computer-intensive. The most efficient way to model an antibody-combining site must be, therefore, to combine the different approaches.[36, 37, 42] CDRs that show a good match with one of the loops already contained in the existing antibody data base should be modelled using the data base loop as a template structure for the new CDR. In most cases, the easiest way to judge the "best fit" is on the basis of the identity of key residues between the two sequences (model and template). The remaining antibody loops in the combining site can then be built using the combined algorithm method.

TARGETING SUITABLE MUTATIONS WITHIN THE CDRs

The residues within an ACS are clearly not all equally suitable candidates for mutagenesis. Engineering antibody affinity by the introduction of individual or grouped mutations across the combining site requires one to assess the suitability of each position within it for modification by protein engineering. A subset of sites within the CDRs can then be defined as being those positions at which the residues can be mutated, with the strong expectation that this will result in a modification of the antigen-binding properties of the molecule, but not a complete loss of affinity. How does one go about targeting such sites and choosing the individual mutations to be made at each?

In the first instance, all those residues that play, or are likely to play, an important role in maintaining the structural integrity of the combining site can be excluded. These include

- The so-called *key* residues within each CDR — identified by Chothia and colleagues[35] as important in determining the canonical structure of the loop.
- Residues involved in strong CDR-CDR interactions in the parent antibody; Roberts and colleagues[14] showed that the mutation of a variable residue (Glu50) at the base of H2, in an antipeptide antibody (Gloop2), resulted in the abolition of antigen binding. In the parent antibody Glu50 (H2) makes two hydrogen bonds, one within the loop and the other to Tyr94 in L3.
- Residues that are conserved in the combining site across a panel of antibodies that recognize overlapping epitopes.

The next step is to identify out of the remaining residues the most appropriate sites at which to target the introduction of mutations with the intention of modifying the antibody-binding affinity. If there is a crystal structure for the antibody-antigen complex, this is relatively straightforward (see below). More likely, however, is the situation where one does not start from a three-dimensional structure of the bound complex. In this event, there are two possible alternatives that can be considered, depending on whether the structure of the antigen moiety is known. If it is, then this can be used in conjunction with the structure of the ACS (either modelled or from x-ray studies) to generate a model for the docked complex (Figure 2-7). The two molecules are docked manually, maintaining both as rigid bodies and using data from epitope mapping experiments[25] as a rough guide in orientating them with respect to one another. The positions of the two molecules can then be adjusted more precisely to optimize their interaction (good setereochemical complementarity and hydrogen bonding), consistent with the general features listed above. The whole procedure can be accomplished within an interactive graphics program such as FRODO. The model should then be subjected to energy minimization, to relieve bad steric clashes and optimize the bonding interactions within the complex. Further refinements to the model might then be made at a later stage, using the results of the protein engineering experiments designed on the basis of it.

With a structure or model of the antibody-antigen complex, the interface between the two molecules can then be examined to look for areas where mutations might be introduced to moderate the interaction. At this stage it is appropriate to list some general observations about the nature of antibody-antigen interactions, made on the basis of the structural studies that have been reported of anti-protein antibodies complexed with their protein antigens. The following appear to be key features of these complexes.

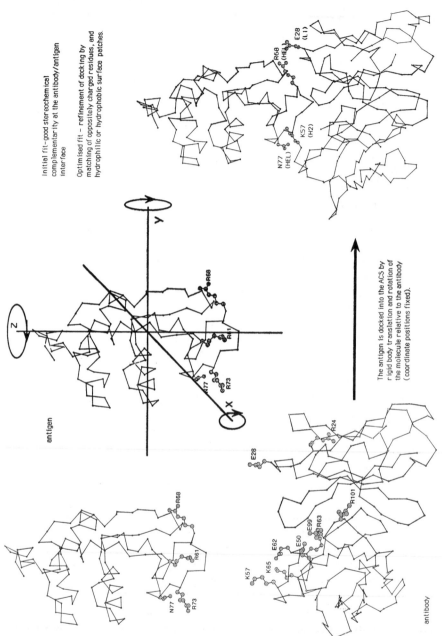

Figure 2-7. Generating a computer model of the antibody-antigen complex. The atoms of the charged residues in the antibody-combining site and the antigen epitope are represented by hatched circles. In this example, the antibody-antigen pair are Gloop2 and hen egg lysozyme, respectively.[51] The outer edges of the epitope on the protein (Asn77 and Arg680) were defined from epitope mapping studies.[25]

- There is extremely high stereochemical complementarity between the surfaces of the bound antigen and the ACS. Depressions in one are filled by protuberances in the other. The tight fit of the two molecules results in the exclusion of water at their interface.
- Many of the CDR residues that are involved in binding to antigen are in highly solvent accessible positions within the ACS.
- Hydrophobic and hydrophilic patches on the surface of the antigen match with comparable areas on the antibody.
- Salt linkages, hydrogen bonds, and Van der Waals interactions all contribute to the enthalpy of binding. Hydrogen bonds contribute to the specificity of the interaction.
- The conformational changes that accompany the binding of the antibody and antigen are small. They mainly involve local adjustments in the side chain positions of interacting residues, but one example of a small but systematic rearrangement in the relative orientation of V_H and V_L domains has also been reported;[17] this is indicative of an induced fit to the antigen rather than a "lock and key" type interaction.

On the basis of these general features, one can identify a number of distinct types of residue change that one may wish to introduce into the combining site:

- Mutations that increase or decrease the bulk of residue side chains. In this way the fit of the antibody to its antigen may be improved or impaired, thus altering the strength of binding. Examples of this type of substitution are Ala to Val, Ser to Thr, Asp to Glu, Lys to Arg, and Ser to Tyr. Note that the hydrophobic/hydrophilic character of the residue is retained in the mutation.
- Mutations that moderate the hydrogen bonding potential of residues in the ACS by introducing or removing side chain groups that can act as hydrogen bonding acceptors or donors. For example, the mutation Tyr to Phe removes the hydrogen bonding capacity of the side chain while retaining the bulk volume.
- Mutations that alter the electrostatic profile of the combining site. The substitution Lys to Gln, for example, has the effect of removing a center of positive charge, while retaining much of the effective side chain volume of the residue and also its capacity to hydrogen bond.
- Mutations confined to surface residues within the ACS, that is, the areas directly involved in antigen contact. Surface residues can be identified by calculating the solvent accessibility of the residues using the algorithm of Lee and Richards.[43]
- Mutations involving buried residues in the CDRs, which have an indirect influence on antigen binding.

In addition, more radical modifications can be identified:

- The insertion or deletion of residues within a CDR.
- The replacement of entire CDRs.

These last two classes of modification might allow one to engineer a more dramatic increase or decrease in the surface area of interaction between the antibody and its antigen than could be achieved by simple residue replacements, or to introduce additional functional properties into the combining site (for example, a metal binding site) while still retaining the antigen binding.

Figure 2-8 demonstrates how a consideration of the factors discussed in this section can be used to identify a set of potential mutation sites in an antibody CDR.

When the structure of the antigen is unknown, the choice of mutations in the first round of protein engineering experiments must be guided solely on the basis of a structural analysis of the antibody itself, supplemented with any information that is available from serological studies pertaining to the nature of the interaction with antigen. In this instance, the first round of mutagenesis experiments can be seen as an opportunity to attain a low resolution working model of the complex, rather than as a directed attempt to engineer antibody affinity. As a consequence, it is probably most efficient to probe the interaction at a number of different positions covering the breadth of the combining site, with a suite of mutations at each ranging from conservative to neoconservative changes. Mutating a glutamic acid residue to Ser, Leu, and Arg in turn, for example, should allow one to establish if that residue is involved in a hydrophilic, hydrophobic, or charged interaction within the antigen bound complex, or none at all.

	24	25*	26	27	a	b	28	29*	30	31	32	33*	34
Gloops 1 & 2	R	A	S	Q	—	—	E	I	S	G	Y	L	S
Gloops 3 & 4	R	S	S	Q	I	I	V	H	F	N	G	N	T
Gloop 5	K	S	S	Q	I	I	Y	S	F	N	Q	K	N

*Key residue as defined by Chothia et al.[35]

☐ Boxed areas show the position of residues in L1 that are conserved between different antibodies in the series.

Figure 2-8. Defining a set of primary mutation sites within a CDR, for the purpose of engineering the antibody affinity. A comparison of the sequences of five anti-peptide antibodies that recognize a set of overlapping epitopes on hen egg lysozyme.[51] Residues that are neither conserved between the different monoclonals nor fall within the key residue definitions given by Chothia and coworkers[35] are good candidates for mutagenesis.

MODELLING THE MUTATIONS INTO THE ANTIBODY CDRs

The starting point for this exercise is the three-dimensional structure of the parent antibody, determined either from x-ray crystallography or by molecular modelling. It is then necessary to select the method that is most appropriate for the modelling of the chosen mutations. This will depend to a large extent on the nature of the changes that are to be made. These can be categorized as follows:

- Amino acid substitutions
- Insertions or deletions in the CDR
- CDR replacement

Amino acid substitutions represent the simplest case, involving the replacement of one or more amino acid residues in the CDR by others. There is good evidence to indicate that, in most instances, the changes within loops as a result of single site mutations tend to be accommodated locally.[44] For residue replacements that involve making conservative substitutions, in particular at surface positions on the CDR, it is only necessary in most cases to consider the placement of the new amino acid side chain in the structure. The MOP method offers one of the easiest means of doing this. A description of the use of this method for mutating residue side chains within a loop *in situ*, that is, within the ACS structure, has already been given in the earlier account of modelling antibody-combining sites by the MOP approach. Implicit in the use of this method is the assumption that the mutation will cause no conformational changes in the backbone of the loop.

If the amino acid substitutions are nonconservative, or involve residues that may be important in CDR-CDR interactions, the MOP can not be used. This is because changes of this type are likely to alter the conformation of the backbone. For example, if a surface hydrophilic residue is mutated to a hydrophobic one, the loop may refold to bury the hydrophobic group and minimize its exposure to solvent. Nonconservative substitutions are best modelled using the combined algorithm method. The basic protocol for doing this can be illustrated by looking at a specific example. Consider the mutation of Q27 and E28 to L27 and S28, respectively, in an 11 residue CDR L1, of sequence R[24] A S I S I S G Y L S.[34]

- Use the L1 structure in the parent antibody to provide a template for the loop construction.
- The section to be reconstructed is then defined to give (1) a full conformational search for the residues that are being mutated and (2) the position of chain closure close to the apex of the loop.

  In the example given, therefore, the construction made would be

R A S [I S (I S G) Y]L S

with residues 27 to 32 deleted from the template structure, full side chain searches for I27, S28, and Y32, and chain closure over the trio I29, S30, and G31 (refer to Figure 2-5). The conformation of the mutated L1 will thus only be restrained toward that in the parent antibody at the junction of the CDR loop with the framework, that is, those regions where the sequence is entirely conserved between parent and mutant.

- Screen the five lowest energy conformations, using the FILTER algorithm, against a set of loops derived from a data base search for an L1 loop of comparable length (11 residues in this case), to give a final structure for the mutant L1.

Insertions and deletions made within a CDR may have a number of different structural consequences. These will depend on both the nature of the residues added or deleted and the position at which they are introduced. Considering the first point, if a glycine residue is introduced, a much greater degree of potential conformational flexibility will be conferred upon the polypeptide backbone of the loop, in the region of the insertion, than if a proline were added. With regard to the position of the insertion or deletion when the modification is made toward the middle of the loop, the changes are likely to be accommodated locally, as with single site mutations, although with somewhat larger conformational adjustments extending into the backbone of the loop. For insertions or deletions made at points closer to the framework junctions, however, the situation becomes more complex. It is then necessary to consider not only the effect of the changes on the conformation of the individual loop in which they are made, but also perturbations to the packing and structure of the neighboring CDRs that surround it within the combining site.

The most appropriate method to model mutant CDRs of this type will therefore depend on the nature of the changes to the sequence:

- Insertions and deletions made in the mid-section of a loop can be modelled manually, using the computer graphics, if the resultant CDR is one for which a suitable template is available in the data base of antibody structures (that is, same length, CDR type, good sequence homology). A MOP-type approach is used, as illustrated in Figure 2-9. It should be remembered, however, that because this method does not account for the possibility of large changes in the backbone conformation of the loop, if the residue composition of the loop is altered drastically by the changes, there is a danger of generating a structure that represents a false, local minimum.

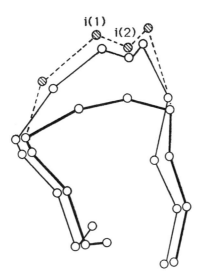

Figure 2-9. Modelling a loop insertion by the maximum overlap procedure (MOP). The template structure (narrow, solid line) for the new CDR is overlayed onto the original CDR (bold, solid line), and two residues {(i) and (i+1)} are built into the loop using the template to guide their placement. The positions of the residues on either side of the insertion must also be changed to accommodate the change in loop length. The final conformation of the modelled mid-section of the loop is shown by dashed lines.

- Where insertions or deletions are made in the middle of the CDR, but no loops of corresponding length or good sequence homology to the mutant are available in the data base, the structure of the loop should be modelled, *ab initio,* in the presence of the other five loops in the combining site. This can be done using the combined algorithm method; details of this procedure can be found in the earlier section on the modelling of antibody-combining sites. Adding or removing residues manually on the graphics, with no template structure as a guide, is highly subjective, and the reproducibility of the results is low.[24, 42]
- Insertions and deletions made toward either the N or C terminus of the CDR should also be modelled using the combined algorithm method. Depending on the nature of the modifications, it may also be necessary to model both the loop into which the mutations are to be introduced, and also to remodel the conformations of those CDRs with which it interacts (for example, if bulky residues, such as isoleucine and tryptophan, were to be inserted close to the base of the loop).

CDR replacements are modelled in the same way that individual loops are constructed onto the F_v framework when generating a model for the entire combining site. As mentioned earlier, when using the MOP method, particular attention should be paid to the nature of the CDR/framework junction. Because the residue in the framework immediately before the N terminus of a CDR influences the take-off angle of the loop relative to the framework, the junction in the engineered antibody should be modelled to correspond with that in the antibody from which the transplanted CDR is derived. Practically, this may necessitate the mutation of a residue in the framework of the engineered antibody in order to accommodate the foreign CDR.[11, 45]

Once the mutations identified as suitable targets for protein engineering have been modelled into the ACS, these structures can be compared with that of the parent antibody. The mutations that are predicted to cause large conformational changes within the backbone of the CDRs, or in their relative packing arrangement, can be rejected because these are likely to abolish antigen-binding completely. The remainder can then be introduced into the combining site by site-directed mutagenesis.

PRODUCTION OF THE ENGINEERED ANTIBODIES *IN VITRO*

Ab initio design of antibody-combining sites does not carry with it an automatic guarantee of success. It is therefore important that any method of production *in vitro* should, first and foremost, allow the outcome of the design process to be assessed rapidly. The *Xenopus* oocyte expression system offers such a route, and Roberts and Rees demonstrated that it could be readily incorporated as part of a general scheme, shown in Figure 2-10, for the production and screening of mutant antibodies.[46, 47] The steps involved can be outlined as follows:

- Full length light chain and heavy chain antibody cDNA clones are subcloned into the M13 mutagenesis vector.
- The designated mutations are then introduced into the CDRs by site-directed mutagenesis* of the appropriate M13 clone using an oligonucleotide mismatch primer.
- RNA transcripts of the mutant cDNA clones in an SP6 expression vector are synthesized.
- Light or heavy chain mutant antibodies are then prepared by comicroinjection of the mutant RNA transcript with that of the appropriate wild-type heavy or light chain into the cytoplasm of *Xenopus* oocytes. Combined light and heavy chain mutant antibodies are prepared by the comicroinjection of two mutant RNA transcripts.

---

* Various methods can be used to perform the *in vitro* mutagenesis, with different levels of efficiency. A useful summary is given in Version 1 of the instruction booklet accompanying the Amersham Mutagenesis System.

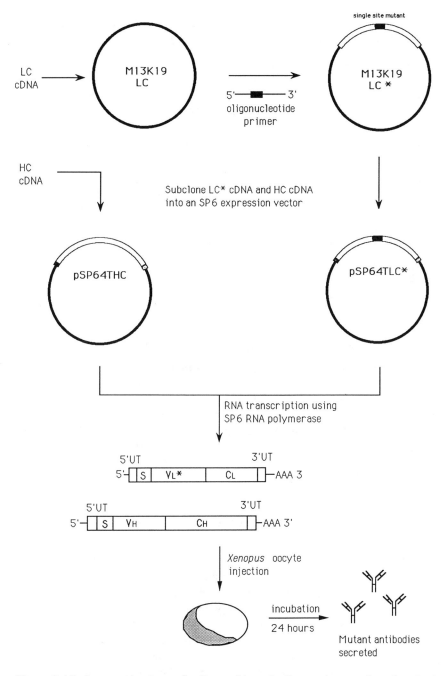

Figure 2-10. A general scheme for the rapid production and screening of mutant antibodies, adapted from Roberts and Rees.[46]

- The antigen-binding characteristics of the secreted antibody are then quantitated by radioimmunoassay using oocyte supernatant.

Full experimental details of the molecular biology manipulations integral to this scheme can be found in references 14, 46, and 48, and a more general description can be found in *Molecular Cloning—A Laboratory Manual* by Sambrook and colleagues.[49] The practical steps involved in the preparation and microinjection of mRNA into *Xenopus* oocytes are discussed in reference 50. Binding assays with the mutant antibodies can be carried out as follows:

- Microtiter plates are coated with goat anti-mouse IgG antibody (affinity purified) at a concentration of 50 μgml^{-1} in PBS for 18 hours at 4°C.
- The plates are then blocked with PBS/0.05% Tween20 for 30 minutes at 4°C, then washed twice for one minute at room temperature.
- Oocyte test supernatant is added and the plates are incubated at room temperature for 6 hours.
- Plates are washed and incubated with ^{125}I-labelled antigen, with and without inhibitor (cold antigen), at room temperature for a further 6 hours.
- Plates are washed with PBS/Tween (3 × 1 minute) and individual wells are cut and counted using a gamma scintillation counter.
- K_D values can then be obtained from Scatchard analysis.

The conditions given above have been optimized for the binding of the Gloop2 antibody and its mutants to peptide and protein antigens,[48,51] but the method should be generally applicable.

Once an antibody with the desired antigen-binding properties has been generated, the cDNA encoding the altered primary sequence can be subcloned into alternative expression systems for over-expression and scaling-up of the production from 2–4 μgml^{-1} to ≥ 100 μgml^{-1} [52, 53] for more detailed studies of structure and function.

AN APPRAISAL OF THE ENGINEERED ANTIBODY AFFINITY

The antigen-binding properties of the mutant antibodies, which incorporate specifically-engineered amino acid changes within their CDRs, provide a direct measure of the success of the design strategy by which the mutations were chosen. As such, they can also provide a basis from which to refine further modifications to the antigen-binding characteristics of an individual antibody. This can be illustrated by reference to some specific examples taken from a study of the anti-peptide antibody Gloop2.[51, 54]

Gloop2 was raised against a peptide immunogen containing the loop determinant of hen egg lysozyme (HEL). It binds to the loop peptide with a

K_D of ~ 10^8 M^{-1}, and to the protein antigen with a tenfold lower affinity.[51] Modelling of the antibody-lysozyme complex,[25] using serological data to define the protein epitope and a MOP-generated model of the ACS, showed that in one of the possible modes of antigen-binding, two charged residues lying at the outer edges of the combining site, Glu28 in L1 and Lys56 in H2, could interact with the surface residues Arg68 and Asn77 in HEL. It was suggested that these, and other charged residues within the combining site, might be crucial for antigen binding, perhaps guiding the relative orientations of the antibody and its antigen prior to formation of the fully bound complex. Three mutation sites within the Gloop2 CDRs were targeted for protein engineering, on the basis of the modelled complex:[14] two charged residues lying at the peripheral edges of the ACS (Glu28 and Lys56), and a third, Glu 50, at the bottom of the antigen-binding cleft. Changes were made at each site to remove the charge from the residue side chain but retain the hydrogen-bonding capacity.

The results (Table 2-2) showed that for the two residues at opposite edges of the combining site, removal of their charges did not abolish antigen binding. For binding to the peptide antigen, both the individual substitutions of Lys56 to Gln in H2, and Glu28 to Ser in L1, gave no measurable change in the antibody affinity. The L1 mutation, however, did produce a fivefold increase in the binding affinity for the protein antigen. When the light and heavy chain mutations were combined, the antibody affinity was enhanced still further, the double mutant (Glu28Ser/Lys56Gln) binding to HEL with a tenfold higher affinity than wild-type Gloop2. Binding to the peptide antigen was also improved (fourfold) in the double mutant. In marked contrast, the substitution of Glu50 (H2) to Ser, in the central region of the combining site, completely abolished binding to both the peptide and protein antigens.

Table 2-2. Affinity Constants of Mutant Antibodies Relative to Wild-type Gloop2

		Antigen	
Mutant	*CDR*	*Peptide*	*Protein*
Glu28Ser	L1	no change	+5 fold
Tyr32Asp	L1	−10 fold	no change
Tyr32Ser	L1	−10 fold	no change
Tyr32Phe	L1	no change	no change
Glu50Ser	H2	no binding	no binding
Lys56Gln	H2	no change	no change
Glu28Ser + Lys56Gln	L1/H2	+4 fold	+10 fold

It is also useful to illustrate the type of behavior that one might observe with an incremental series of mutations at one position in the CDR loop, designed to probe the specific role of a residue in antigen binding. Three different amino acid substitutions were made at Tyr 32 in Gloop2 L1, to Phe, Ser, and Asp.[55] Removal of the hydrogen-bonding group in the side chain had no measurable effect on the antigen affinity. The loss of the aromatic ring (Tyr32Ser and Tyr32Asp), however, caused a tenfold reduction in peptide affinity (see Table 2-2). These data suggest that Tyr32 plays a hydrophobic role in peptide binding.

Thus, from the results of the first round of mutagenesis experiments with Gloop2, a number of useful points emerge that should be considered when deciding upon a second round of protein engineering experiments.

- The peptide and protein antigens appear to be recognized somewhat differently. Mutations that affect the affinity of the antibody for one antigen form need not affect the binding of the other.
- To preferentially enhance the binding of the protein antigen, efforst might be focused, in general, on residues lying at the outer edges of the ACS, and in particular on the L1 loop around residue 28.
- Changing residues that are located in the center of the combining site, and which may be structurally determining as a result of CDR-CDR interactions, is likely to abolish antigen binding.

Additional protein engineering experiments carried out with Gloop2 have confirmed that these preliminary observations do provide a useful set of working guidelines on which to base further mutation studies.[55, 56]

Generating antibodies with preselected antigen-binding affinities by direct manipulation of residues within the CDRs has still to come of age. An important limitation is the current small size of the data base describing the molecular and structural origins of antibody specificity. Protein engineering methods, however, offer a relatively rapid means by which to evaluate the contributions of individual residues with the ACS to antigen binding. One can therefore expect to see the addition of a significant amount of data to our knowledge base from this source in the coming years, as the general level of interest in engineering antibody molecules grows. In parallel with this, the task of generating antibody affinities by design should become more routine, and the guarantee of success more certain.

REFERENCES

1. Tonegawa, S. 1983. Somatic generation of antibody diversity. *Nature* 302:575.
2. Lerner, R.A. and Benkovic 1988. Principles of antibody catalysis. *Bioessays* 9:107.

3. Shokat, K.M., and Schultz, P.G. 1990. Catalytic antibodies. *Ann. Rev. Immunol.* 8:335.
4. Novotny, J., Bruccoleri, R.E., Newell, J., Murphy, D., Haber, E., and Karplus, M. 1983. Molecular anatomy of the antibody binding site. *Journal of Biological Chemistry* 258:14433.
5. Lesk, A. and Chothia, C. 1982. Evolution of proteins formed by β-sheets. II. The core of the immunoglobulin domains. *J. Mol. Biol.* 160:325.
6. Chothia, C., Novotny, J., Bruccoleri, R., and Karplus, M. 1985. Domain association in immunoglobulin molecules: The packing of variable domains. *J. Mol. Biol.* 186:651.
7. Wu, T.T. and Kabat, E.A. 1970. An analysis of the sequences of the variable regions of Bence Jones proteins and myeloma light chains and their implications for antibody complementarity. *J. Exp. Med.* 132:211.
8. Alzari, P.M., Lascombe, M.-B., and Poljak, R.J. 1987. Three-dimensional structure of antibodies. *Ann. Rev. Immun.* 6:555.
9. Jones, T.P., Dear, P.H., Foote, J., Neuberger, M., and Winter, G. 1986. Replacing the complementarity-determining regions in a human antibody with those from a mouse. *Nature* 321:522.
10. Verhoeyen, M., Milstein, C., and Winter, G. 1988. Reshaping human antibodies: Grafting an antilysozyme activity. *Science* 239:1534.
11. Riechmann, L., Clark, M., Waldmann, H., and Winter, G. 1988. Reshaping human antibodies for therapy. *Nature* 332:323.
12. Iverson, B., Iverson, S.I., Roberts, V.A., Getzoff, E.D., Tainer, J.A., Benkovic, S.J., and Lerner, R.A. 1990. Metalloantibodies. *Science* 249:659.
13. Roberts, V., Iverson, B., Benkovic, S., Lerner, R.A., Getzoff, E.D., and Tainer, J.A. 1990. Antibody remodelling: A general solution to the design of a metal coordination site in an antibody binding pocket. *Proc. Nat. Acad. Sci. USA* 87:6654.
14. Roberts, S., Cheetham, J.C., and Rees, A.R. 1987. Generation of an antibody with enhanced affinity and specificity for its antigen by protein engineering. *Nature* 328:731.
15. Sharon, J., Gefter, M.L., Manser, T., and Ptashne, M. 1986. Site-directed mutagenesis of an invariant amino acid residue at the variable diversity segments junction of an antibody. *Proc. Nat. Acad. Sci. USA* 83:2628.
16. Stanfield, R.L., Fieser, T.M., Lerner, R.A., and Wilson, I.A. 1990. Crystal structures of an antibody to a peptide and iys complex with peptide antigen at 2.8Å. *Science* 248:712.
17. Bhat, T.N., Bentley, G.A., Fischmann, T.O., Boulot, G., and Poljak, R.J. 1990. Small rearrangements in structures of F_V and Fab fragments of antibody D1,3 on antigen binding. *Nature* 347:483.
18. Smith-Gill, S.J., Wilson, A.C., Potter, M., Feldmann, R.J., and Mainhart, C.R. 1982. Mapping the antigenic epitope for a monoclonal antibody against avian lysozyme. *J. Immunol.* 128:314.
19. Jemmerson, R. and Paterson, Y. 1986. Mapping epitopes on a protein antigen by the proteolysis of antigen–antibody complexes. *Science* 232:1001.

20. Burnens, A., Demotz, S., Corradin, G., Binz, H., and Bosshard, M.R. 1987. Epitope mapping by chemical modification of free antibody-bound protein antigen. *Science* 235:780.

21. Chothia, C. and Lesk, A.M. 1987. Canonical structures for the hypervariable regions of immunoglobulins. *J. Mol. Biol.* 196:901.

22. Davies, D.R., Padlan, E.A., and Segal, D.M. 1975. Three-dimensional structure of immunoglobulins. *Ann. Rev. Biochem.* 44:639.

23. Bernstein, F.C., Koetzle, T.F., Williams, G.J.B., Meyer, E.F., Brice, M.D., Rodgers, J.R., Kennard, O., Shimanouchi, T., and Tasumi, M. 1977. The Protein Data Bank: A computer-based archival file for macromolecular structures. *J. Mol. Biol.* 112:535.

24. Martin, A.C.R. 1990. D. Phil. Thesis, University of Oxford.

25. de la Paz, R., Sutton, B.J., Darsley, M.J., and Rees, A.R. 1986. Modelling of the combining sites of three anti-lysozyme monoclonal antibodies and of the complex between one of the antibodies and its epitope. *EMBO J.* 5:415.

26. Padlan, E.A., Davies, D.R., Pecht, I., Givol, D., and Wright, C. 1976. Model-building studies of antigen binding sites: The hapten-binding site of MOPC-315. *Cold Spring Harbor Quantitative Symposia in Biochemistry* 41:627.

27. Jones, T.A. 1985. Interactive computer graphics: FRODO. *Methods Enzymol.* 115:157.

28. Hubbard, R.E. 1984. The representation of protein structure. In: *Proceedings of the Computer-Aided Design Conference* 99.

29. Hermans, J. and McQueen, J.E. 1974. Computer manipulation of (macro)molecules with the method of local change. *Acta. Cryst.* A30:730.

30. Brooks, B., Bruccoleri, R.E., Olafson, B.D., States, D.J., Swaminathan, S., and Karplus, M. 1983. CHARMM: A program for macromolecular energy, minimization, and dynamics calculations. *Comp. Chem.* 4:187

31. Aqvist, J., van Gunsteren, W.F., Leifonmark, M., and Tapia, O. 1985. A molecular dynamics study of the C-terminal fragment of the L7/L12 ribosomal protein. *J. Mol. Biol.* 183:461.

32. Thornton, J.M., Sibanda, B.L., Edwards, M.S., and Barlow, D.J. 1988. Analysis, design and modification of loop regions in proteins. *Bioessays* 8:63.

33. Martin, A.C.R., Cheetham, J.C., and Rees, A.R. 1989. Modelling antibody hypervariable loops: A combined algorithm. *Proc. Natl. Acad. Sci. USA* 86:9268.

34. Cheetham, J.C., Unpublished work.

35. Chothia, C., Lesk, A.M., Tramontano, A., Levitt, M., Smith-Gill, S.J., Air, G., Sheriff, S., Padlan, E.A., Davies, D., Tulip, W.R., Colman, P.M., Spinelli, S., Alzari, P.M., and Poljak, R.J. 1989. Conformations of immunoglobulin hypervariable regions. *Nature* 342:877.

36. Gregory, D.S., Staunton, D., Martin, A.C.R., Cheetham, J.C., and Rees, A.R. 1991. Antibody-combining sites: prediction and design. *Biochem. Soc. Symp.* 57:147.

37. Cheetham, J.C., Martin, A.C.R., Chothia, C., Lesk, A.M., and Rees, A.R. Unpublished work.

38. Bruccoleri, R.E. and Karplus, M. 1987. Prediction of the folding of short polypeptide segments by uniform conformational sampling. *Biopolymers* 26:137.

39. Martin, A.C.R., Cheetham, J.C., and Rees, A.R. 1991. Use of an all-protein database in antibody loop modelling. *Prot. Eng.* In press.
40. Jones, T.A. and Thirup, S. 1986. Using known sub-structures in protein model building and crystallography. *EMBO J.* 5:819.
41. Sutcliffe, M.J., Hayes, F.R.F., and Blundell, T.L. 1987. Knowledge based modelling of homologous proteins. Part 1: Three dimensional frameworks derived from simultaneous superposition of multiple structures. *Prot. Eng.* 1:377.
42. Martin, A.C.R., Cheetham, J.C., and Rees, A.R. 1991. Modelling antibody combining sites. *Methods Enzymol.* In press.
43. Lee, B.K. and Richards, F.M. 1971. The interpretation of protein structures: Estimation of static accessibility. *J. Mol. Biol.* 55:379.
44. Greer, J. 1981. Comparative model-building of the mammalian serine proteases. *J. Mol. Biol.* 153:1027.
45. Cheetham, J.C. 1988. Reshaping the antibody combining site by CDR replacement—tailoring or tinkering to fit? *Prot. Eng.* 2:170.
46. Roberts, S. and Rees, A.R. 1986. The cloning and expression of an anti-peptide antibody: A system for rapid analysis of the binding properties of engineered antibodies. *Prot. Eng.* 1:59.
47. Rees, A.R. and de la Paz, P. 1986. Investigating antibody specificity using computer graphics and protein engineering. *TIBS* 11:144.
48. Roberts, S. 1986. D. Phil. Thesis, University of Oxford.
49. Sambrook, J., Fritsch, E.F., and Maniatis, T. 1989. *Molecular Cloning: A Laboratory Manual.* Second ed. Cold Spring Harbor, NY: Cold Spring Harbor Laboratory Press.
50. Colman, A. 1984. In: *Transcription and Translation—A Practical Approach.* Hames, D. and Higgins, S., eds. Oxford: IRL Press.
51. Darsley, M.J. and Rees, A.R. 1985. Three distinct epitopes within the loop region of hen egg lysozyme defined with monoclonal antibodies. *EMBO J.* 4:383.
52. Pluckthun, A. 1990. Antibodies from *Escherichia coli. Nature* 347:497.
53. Field, H., Yarrington, G.T., and Rees, A.R. 1989. Expression of mouse immunoglobulin light and heavy chain variable regions in *Escherichia coli* and reconstitution of antigen-binding activity. *Prot. Eng.* 3:641.
54. Darsley, M.J. and Rees, A.R. 1985. Nucleotide sequences of five monoclonal anti-lysozyme antibodies. *EMBO J.* 4:383.
55. Hilyard, K.L. 1991. D. Phil. Thesis, University of Oxford.
56. Roberts, S., Hilyard, K.L., McKeowen, S., and Rees, A.R. Unpublished results.
57. Go, N. and Scheraga, H.A. 1980. Ring closure and local conformational deformation of chain molecules. *Macromolecules* 3:178.

CHAPTER 3

Engineering the Hinge Region to Optimize Complement-induced Cytolysis

Inger Sandlie, Terje E. Michaelsen

The classical complement pathway is a cascade system generating a variety of potent biologic molecules. The pathway is triggered by the interaction of the first complement protein complex, C1, with antigen-complexed IgG. C1 is composed of C1q, C1r, and C1s, and the C1q subunit interacts with the second domain of the heavy chain (C_H2) on IgG. The residues Glu 318, Lys 320, and Lys 322 on C_H2 are involved in the binding.[1] This core binding motif is conserved in the four human IgG subclasses, both the lytic and the nonlytic molecules. Therefore, further structural determinants must be involved in the lysis mechanism. C1q has a molecular weight of approximately 460,000 and has the appearance of a bunch of tulips.[2] The molecule is multivalent in its binding to IgG, and binding to monomeric IgG is weak (Ka 10^4M^{-1}). When several IgGs bind to multiple epitopes on an antigenic surface, the resulting aggregation of IgG molecules allows the binding of two or more tulip heads, leading to a tight binding (Ka 10^8M^{-1}) that is necessary for the activation process to proceed.

It is possible that an exact alignment of antibodies and C1q is required for full activation and also that some degree of flexibility in the molecules is necessary. Clearly, this would reduce the stringency of the steric requirements when C1q binds to an array of IgG molecules. Some flexibility is detected in the C1q molecule,[3] and several modes of flexibility have been demonstrated for IgG molecules.[4]

X-ray diffraction analysis of whole IgG crystals has been characterized by a lack of electron density associated with part of the hinge and the whole of Fc; this phenomenon has been attributed to hinge flexibility.[5] The hinge can be divided into three regions: the upper, middle, and lower hinge. The upper hinge has been defined by Burton[6] as the number of amino acids between the end of the first domain of the heavy chain (C_H1) and the first cysteine forming an interheavy chain disulfide bridge. The middle hinge contains the interheavy cysteine disulfide bridges and a high content of proline. The lower hinge connects the middle hinge to the C_H2 domain.

Dangl and colleagues[7] have generated a family of nine chimeric IgG molecules with identical antigen-combining sites for the hapten dansyl (DNS) and heavy chain constant regions of human, mouse, and rabbit origin, respectively. The segmental flexibility of the molecules was measured and was found to correlate with the length of the upper hinge.

A long upper hinge will allow the angle between the Fab arms to vary widely, whereas a short upper hinge allows for little Fab arm motion. This hinge flexibility allows divalent recognition of variably spaced antigenic determinants. The ability of Ig molecules to change their conformation from Y to T shape[4] greatly facilitates the capacity of antibodies to link to antigens.

The information to date concerning the conformation of the middle hinge indicates that it has the characteristics of a polyproline helix.[8–10] This is a relatively rigid, rod-like double-stranded structure. All the IgG middle hinge sequences have similar polyproline cores (Table 3-1) and probably adopt the same polyproline structure. The length of the middle hinge, however, varies widely among the human IgG subclasses, and is 50 amino acids for IgG_3 and 5 amino acids for IgG_1. The middle hinge may have several functions; it contains the cysteines participating in disulfide bridges and thus contains the residues keeping the two C_H2 domains together in the N-terminal end,[11] the rod shaped core provides spacing or distance between the antigen-binding and biologic effector domains, and the polyproline double helix possibly maintains an appropriate spatial relationship between these two parts of the molecule.

The lower hinge may be the site for Fc motion relative to Fab. There is little amino acid variation in the lower hinges of the human IgGs.

Segmental flexibility has been correlated with effector functions of IgG. Of the nine different IgG molecules studied by Dangl and colleagues, the more flexible antibodies were able to fix complement most effectively, and the efficiency correlated with the length of the upper hinge.

Table 3-1. Comparison of Hinge Sequences of Human
and Mouse Immunoglobulins

	Upper Hinge *216*	*Middle Hinge*	*Lower Hinge* *238*
Human IgG$_1$	EPKSCDKTHT	CPPCP	APELLGGP
Human IgG$_2$	ERK	CCVECPPCP	APPVAGP
Human IgG$_3$	ELKTPLGDTTHT	CPRCP (EPKSCDTPPPCPRCP)$_3$	APELLGGP
Human IgG$_3$M15	EPKS	CDTPPPCPRCP	APELLGGP
Human IgG$_4$	ESKYGPP	CPSCP	APEFLGGP
Mouse IgG$_1$	VPRDCG	CKPCICT	VPSEVS
Mouse IgG$_{2a}$	EPRGPTIKP	CPPCKCP	APNLLGGP

To study the proposed association between hinge length, flexibility, and effector function, mutants of human IgG$_3$ were made, varying the length of the hinge, while the rest of the molecule was kept unaltered.[12] Thus, the effect of manipulating the hinge could be studied independently of any effects due to isotype differences in C$_H$1, C$_H$2, and C$_H$3. The new antibodies were tested for their ability to activate complement and to initiate complement-mediated lysis (CML) and antibody-dependent cell-mediated cytotoxicity (ADCC). Five different deletion mutants were constructed, as shown in Figure 3-1, deleting one or more hinge exons. The resulting antibodies have hinges of 47, 45, 32, 15, and 0 amino acids, respectively. The length of the upper hinges of mutant M47 and M32 are identical to that of IgG$_3$ wild type, namely 12 amino acids, whereas the upper hinge of M45 and M15 consists of 4 amino acids. Both M45 and M15 activated complement. M45 was equally efficient

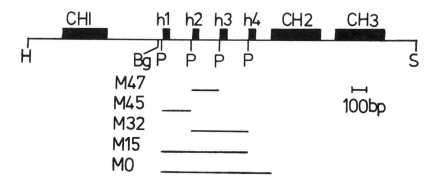

Figure 3-1. Restriction map of the human γ$_3$ gene. Exons are shown as boxes. Lines indicate the size of deletions in the hinge region in the various mutants. H = Hind III, Bg = Bg1 II, P = Pst I, S = Sph I.

as wild type IgG$_3$, while M15 was more efficient.[13] Therefore, a long upper hinge is not necessary for complement activation. Also, it seems that the long hinge of IgG$_3$ downregulates the lytic potential of this subclass. Tan and coworkers[14] made similar IgG$_3$ mutants with specificity for the DNS hapten. Segmental flexibility of the antibodies was measured and found to be low. These rigid antibodies were also shown to activate complement efficiently. Thus, complement activation does not depend on a high degree of segmental flexibility. However, in several species there is a correlation between segmental flexibility of naturally occurring antibodies and ability to fix complement. Possibly, the organisms have an advantage when the molecules most active in complement activation are able to do extensive Fab arm waving, and thereby bind variably spaced epitopes, while the nonlytic molecules are limited in this respect.

IgG$_4$ is completely inactive in complement activation. To determine whether the amino acid sequence of the genetic IgG$_4$ hinge is responsible for its lack of effector function, the hinge exon of M15 was mutated by *in vitro* mutagenesis to become identical to that of IgG$_4$.[15] Instead of losing effector function, the IgG$_3$-derived molecule M15C (Figure 3-2) activated complement even better than IgG$_3$ M15, and was found to be 20 times more efficient that IgG$_3$ wild type in CML. Thus, the amino acid sequence of the hinge modulates the lytic ability of IgG. However, an IgG$_4$ hinge sequence in an

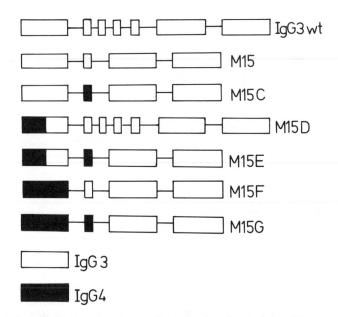

Figure 3-2. Schematic drawing of the IgG$_3$-derived antibody genes. Exons are shown as boxes.

otherwise intact IgG_3 molecule does not abolish its efficient complement activation, and the amino acid sequence of the IgG_4 hinge alone cannot be the reason that IgG_4 is nonlytic. IgG_3 molecules with the hinge of IgG_4 were also made by Tan and coworkers[14] as well as IgG_4 molecules with the hinge of IgG_3. Functional studies performed on these antibodies also demonstrate that the amino acid sequence of the IgG_4 hinge is not the reason that IgG_4 does not activate complement.

Molecules that are IgG_4-like in C_H1 and the hinge, and IgG_3-like in C_H2 and C_H3 have also been made (Figure 3-3). These molecules activate complement as efficiently as IgG_3M15. This result is unexpected, because Fc fragments from human IgG_4 have been shown to bind C1q with an affinity comparable to that of the corresponding fragment from IgG_1.[16] The result was interpreted to suggest that Fab may modulate the activity of the C1q binding site. It has been shown that Fab from IgG_4 does not negatively modulate the C1q binding site on IgG_3. Clackson and Winter[17] have created hybrids of lytic and nonlytic murine antibodies and have shown that the C_H2 exon of the IgG_{2b} antibody active in CML can confer lytic ability when replacing the C_H2 exon on the usually inactive IgG_1. This also argues against the hypothesis that the length of the upper hinge determines the ability of an antibody to activate complement.

The carbohydrate bound to Asn 297 in C_H2 is necessary for C1q-binding,[1] as aglycosylated antibodies produced by a Asn/Ala amino acid substitution at res 297 show a threefold lower association constant for C1q and do not activate C1. Studies by Lund and coworkers[18] suggest that aglycosylation results in very localized structural changes in the lower hinge. It is suggested that C1q interacts both with the "core" binding motif and the lower hinge, and that aglycosylation results in loss of accessibility to the hinge. Tight C1q binding, however, is not sufficient for complement activation and CML to occur, because both wild-type antibodies and mutant variants possessing strong C1q binding activity can be nonlytic.[1, 19]

When comparing the four human IgGs in CML, it was found that IgG_3 was the most efficient in complement activation as well as lysis.[20, 21] The activity of the different subclasses was measured whiie varying the epitope number

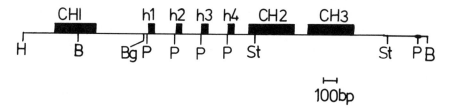

Figure 3-3. Restriction map of the human γ gene. Exons are shown as boxes. H = Hind III, B = Bam HI, Bg = Bg1 II, P = Pst I, St = Sty I.

and also the epitope density on target cells. It was indeed found that the activity of the different subclasses does depend on these features. IgG_1, which is generally believed to be highly active in CML, was found to have a low activity at low epitope number and low epitope density. IgG_3 was the most active at a wide range of conditions tested. It is noteworthy that the short hinge mutant IgG_3M15 proved more active that IgG_3 wild type at all conditions tested.[13] Work by others[22,23] suggests that IgG_1 is superior in CML due to better activity at a later stage in the complement cascade, namely C4 activation. Our work does not confirm these findings, and the discrepancy probably reflects the differences in the *in vitro* experimental conditions employed.

Experiments *in vivo* will eventually determine how efficient the various antibodies are in lysing target cells. Work with a matched set of rat antibodies of the CAMPATH-1 family recognizing human lymphocytes shows that IgG_{2a}, which is lytic with human complement, but inactive in ADCC, gave transient depletion of blood lymphocytes in patients with lymphoid malignancies. IgG_{2b}, which is also active in ADCC, produced long-lasting depletion of lymphocytes from both blood and marrow.[24] Humanized antibodies with the same antigen specificity and of the IgG_1 subclass have been shown to be potent *in vivo*.[25]

ADCC is mediated through Fc-receptors (FcR) on the membrane of effector cells such as K-cells, NK-cells, monocytes, and neutrophils.[26] There are three well-known FcR (FcRI, FcRII, and FcRIII), which are unevenly distributed on different cell types, and all of them probably have the potential to participate to a variable degree in the ADCC activity.[27] Of the human subclasses, IgG_2 does not bind FcR1, whereas IgG_1 and IgG_3 bind FcR1 with high affinity, and IgG_4 binds FcR1 with a tenfold lower affinity constant. A mutant IgG_2 with C_H2 from IgG_3 shows a dramatic increase in FcR1 binding, but the affinity constant is still five times lower than that of IgG_3. Exchanging C_H3 domains between the two subclasses has no influence on the isotype pattern (Morrison, S.L., personal communication). Therefore, even though C_H2 contains the features most important for FcR1 binding, other parts of the molecules other than C_H3 are also involved in optimizing the binding.

When the IgG_3 mutants with truncated hinge region and the one with the hinge of IgG_4 were tested in an ADCC assay, it was found that the ADCC activity was mainly unaltered in all the mutants except the one with deletion of all the hinge exons. This showed a lower ADCC activity than the wild type.[28] The binding of the molecules to FcR1 in particular has not been measured.

To introduce the changes in the IgG_3 heavy chain gene, two different methods have been employed: that of partial restriction enzyme digestion, and *in vitro* mutagenesis. The gene used in our studies codes for a G3m (b°)

variant.[29] The full length gene is cloned into the polylinker of the plasmid pUC19 (see Figure 3-3). The plasmid was partially digested with Pst I, ligated, and introduced in competent *Escherichia coli* JM85. Plasmid preparations of individual colonies were analyzed by digestion with Bgl II and BamHI. One that had deleted the first three hinge exons, while retaining h4, C_H2, and C_H3, was introduced as a 2 kb Hind III-BamHI fragment downstream from a V_H gene in the pSVgpt derived vector pSV-V_{NP}.[30] The vector was introduced by electroporation[31] into J558L, a mouse myeloma cell line producing a λ1 light chain. Approximately 10^7 cells and 20 μg plasmid in 0.8 ml PBS at 0°C were subjected to an electric field of 3.5 kV/cm using a capacitance setting of 25 uF. About 50% of the cells survived electroporation. They were diluted in growth medium to 10^5 cells/ml, and 1-ml portions were plated in 24 wells tissue culture dishes. After incubation at 37°C for 48 hours, 1 ml of growth medium supplemented with 2 μg/ml mycophenolic acid (Gibco) and 500 μg/ml xanthine was added to select for transfected cells. Clones were visible after 1 to 2 weeks. Individual clones were selected by limiting dilution.

To further modify the hinge region of γ3 by *in vitro* mutagenesis, a 1.3 kb Pst I fragment containing h4, C_H2, and C_H3 was subcloned into the polylinker of M13 mp19. Direction of the insert in the vector was determined by restriction enzyme mapping.

In *in vitro* mutagenesis, the DNA fragment to be mutated is cloned into a vector whose DNA can exist in both single- and double-stranded forms. To single-stranded DNA, a mutagenic primer is annealed. Complete double-stranded DNA is synthesized *in vitro* from the primer by the use of DNA polymerase. Covalently closed circles are made by the addition of DNA ligase, and DNA is transformed into competent bacterial cells. The vector multiplies within the bacteria and progeny containing the desired mutation can be obtained. The mutation can be verified by sequencing DNA in the single-stranded form. A mixture of wild-type and mutated progeny is obtained. *In vitro* mutagenesis reagents from Bio Rad Laboratories were employed in these studies.

INTRODUCTION TO M13 CLONING (METHOD 1)

The vectors employed are of the M13mp strains, which are prepared by Messing to be useful in DNA cloning.[32] M13 is a single-stranded filamentous phage. The phage enters the host cells (*E coli* F') by way of the F-pilus. Once inside the cell, the phage single-stranded DNA is converted to the replicative double-stranded form. DNA replication proceeds to create about 100 progeny double-stranded DNA molecules. Thus, double-stranded M13 DNA can be purified from infected bacterial cells and used for restriction enzyme digestion and subcloning. From the double-stranded DNA, single-stranded DNA is synthesized in the bacteria and packaged into viral protein coats. Phages are extruded from the hosts without cell lysis. However, bacterial growth is severely retarded by the infection, and after plating, turbid plaques are visible on a lawn of uninfected cells. Phage particles can be collected from the growth medium when infected bacteria are grown in culture. Single-stranded DNA can then readily be isolated from the phages and used for sequencing or further manipulation.

The following host bacteria were used for growing M13: *E coli* MV1190Δ (*lac-pro* AB), *thi, sup*E, Δ (*sr*1-*rec*A) 306::Tn10(*tet*^{r}) (F′:*tra*D36, *pro* AB, *lac* I^{q}Z M15). M13 vectors of the mp series carry a short segment of *E coli* DNA containing coding information for a piece of the galactosidase gene (*lac* Z). *E coli* MV1190 has a mutation in the lac gene, while its F′ plasmid carries information for a truncated galactosidase protein that can complement the protein encoded by M13. Synthesis of the protein from M13 is induced by isopropylthio-β-D-galactosidase (IPTG). If IPTG is added to the infected bacteria together with X-gal (5-bromo-4-chloro-3-indolyl-β-D-galactoside), which is a substrate for galactosidase, X-gal will be cleaved to form a blue colored product, and blue plaques are formed.

Foreign DNA is inserted into M13mp vectors in a polylinker that carries numerous restriction enzyme recognition sites with the *lac*Z region. This disrupts the DNA coding for the galactosidase fragment, and complementation is thereby eliminated. Consequently, recombinant M13mp vectors will give rise to colorless, or white, plaques.

E coli MV1190 is defective in proline biosynthesis. The F′ plasmid also carries the proline synthesis genes. To select for bacteria with F′ plasmid, MV1190 are grown on minimal medium plates.

M13mp18 and M13mp19 differ only in the orientation of the poly linker. Thus, a double-stranded DNA fragment cleaved with two different restriction enzymes can be ligated into these two vectors in opposite orientations. Because both phages pack single-stranded DNA of the + type in viral protein coats, M13mp18 will have one of the two strands of the fragment inserted, and M13mp19 will carry its complementary sequence. This is important when designing oligonucleotide probes for mutation and sequencing (Figure 3-4).

M13 DNA and target Ig DNA are cut with appropriate restriction enzymes. The cut DNA is size fractionated on an 0.8% agarose gel, and the DNA fragment of interest is cut out and purified from the gel before it is ligated into the linearized M13 vector. The molar ratio between fragment and vector in the ligation mixture should be approximately 3:1, and 20 ng cut vector is used in a total ligation mixture volume of 10 μl. Competent cells to be transformed with the ligation mixture are prepared as described in the following section.

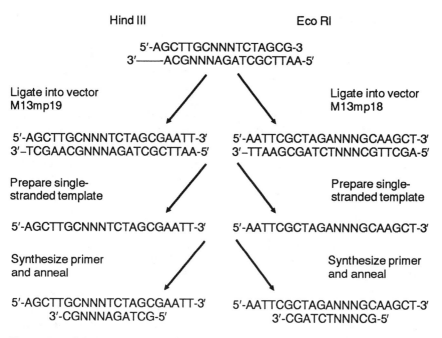

Figure 3-4. Cloning in M13mp18 and M13mp19. NNN indicates a long stretch of nucleotides. The arrows show direction of DNA synthesis.

Preparation of Competent Cells

MV1190 carrying the F-factor are selected on glucose/minimal medium plates. (It generally takes at least two days for bacteria to show visible colonies on these plates). A single colony is picked and an overnight culture (ONC) is grown in Luria broth (LB). The next day 250 ml LB is inoculated with ONC so that Abs590 is 0.1, and the bacteria are grown exponentially at 37°C with aeration until Abs590 reaches 0.8–0.9. Then, the culture is centrifuged in the cold for 15 minutes at 5000 rpm, the supernatant is removed, and the pellet is resuspended in 50 ml ice-cold 100 mM $MgCl_2$. (It is crucial that all solutions are really ice-cold and that the bacteria are kept on ice throughout the entire procedure). The bacteria are harvested by centrifugation as before and carefully resuspended in 10 ml ice-cold 100 mM $CaCl_2$. Then, 100 ml 100 mM $CaCl_2$ is added and the bacteria are left on ice for 45 minutes. After centrifugation they are carefully resuspended (at this stage the cells are very fragile) in 12.5 ml 85 mM $CaCl_2$, 15% glycerol. The resulting component cells are pipetted into prechilled eppendorf tubes in small aliquots and stored at –70°C. They are ready for transformation and can be stored for several months. The competent cells are thawed on ice before use.

Transformation

300 µl competent *E coli* MV1190 in eppendorf tubes are mixed with 2 µl (1–10 ng) of the ligation mixture, left on ice for 45 minutes, heatshocked (3 minutes at 42°C), and returned to the ice bath. 100 µl of each of the transformation mixtures are transferred to tubes containing freshly made ice-cold mixtures of 300 µl MV1190 ONC, 50 µl X-gal, 2% in dimethyl formamide, and 20 µl 100 mM IPTG. IPTG is diluted from a frozen stock solution of 1 M. X-gal in 2% dimethyl formamide can be kept frozen for several months. After mixing, 2.5 ml molten top agar at 45°C is added to each tube, and the contents are mixed by rolling and are poured onto prewarmed H-plates. The H-plates are left to set, inverted, and incubated at 37°C overnight. The next day, plaques should be visible.

Controls should also be included, consisting of competent cells transformed with (1) 1 ng uncut M13 DNA and (2) 10 ng cut and unligated vector. Uncut M13 DNA should give approximately 200 blue plaques. There should be few plaques on the plate with the cut and unligated vector.

A few white plaques from the plates with recombinant M13 are picked with sterile Pasteur pipettes and the small agar plugs are blown into eppendorf tubes containing 1 ml TE buffer. These are vortexed for 1 minute to release the phages from the agar, stored in the cold, and used as a source for making double-stranded and single-stranded M13 DNA.

Preparation of Double-stranded M13 DNA

Double-stranded recombinant M13 DNA samples are prepared by mixing 300 µl ONC MV1190, 100 µl phages in TE buffer, and 5 ml LB in tubes that are shaken at 300 rpm for 5 hours at 37°C. 1.5 ml from each tube is transferred to eppendorf tubes and the bacteria are pelleted by centrifugation for 30 seconds in a microcentrifuge. The supernatant is discarded and the bacteria are resuspended in 100 µl STE buffer. 100 µl phenol:chloroform (1:1) is added and the tubes are vortexed for 30 seconds before centrifugation for 5 minutes. The upper aqueous phase is transferred to a new eppendorf tube and ethanol is precipitated. The pellet is thoroughly washed in ice-cold 70% ethanol, dried, and resuspended in 10 µl dH$_2$O. The yield of DNA should be at least 1 µg and sufficient for four restriction enzyme reactions. We have included 1 µl of RNAse (10µg/µl) in the cutting reactions to remove RNA before running cut DNA on an agarose gel.

To check that M13 are carrying the fragment of interest, double-stranded M13 DNA has to be prepared from the colorless plaques and cut with restriction enzymes that will release the fragment. This can be visualized after size fractionation on an agarose gel. If the fragment has been prepared with a single restriction enzyme, its direction of insertion in M13 will have to be determined by cutting with additional restriction enzymes, which cuts both in the fragment and in the vector. The restriction enzyme must be selected so that the length of the restriction fragments obtained will differ, depending on the direction of the insert.

Inserts in M13 longer than 5 kb tend to be unstable. Also, during *in vitro* DNA synthesis, replication errors may be obtained, so that alterations other than the desired mutation may be introduced in the target DNA. Therefore, target DNA should be sequenced in full after mutation. Thus, the size of the insert ideally selected for cloning in M13 is considerably less than 5 kb, to facilitate sequencing.

INTRODUCTION TO M13 CLONING (METHOD 2)

Preparation of Template DNA

The *in vitro* mutagenesis method described by Kunkel[33] provides a very strong selection against the nonmutagenized strand of a heterologous double-stranded DNA. The template DNA is grown in a *dut-*, *ung-* bacterium. The *dut* mutation inactivates the enzyme dUTPase and results in high intracellular levels of dUTP. Consequently, the nascent DNA carries a number of uracils in thymine positions. The *ung* mutation inactivates uracil N-glycosylase, which cleaves uracil residues from DNA; therefore, uracil is allowed to remain in the DNA. Uracil basepairs with adenine in the complementary strand and may be used as a template for *in vitro* synthesis of an oligonucleotide primed nonuracil-containing mutant strand. When the double-stranded DNA is transformed into a strain with a functional uracil N-glycosylase, the uracil-containing template strand without mutations is cleaved and degraded, while the mutated strand is replicated. Mutation frequencies of more than 70% are routinely obtained when employing this method.

The following strain for template synthesis has been used: *E coli* CJ236 *dut*, *ung*, *thi*, *rel*A; pCJ105 (Cm^r). The strain carries the plasmid pCJ 105, which has information for F′ pilus construction and also a gene for chloramphenicol resistance. The strain is grown in the presence of chloramphenicol to ensure that the plasmid is not lost. M13 vectors such as M13mp8, which is carrying an amber mutation, cannot grow in CJ236.

Preparation of Single-stranded Template DNA

The number of phage particle (pfu) in the plaques sampled into TE buffer is titered as follows before single-stranded M13 DNA template is prepared: 10^3, 10^5, 10^6, 10^7, and 10^8 dilutions of the phage solution are made in TE buffer.

100µl from each phage dilution are mixed with 300 µl ONC of MV1190, portions of 2.5-ml molten top agar at 45°C are added, and the mixture is poured onto LB plates. The plates are inverted and stored at 37°C overnight. An ONC of CJ236 in LB containing 30 µg/ml chloramphenicol is also prepared.

The next day, 10 ml LB with 30 µg/ml chloramphenicol is mixed with 10 µl ONC of CJ236 and shaken at 37°C for 6 hours. Then, 3×10^6 recombinant phages in TE buffer are added and the infection is allowed to proceed overnight at 37°C with shaking. The following day, the bacteria are pelleted for 10 minutes by spinning at 10,000 rpm for 10 minutes. The supernatant is transferred to a new tube carefully so that the bacterial pellet is not disturbed, centrifuged again, and transferred to a new tube.

To isolate single-stranded M13 DNA, 1/4 vol of a solution of 20% PEG 6000/2.5M NaCl is added to the supernatant. The mixture is shaken thoroughly and left on ice for 30 minutes. The phages are then collected by centrifugation for 15 minutes at 12,000 rpm. The supernatant is removed carefully and the tubes are inverted and left to drain for 20 minutes. The edges of the tubes are wiped clean of traces of PEG and the phage pellet is suspended in 200 µl TE buffer and transferred to an eppendorf tube. The phage particles are opened and the single-stranded DNA is extracted by two subsequent phenol extractions as described below. 200 µl phenol:chloroform (1:1) is added. The tubes are vortexed for 30 seconds and left on the bench for 15 minutes. After a new vortex, the tubes are spun in a microcentrifuge, the aqueous phases are transferred to new eppendorf tubes, and the procedure is repeated. The aqueous phases are then extracted with chloroform and transferred to new eppendorf tubes. The DNA is ethanol precipitated by addition of 1/10 vol 3 M KAc (pH = 4.8) and 2.5 vol ice-cold 96% ethanol, and kept at 70°C for at least 30 minutes. After centrifugation, the pellet is resuspended in 10 µl TE buffer. The pellet is usually very small and hardly visible.

To estimate the concentration of DNA, 2 µl is run on an agarose gel with a known amount of single-stranded M13 DNA as standard.

After growing recombinant M13 in CJ236, the supernatant should contain phage particles with single-stranded DNA with a number of uracil residues incorporated in place of thymine. It is important to start the infection of CJ236 with a low number of phage particles. This ensures that the progeny obtained have been grown through the *dut-*, *ung-* strain, and are not contaminated by unadsorbed phage from the inoculum.

If the infection of CJ236 was efficient, the supernatant should contain about 5×10^{11} pfu/ml when titered in CJ236, and if the template DNA contains enough uracil to be degraded in MV1190, the phage titer in MV1190 should be smaller than that in CJ236 by at least four orders of magnitude. Before proceeding to the *in vitro* DNA synthesis step, therefore, the phages should be titered in MV1190 and in CJ236: 10^3, 10^5, 10^6, 10^7, and 10^8 dilutions of the phages are made in TE buffer. 100 µl from each phage solution are mixed with 300 µl MV1190, and 1 µl from each dilution is mixed with 300 µl CJ236 ONC. Top agar is added and the mixtures are plated as already described.

INTRODUCTION TO M13 CLONING (METHOD 3): *IN VITRO* DNA SYNTHESIS

Primer Design

The sequence of the primer is made complementary and antiparallel to the template strand (see Figure 3-4). The nucleotide sequence of the four human IgGs is shown in Figure 3-5. Primers conferring substitutions, additions, or deletions may be employed. For a simple substitution reaction, a primer of 16 to 18 nucleotides with the mutation situated near the center of the oligonucleotide is sufficient. Ideally, the Tm of the two "arms" of the primer should be similar, and their (G+C) content should be around 50%. The ends of the primers should have G or C residues, to ensure tight hybridization to the template at these regions. Primers containing stretches of G or C residues should be avoided, as these may hybridize strongly out of phase with the template. Also, primers should not be able to form secondary structures. Computer programs exist for the selection of primers.

Several substitutions may be done in the same reaction by employing primers with several mismatches. In this case, any mismatch to the target sequence should be distanced at least 10 nucleotides from the 3' end of the primers. Larger alterations, such as the addition or deletion of several bases, require longer oligonucleotide primers. To delete or add up to 30 nucleotides, primers of about 35 nucleotides have been used.

Phosphorylation of Primers

Before the template DNA is hybridized to the oligonucleotide primer containing the mutation, the oligonucleotide, which has a terminal OH-group in both ends, must be phosphorylated: The oligonucleotide is lyophilized after synthesis and resuspended in dH_2O at 10–20 pmol/µl. 200 pmol nucleotide is mixed with the following:

1 M Tris-HCl (pH = 8.0)	3 µl
0.2 M MgCl$_2$	1.5 µl
0.1 M DTT	1.5 µl
1mM ATP	13 µl

```
        .                                    50              .                      100
Cγ3  ACCTTTCTGGGGCAGGCCAGGCCTGACTTTGGCT*GGGGCAGGGAGGGGGCTAAGGTGACGCAGGTGGCGCCAGCCAGGCGGCACACCCAATGCCCGTGAGCCCAGACACTGGACCCTGCCTGGACCCTC
Cγ1  ------------------------------------------TT---------------------G--------------------*--I----------------A-----------------G---*****-A----
Cγ2  ------------GA----------TT-------T------G--------------------------------------------------------------------------------A--------
Cγ4  -------------------------------------------*---------------------------------T-------------------G---------------------A------A---
```

```
                                                                              A  S  T  K  G  P  S  V  F  P  L  A  P  C  S
       .                 150            .                  200             .                       250
GTGCATAGACAAGAACCCAGGGGCCTCTGCGCCCTGGGCCCAGCTCTGTCCCACACCGCAGTCACATGGCGGCCATCTCTTGCAGCTTCCACCAAGGGCCCATCGGTCTTCCCCCTGGCGCCCTGCTCC
-C----C---TT-----C---------------------------------------U-------------A--C----------------------------C--------------------A---C----
-C-----------------C-----------------------------*---------G-----------A--C-------------------------------------------------------
-----G-----------------*-----------------------------------G------------A--C----------------------------C------------------------
```

```
    K  S  T  S  G  G  T  A  A  L  G  C  L  V  K  D  Y  F  P  E  P  V  T  V  S  W  N  S  G  A  L  T  S  G  V  H  T  F  P  A  V  L  Q  S
       .                300             .                 350                .
AGGAGCACCTCTGGGGGCACAGCCGGCCCTGGGCTGCCTGGTCAAGGACTACTTCCCCGAACCGGTGACGGTGTCGTGGAACTCAGGCGCCCTGACCAGCGGCGTGCACACCTTCCCGGCTGTCCTACAGT
-A-----------------------------------------------------------------------------------------------T--------------------A----------
----------C-A-A-------C---------------------------------------------------------------------------------------------------------
----------C-A-A-------C------------------------------------------------------------------------------T--------------------A------
```

```
    S  G  L  Y  S  L  S  S  V  V  T  V  P  S  S  S  L  G  T  Q  T  Y  T  C  N  V  N  H  K  P  S  N  T  K  V  D  K  R  V
       .           400        .                450             .              500
CCTCAGGACTCTACTCCCTCAGCAGCCTGGTGACCGTGCCCTCCAGCAGCTTGGGCACCCAGACCTACACCTGCAACGTGAATCACAAGCCCAGCAACACCAAGGTGGACAAGAGAGTTGGTGAGAGGGC
----------------------------------------------------------------------T-----------------------------------------A----------------
-------------------------------------------------A---C--------------------AG------------------------------------A----------------
-------------------------------------------GA-----------G--------------------AG------------------------------------C--------------
```

```
       .                550             .                 600             .                 650
ACCGCAGGCAGGGAGGGTGTCTGCTGGAAGCCAGGCTCAGCCCTCCTGCCTGGACGCATCCGGGCTGTCCAGTCCCAGGCCAGCAAGGCAGGCCCCGTCTGACTCCTCACCCGGAC*CCTCTGCC
---A----------------------------*--------------------------A-----C------A------------------------------C---T----------------------
---T----------------------------------------------C---------------------A-----------------------------------A----T-----------------
---A----------------------------A------------------------------C----------------A----------------T----A-----T--------------A-------
```

```
       .                 700            .              750             .
CGGCCCACTCATCGCTCAGGGAGAGGGTCTTCTGGCCTTTTCCACCAGGCTCCGGGCAGGCACAGGCTGGATGCCCGTACCCCAGGCCCTTCACACACACGGGCAGGTGCTGCGGCTGCAGCTGCCAAAAG
----------------------------------------**-----------C----------A--G---------A----------------C---A---------------G--------G------
----------------------------------------------------------C--------A------------G---------------------------------TG---------C-----
---A-------------------------A-----------------C----C*--------------------------------------------G--G--T--*---*-----------G-----
```

```
       .             800           .                850               .            900
CCATATCCAGGAGGACCCTGCCCCTGACCTAAGCCCACCCAAAGGCCAAACTCTCTACTCACTCAGCTCAGACACCTTCTCTCTTCCCAGATCTGACTAACTCCCAATCTTCTCTCTGCA
--------------G---------------------------------------------C----C------G----------C------------TCC------------------
--------------G------------------------G---------------------G--C--C----------------C------------------------------
---------------------------------------------------------------C----C----------------C-------------------------------
```

```
    E  L  K  T  P  L  G  D  T  T  H  T  C  P  R  C  P
     902          .              950                .              1000
Cγ3 GAGCTCAAAACCCCACTTGGTGACACAACTCACACATGCCCACGGTGCCCAGGTAAGCCAGCCCAGGACTCGCCCTCTCAGCTCAAGCCGGGACAAGAGCCCTAGAGTGGCCTGAGTCCAGGGACAGGGCCC
```

```
                                              E  P  K  S  C  D  T  P  P  P  C  P  R  C  P
                      .          1050        .             1100                .              1150
CAGCAGGGTGCTGACGGCATCCACCTCCATCCCAGATCCCCGTAACTCCCAATCTTCTCTCTGCAGAGCCCAAATCTTGTGACACACCTCCCCCGTGCCCACGGTGCCCAGGTAAGCCAGCCCAGGCCTCA
```

```
                                                                                          E  P  K
                      .              1200           .                 1250              .
CCCTCCAGCTCAAGCGCAGGACAAGAGCCCTAGAGTGGCCTGAGTCCAGGGACAGGCCCCAGCCAGGGTGCTGACGGGTCCACCTCCATCCCAGATCCCCGTAACTCCCAATCTTCTCTCTGCAGAGCCCAA
```

```
    S  C  D  T  P  P  P  C  P  R  C  P
                      .             1300            .            1350             .              1400
ATCTTGTGACACACCTCCCCCATGCCCACGGTGCCCAGGTAAGCCAGCCCAGGCCTCGCCCTCCAGCTCAAGGCGGGACAAGAGCCCTAGAGTGGCCTGAGTCCAGGGACAGGCCCCAGCAGGGTGCTGA
```

```
                                   E  P  K  S  C  D  T  P  P  P  C  P  R  C  P
                      .             1450            .            1500             .              1550
CGGCATCCACCTCCATCCCAGATCCCCGTAACTCCCAATCTTCTCTCTGCACAGCCCAAATCTTGTGACACACCTCCCCCGTGCCCAAGGTGCCCAGGTAAGCCAGCCCCAGGGCCTCGCCCTCCAGCTCAAG
```

```
                      .                 1600          . 1634
GCAGGACAGGTGCCCTAGAGTGGCCTGCATCCAGGGACAGGTCCCAGTCGGGTGCTGACACATCTGCCTCCATCTCTTCCTCA
```

```
    A  P  E  L  L  G  G  P  S  V  F  L  F  P  P  K  P  K  D  T  L  M  I  S  R  T  P  E  V  T  C  V  V  V  D  V  S  H  E  D  P  E  V  Q
     1635         .    1650          .                1700             .                1750
Cγ3 GCAACTGAACTCCTGGGAGGACCGTCAGTCTTCCTCTTCCCCCCAAAACCCAAGGATACCCTTATGATTTCCCGGACCCCTGAGGTCACGTGCGTGGTGGTGGACGTGAGCCACGAAGACCCCGAGGTCC
Cγ1 --------------------G---------------------------------------------------------------------A----------------------------T-----A--
Cγ2 ***--CTG---C---------------------------------------------------------------------------------------------------------------------
Cγ4 ---GT----G------A--------G----------------------------------C--T--C--------------------------------------------------------------
```

```
    F  K  W  Y  V  D  G  V  E  V  H  N  A  K  T  K  P  R  E  E  Q  Y  N  S  T  F  R  V  V  S  V  L  T  V  L  H  Q  D  W  L  N  G  K
                      .             1800             .                1850             .
AGTTCAAGTGGTACGTGGACGGCGTGGAGGTGCATAATGCCAAGACAAAGCCGCGGGAGGAGCAGTACAACAGCACGTTCCGTGTGGTCAGCGTCCTCACCGTCCTGCACCAGGACTGGCTGAACGGCAA
-------------C------------------------------------------A---G-------------------------------------------------------------T-----
-------------C---------------------------------------A-----------------T-------------------------TG-----------------------------
-------------C-------------------T---------------------A-----------------T----------------------------------------------A-------
```

```
    E  Y  K  C  K  V  S  N  K  A  L  P  A  P  I  E  K  T  I  S  K  T  K
     1900            .             1950             .                 2000
GGAGTACAAGTGCAAGGTCTCCAACAAAGCCCTCCCAGCCCCCATCGAGAAAACCATCTCCAAAACCAAAGGTGGGACCCGCGGGGTATGAGGGCCACATGGACAGAGGCCAGCTTGACCCACCCTCTGC
---------------------------------------------------------------------------------T-----GC--------------------------G---C-G-----
--------------------G------------------------------------------------------------G--------------------------------------G---C-G----
------------------GT--T----------------------------------------------------G-----GC------------A-------------------------G---C-G----
```

```
                                   G  Q  P  R  E  P  Q  V  Y  T  L  P  P  S  R  E  E  M  T  K  N  Q  V  S  L  T  C  L  V  K  G
                      .             2050           .                2100              .              2150
CCTGGGAGTGACCGCTGTGCCAACCTCTGTCCCTACAGGACGAGCCCCGAGAACCACAGGTGTACACCCTGCCCCCATCCCGGGAGGAGATGACCAAGAACCAGGTCAGCCTGACCTGCCTGGTCAAAGGC
----A-----------------------------------*---------------------------------------T--C-----------------------------------------
------------------------------------------------------------------------------------------------------------------------------
------------------------------------------------------------------------------------------------------------------------------
```

```
    F  Y  P  S  D  I  A  V  E  W  E  S  S  G  Q  P  E  N  N  Y  N  T  T  P  P  M  L  D  S  D  G  S  F  F  L  Y  S  K  L  T  V  D  K  S
                      .             2200             .                2250             .
TTCTACCCCAGCGACATCGCCGTGGAGTGGGAGAGCAGCGGGCAGCCGGACAACAACTACAACACCACGCCTCCCATGCTGGACTCCGACGGCTCCTTCTTCCTCTACAGCAAGCTCACCGTGGACAAGA
-------T-----------A--------------AT---------------------G---------A--------------------------------------------------------
--------------------------------AT-------------------------G---------A---------------------------------------------------------
--------------------------------AT-------------------------G---------A---------------------------------------------------------
```

```
    R  W  Q  Q  G  N  I  F  S  C  S  V  M  H  E  A  L  H  N  R  F  T  Q  K  S  L  S  L  S  P  G  K  *
                      .      2300             .              2350              .              2400
GCAGGTGGCAGCAGGGGAACATCTTCTCCATGCTCCGTGATGCATGAGGCTCTGCACAACCGGCTTCACGCAGAAGAGCCTCTCCCTGTCTCCGGGTAAATGAGTGCGACAGCCGGCAACCCCCCGCTCCC
--------------G------------------------------------------------------A--A--A---------------------------------C--G------
-----------------G------------------------------------------------A--A--A-----------------------------------------C---G---
-----------------TG----------------------------------------------A--A--A---------------------T----------------------C-GG----
```

```
                      .              2450             .              2500
GGGCTCTCGGGGTCGGGGCAGGGATGCTTTGGCACGTACCCCGTGTACATACTTCCCGGGCACCCAGCATGGAAATAAAGCACCCAGCGCTGCCCTGGGCCCCTGTGAGCACTGTGATGGTTCTTTCCACGGG
------C-----A-------------------------------------------------------C---------------------------
A----------T---------------------A----------------------------------------------------------GT---
----------------------------------------C-A----------------------------------------------------
```

```
      2550
TCAGGCCCGAGTCTGAGGCCTGAGTGACATGAGGGAGGCAGAGCGGGTC
---------G----------------------
---------G----------------------T-----
```

Figure 3-5. Sequence of a human γ3 constant region gene and alignment with γ1, γ2, and γ4 genes. Deduced amino acid sequence from the γ gene is shown above the nucleotide sequence. Dashes represent identity of the γ gene to the other γ sequences. Gaps introduced to maintain sequence homology are indicated by asterisks. The presumptive poly(A) addition signal sequence is underlined.

dH$_2$O is added to a total volume of 30 µl. 4.5U T4 polynucleotide kinase is added. After 45 minutes incubation at 37°C, the reaction is stopped by heating to 65°C for 10 minutes.

In Vitro DNA Synthesis

Template DNA is mixed with the primer and annealing buffer in an eppendorf tube as follows:

Template DNA	0.2 pmol
Mut. primer	2-3 pmol
10x annealing buffer	1 µl
dH$_2$O	to a total volume of 10 ml

10x annealing buffer consists of:

200 mM Tris-HCl (pH = 7.4)
100 mM MgCl$_2$
500 mM NaCl

A control reaction without the mutation primer should be included to test for nonspecific priming. The tubes are placed in a 70°C water bath for 3 minutes and are then allowed to cool slowly to room temperature in the water bath for approximately 45 minutes. After a short spin in a microcentrifuge, the tubes are kept on ice. To each of the tubes is added the following reaction mixture:

10x synthesis buffer	1 µl
T4 ligase	2 µl (2 units)
diluted T4 polymerase	1 µl (1 unit)

T4 polymerase is diluted 1:5 in cold dilution buffer consisting of:

20 mM K phosphate (pH = 6.5)
5 mM DTT
50% glycerol

The 10x synthesis buffer is made of:

5 mM each of the four deoxynucleoside triphosphates
10 mM ATP
100 mM Tris-HCl (pH = 7.4)
50 mM MgCl$_2$
20 mM DTT

The ingredients are collected at the bottom of the tubes by a short spin in a microcentrifuge and incubated for 5 minutes on ice, 5 minutes in a 25°C water bath, and 90 minutes in a 37°C water bath. The tubes are given a short spin and samples of 7 µl are removed from each reaction and run on an agarose gel to monitor DNA synthesis. Single-stranded template DNA is included as a control. Double-stranded DNA runs behind single-stranded DNA on the gel. The control reaction without a mutation primer should not show signs of double-stranded DNA. To the remaining 7 µl of the DNA synthesis reaction, 43 µl TE buffer is added. The reactions can be stored for at least a month at –20°C before transformation. MV1190, made competent as already described, are transformed with double-stranded DNA by mixing 300 µl competent cells with 7.5 µl of the DNA synthesis reaction. The remaining 42.5 µl are stored at –20°C. The transformation and plating of bacteria has already been described. (X-gal and IPTG are not included.) The plates are inverted and incubated overnight at 37°C.

The next day, plaques should be visible. A number of plaques are picked with sterile Pasteur pipette, depending on the expected mutation frequency (we have usually picked 10 plaques), and blown into 1 ml TE buffer and vortexed for 1 minute. The tubes are marked carefully.

If the competent cells were transformed by more than one M13 molecule, each plaque may consist of different phages. Therefore, it is necessary to plaque-purify the phage isolates before single-stranded DNA purification and sequencing. The phage suspension is diluted by a factor of 10_3, and 100 µl are plated as before. The next day, single plaques are picked again into 1 ml TE buffer.

Single-stranded DNA is prepared after infection of MV1190. The procedure is the same as for infection of CJ 236 and isolation of template DNA. After the DNA content of the phages is analyzed by sequencing, double-stranded DNA is prepared as described previously, and the mutated gene fragment is cut out of the M13 vector and subcloned to reconstitute a full-length heavy chain gene.

To synthesize the mutant strand, T4 DNA polymerase was used. The enzyme exhibits 5' to 3' polymerase and 3' to 5' exonuclease activities, but no 5' to 3' exonuclease activity. Also, it does not perform strand displacement. This is important, because strand displacement activity may lead to the mutagenic primer being "peeled off" during the *in vitro* DNA synthesis reaction, and may thereby lead to a decrease in the mutation efficiency.

If double-stranded DNA is not visible on the agarose gel after *in vitro* DNA synthesis, the primer may not have hybridized to the template DNA, and other hybridization conditions must be found. A short oligonucleotide primer may require a lower annealing temperature. Temperatures as low as 55°C may be tried for 16 nucleotide primers.

CONCLUSION

Partial restriction enzyme digestion and *in vitro* mutagenesis were used to manipulate the hinge region of IgG_3. By doing this, antibodies that show a dramatic increase in CML while retaining the ADCC activity of the native antibodies were produced. The antibodies were thereby engineered to enhance a desired effector function.

The site of interaction between Clq and mouse IgG_{2b} has been mapped to the amino acid sequence Glu 318, Lys 320, Lys 320 on C_H2. Mutating any one of these amino acids to Ala results in antibodies with at least a 30-fold reduction in the affinity for Clq and a concomitant loss of activity in CML.[1] Thus, *in vitro* mutagenesis can also be employed to abolish an effector function from an antibody.

Neither mouse IgG_{2b} nor human IgG_2 bind FcR1, and both lack Leu in position 235 in C_H2. By substituting Glu (mouse IgG_{2b}) with Leu in this position, IgG_{2b} became able to bind to FcR1.[34] This knowledge might also be employed to abolish FcR1 binding in antibodies. Morrison has substituted Leu with Glu in position 235 of IgG_3 and obtained an antibody with a 100-fold reduction in binding affinity for FcR1 (personal communication). Generally, when introducing mutations in proteins, one must be aware of the possibility that the changes may severely alter the folding or stability of the entire protein. In antibodies, individual exons encode independently folding polypeptide domains, and altering amino acids in domains, or even removing entire domains, may often conserve effector functions when the binding site for effector molecules are located to other domains.

This was demonstrated by Traunecker and coworkers,[35] who fused the gene coding for the first two N-terminal domains of CD4 with the hinge C_H2, and C_H3 exons from mouse IgG_{2a}. Thus, the antigen-binding site of IgG was replaced by CD4, and dimeric molecules were secreted without light chains. The functions of the Fc portion of the CD4-Ig molecules were intact; the molecules retained the ability to bind Clq and FcR. A similar construct made with C_H1, hinge, C_H2, and C_H3 from human IgG_1 did not bind Clq, whereas FcR binding was intact,[36] as well as long half-life and placental transfer.[37] It is not known which conformational features of this molecule are responsible for the lack of Clq binding. However, removing the C_H3 domain from antibodies leaves them unable to bind FcR1 and greatly reduces complement activation. This domain is important for maintaining quaternary structure of the C_H2 domain. Hingeless mutants of IgG are not active in CML and have a greatly reduced ADCC activity.[13, 28]

REFERENCES

1. Duncan, A.R. and Winter, G. 1988. The binding site for C1q on IgG. *Nature* 332:738.
2. Reid, K.E.M. and Porter, R.R. 1981. The proteolytice activation systems of complement. *Annu. Rev. Biochem.* 50:433.
3. Poon, P.H., Schumaker, V.N., Phillips, M.L., and Strang, C.J. 1983. Conformation and restricted segmental flexibility of C1, the first component of human complement. *J. Mol. Biol.* 168:563.
4. Nezlin, R. 1990. Internal movements in immunoglobulin molecules. *Adv. Immunol.* 48:1.
5. Huber, R., Deisenhofer, J., Colman, P.M., Masaak, M., and Palm, W. 1976. Crystallographic structure studies of an IgG molecule and a Fc fragment. *Nature* 264:415.
6. Burton, D.R. In: *Molecular Genetics of Immunoglobulin.* 1987. Calabi, F. and Neuberger, M.S., eds. New York, Elsevier, pp 1–50.
7. Dangl, J.L., Wensel, T.G., Morrison, S.L., Stryer, L., Herzenberg, L.A., and Oi, V.T. 1988. Segmental flexibility and complement fixation of genetically engineered chimeric human, rabbit, and mouse antibodies. *EMBO J.* 7:1989.
8. Johnson, P.M., Michaelsen, T.E., and Scopes, P.M. 1975. Conformation of the hinge and various fragments of human IgG3. *Scand. J. Immunol.* 4:113.
9. Endo, S. and Arata, Y. 1985. Proton nuclear magnetic resonance study of human IgG$_1$ and their proteolytic fragments: Structure of the hinge region and effects of a hinge region deletion on internal flexibility. *Biochemistry* 24:1561.
10. Ito, W. and Arata, Y. 1985. Proton nuclear magnetic study of the dynamics of the conformation of the hinge segment of human G1 immunoglobulin. *Biochemistry* 24:6467.
11. Michaelsen, T.E. 1976. Indications that the C$_H$2 homology region is not a regular domain. *Scand. J. Immunol.* 5:1123.
12. Sandlie, I., Aase, A., Westby, C., and Michaelsen, T.E. 1989. C1q binding to chimeric monoclonal IgG3 antibodies consisting of mouse variable regions and human constant regions with shortened hinge containing 15 to 47 amino acids. *Eur. J. Immunol.* 19:1599.
13. Michaelsen, T.E., Westby, C., Aase, A., and Sandlie, I. 1990. Enhancement of complement activation and cytolysis of human IgG3 by deletion of hinge exons. *Scand. J. Immunol.* 32:517.
14. Tan, L.K., Shopes, R.J. Oi, V.T., and Morrison, S.L. 1990. Influence of the hinge region on complement activation, C1q binding, and segmental flexibility in chimeric human immunoglobulins. *Proc. Natl. Acad. Sci. USA* 87:162.
15. Sandlie, I., Norderhaug, L., Brekke, O.H., Bremnes, B., Sandin, R., Aase, A., and Michaelsen, T.E. Chimeric mouse/human IgG3 antibodies with an IgG4–like hinge region induce complement mediated lypis more efficiently than IgG3 wild type. *Eur. J. Immunol.* In press.
16. Isenmann, D.E., Dorrington, K.J., and Painter, R.H. 1975. The structure and function of immunoglobulin domains. II. The importance of interchain disulfide bonds and the possible role of molecular flexibility in the interaction between immunoglobulin and complement. *J. Immunol.* 114:1726.

17. Clackson, T. and Winter, G. 1989. "Sticky-feet"-directed mutagenesis and its application to swapping antibody domains. *Nucleic Acids Res.* 17:10163.

18. Lund, J., Tanaka, T., Takahashi, N., Sarmay, G., Araka, Y., and Jefferis, R. 1990. A protein structural change in aglycosylated IgG3 correlates with loss of human FcRI and human FcRIII binding and/or activation. *Mol. Immunol.* 27:1145.

19. Bindon, C.I., Hale, G., and Waldman, H. 1990. Complement activation by immunoglobulin does not depend solely on C1q binding. *Eur. J. Immunol.* 20:277.

20. Michaelsen, T.E., Garred, P., and Aase, A. 1991. Human IgG subclass pattern of inducing complement-mediated cytolysis depends on antigen concentration and to a lesser extent on epitope patchiness, antibody affinity and complement concentration. *Eur. J. Immunol.* 21:11–16.

21. Garred, P., Michaelsen, T.E., and Aase, A. 1989. The IgG subclass pattern of complement activation depends on epitope density, antibody- and complement concentration. *Scand. J. Immunol.* 30:379.

22. Bruggemann, M., Williams, G.T., Bindon, C.I., Clark, M.R., Walker, M.R., Jefferis, R., Waldmann, H., and Neuberger, M.S. 1987. Comparison of the effector functions of human immunoglobulins using a matched set of chimeric antibodies. *J. Exp. Med.* 166:1351.

23. Bindon, C.I., Hale, G., Bruggemann, M., and Waldmann, H. 1988. Human monoclonal IgG isotypes differ in complement activating function at the level of C4 as well as C1q. *J. Exp. Med.* 168:127.

24. Dyer, M.J.S., Hale, G., Hayhoe, F.G.J., and Waldmann, H. 1989. Effects of CAMPATH-1 antibodies *in vivo* in patients with lymphoid malignancies: Influence of antibody isotype. *Blood* 6:1431.

25. Cobbold, S.P., Hale, G., Clark, M.R., and Waldmann, H. 1990. Purging in auto- and allografts: Monoclonal antibodies which use human complement and other natural effector mechanisms. *Progr. Clin. Biol. Res.* 333:139.

26. Anderson, C.L. and Looney, R.J. 1986. Human leukocyte IgG Fc receptors. *Immunology Today* 7:264.

27. Shen, L., Graziano, R.F., and Fanger, M.W. 1989. The functional properties of FcRI, II and III on myeloid cells: A comprehensive study of killing of erythrocytes and tumor cells mediated through different Fc receptors. *Mol. Immunol.* 26:959.

28. Michaelsen, T.E., Aase, A., Norderhaug, L., and Sandlie, I. Antibody dependent cell-mediated cytotoxicity of human NK/K cell induced by chimeric mouse-human IgG subclasses and IgG3 antibodies with altered hinge region. Submitted.

29. Huck, S., Fort, P., Crawford, D.H., Lefranc, M.-P., and Lefranc, G. 1986. Sequence of a human immunoglobulin gamma 3 heavy chain constant region gene: Comparison with the other human Cj genes. *Nucleic Acids Res.* 14:1779.

30. Neuberger, M.S., Williams, G.T., Mitchell, E.B., Jouhal, S.S., Flanagan, J.G., and Rabbitts, T.H. 1985. A hapten-specific chimaeric IgE antibody with physiological effector function. *Nature* 314:268.

31. Potter, H., Weir, L., and Leder, P. 1984. Enhancer-dependent expression of human K immunoglobulin genes introduced into mouse pre-B lymphocytes by electroporation. *Proc. Natl. Acad. Sci. USA* 81:7161.

32. Messing, J. 1983. New M13 vectors for cloning. *Methods Enzymol.* 101:20.
33. Kunkel, T.A., Roberts, J.D., and Zakour, R.A. 1987. Rapid and efficient site-specific mutagenesis without phenotypic selection. *Methods Enzymol.* 154:367.
34. Duncan, A.R., Woof, J.M., Partridge, L.J., Burton, D.R., and Winter, G. 1988. Localization of the binding site for the human high-affinity Fc receptor on IgG. *Nature* 7:563.
35. Traunecker, A., Schneider, J., Kiefer, H., and Karjalainen, K. 1989. Highly efficient neutralization of HIV with recombinant CD4-immunoglobulin molecules. *Nature* 339:68.
36. Capon, D.J., Chamow, S.M., Mordenti, J., Marsters, S.A., Gregory, T., Mitsuya, H., Byrn, R.A., Lucas, C., Wurm, F.M., Groopman, J.E., Broder, S., and Smith, D.H. 1989. Designing CD4 immunoadhesins for AIDS therapy. *Nature* 337:525.
37. Byrn, A.R., Mordenti, J., Lucas, C., Smith, D., Marsters, S.A., Johnson, J.S., Cossum, P., Chamow, S.M., Wurm, F.M., Gregory, T., Groopman, J.E., and Capon, D.J. 1990. Biological properties of a CD4 immunoadhesin. *Nature* 344:667.

CHAPTER 4

Amplification of Rearranged Ig Variable Region DNA from Single Cells

Lena Danielsson, Carl A.K. Borrebaeck

The polymerase chain reaction (PCR) is an *in vitro* methodology that allows enzymatic amplification of genomic or cloned DNA sequences. Due to the exponential amplification rate of the methodology, the amplification of a single copy DNA, in a complexed mixture, results in microgram quantities of specific target DNA. The sensitivity, specificity, and rapidity of the PCR technology, when the reaction is performed with a thermostable DNA polymerase, has revolutionized molecular biology and opened up a number of new fields. The applications include, for example, direct sequencing, genomic cloning, site-directed mutagenesis, molecular diagnosis of heritable disorders, detection of infectious microorganisms, DNA typing, analysis of allelic variants, and antibody engineering.

Antibody engineering has been greatly facilitated by the introduction of PCR, because the gene segments encoding the variable regions of the heavy and light chains simply and rapidly can be amplified several million times, using degenerate primers. Consequently, this has increased the accessibility of sequence information for antigen-binding regions, which in turn is important for homology studies and the possible design of "synthetic antibodies."

Furthermore, sequence information is of crucial importance when studying the restriction of a human humoral immune response against a defined hapten, peptide, vaccine, and so on. The successful application of PCR on the gene segments encoding the variable regions was based on the fact that degenerate primers were introduced. A degenerate primer implies that several different nucleotides can be found at a particular position in the primer sequence, that is, the resulting primer obtained from the DNA synthesizer is rather a mixture of several primers, with oligonucleotide sequences differing at one or more positions.[1] This type of degeneracy can be very high and the use of mixtures of up to 4096 primers has recently been reported for the successful amplification of variable regions of a human heavy chain.[2] In the ideal case when constructing designer antibodies, the mature specificity of a single immune peripheral blood lymphocyte would be cloned, by inserting the PCR amplified gene segments coding for the antibody variable regions, directly into a prokaryotic expression vector. An expression system, based on *Escherichia coli*, will be used as a selection box to decide which clones are worth cloning further using an eukaryotic host, which will give antibodies with a proper glycosylation. It is, therefore, of the utmost importance to have a mixture of PCR primers that will amplify gene segments, encoding the antibody variable regions from any of the selected B cells. A high degree of degeneracy increases the probability of designing a "consensus" primer of this type of Ig cloning. The immunologic specificity in the starting material can be found directly in peripheral blood of patients or, more commonly, generated by *in vitro* immunization or by the use of the SCID mouse.[3] The general strategy that currently is the most promising for the production of human recombinant antibodies/antibody fragments is outlined in Figure 4-1.

A step-by-step procedure that will allow easy and quick sequence determination of gene segments, encoding the antibody variable regions, amplified by PCR from a single hybridoma cell, is described next. This procedure also briefly describes a prokaryotic expression of antibody fragments for the purpose of selecting antibody specificities, improving the antibody specificity/affinity by mutagenesis, or adding new effector functions to the antibody.

SELECTION OF STARTING MATERIAL FOR AMPLIFICATION OF VARIABLE REGION ENCODING SEQUENCES

In order to clone DNA encoding variable regions of antibodies, mRNA transcripts of the rearranged immunoglobulin genes that are expressed in antibody-producing cells should be used as a template for a PCR. The thermostable DNA polymerase used in a normal PCR will require a single-stranded DNA as a template, and therefore cDNA copies must be synthe-

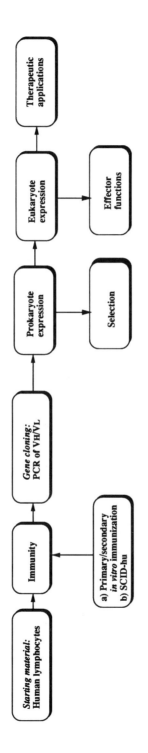

Figure 4-1. A general outline of the strategy involved in the generation of therapeutically optimal recombinant human antibodies/antibody fragments, by the combination of cell-derived immunologic specificity and PCR-based cloning of the Ig genes.

sized from the RNA. There is, however, no need to purify the RNA in order to obtain messenger RNA. Generally, any tissue containing antibody-producing cells can be used as a source of RNA. Mouse spleen has been used by several groups[4, 5] for the isolation of RNA. In order to get good results, the tissue needs to be fresh. Cultured cells have the advantage that they can be lysed and used for RNA isolation immediately. For this reason, hybridoma cell lines have been used as starting material when setting up a system for the amplification of variable region encoding sequences.[1] For the same purpose, Epstein-Barr virus (EBV)-transformed lymphoblastoid cell lines and peripheral blood lymphocytes have also been used.

SINGLE CELLS AS STARTING MATERIAL FOR AMPLIFICATION

It has been demonstrated that it is possible to amplify DNA encoding variable regions from a single cell.[2] This is important because it means that generation of hybridomas is not necessary to obtain monoclonal antibodies. Instead, variable region encoding DNA could be amplified from single cells, directly cloned in expression vectors, and produced in a suitable expression system. The main problem with this technique is not choosing a single cell (see below) but detecting the cell of interest, for example, from peripheral blood cells after *in vitro* immunization. Methods to detect antigen-specific surface Ig on antibody-producing cells is beyond the scope of this chapter, but our best experience has been to use biotinylated antigen together with FITC-streptavidin for this purpose. Cells stained with these reagents are diluted in culture medium and placed in a petri dish. Single flourescent cells can then be picked out, using a florescence microscope, with the aid of a glass micropipette, made from a drawn-out standard Pasteur pipette. Hybridoma cells and lymphoblastoid cells can be picked directly, using a light microscope. This procedure will produce the best starting material for single cell PCR, as compared to antigen-specific FACS sorting or the use of antigen-coated magnetic beads. The latter methodology will both result in the isolation of cell populations that contain a high percentage of antigen–*non*specific B cells.

RNA ISOLATION

When larger quantities of tissue or cells are available, a simple and fast procedure, as the one described by Chomczynski and Sacchi,[6] is recommended for RNA isolation, which improves the chance to isolate undegraded RNA. The high sensitivity of the PCR method, allowing amplification of sequences present in single copy templates, means that RNA from a single cell is sufficient for amplification. This has indeed been accomplished, using RNA from a single hybridoma cell or from a single mouse blastocyst, as PCR template source.[2, 7] The procedure routinely used for RNA isolation from small numbers of cells, including micro-scale CsCl centrifugation,[7] is described in the following section. For good yields, in small-scale isolation of RNA, it is essential to work in the presence of an excess of exogenous RNA, which is added in the initial step of the procedure.

Micropreparation

1. The cell is pelleted in a microfuge at 6500 rpm for five minutes, and the supernatant is aspirated.
2. The cell is then lysed with 100 µl of 4 M guanidium isothiocyanate, 10 mM Tris-HCl, pH 7.5, containing 5 µg ribosomal RNA from *E coli* (16S- and 23S-rRNA, Boehringer-Mannheim GmbH, FRG).
3. The lysis solution is layered on top of 100 µl of 5.7 M CsCl in a 200 µl ultracentrifuge tube and centrifuged using a TLA-100 rotor in a benchtop ultracentrifuge (TL-100, Beckman Instruments AB, Stockholm, Sweden) at 95,000 rpm, for 2 hours.
4. The supernatant is carefully aspirated and the pelleted RNA is suspended in 100 µl of diethylpyrocarbonate (DEPC)-treated water by vortexing.
5. RNA is precipitated with 0.1 volumes of 2 M KAc, pH 5.5, and 2.5 volumes of ethanol, usually overnight at –20°C, or on dry ice for one hour. The RNA is then pelleted using a microfuge, washed with 80% ethanol, and dried.

cDNA SYNTHESIS

The PCR will require cDNA copies of the mRNA as template for amplification. Single-stranded copies will be sufficient and these can be synthesized directly from mRNA present in the total RNA preparation, without the isolation of mRNA. The following procedure is the standard first-strand cDNA synthesis protocol.[8]

The cDNA synthesis is performed in a 10 µl reaction volume, which is enough for up to about 10^5 cells. The dried RNA is resuspended in 5.6 µl of DEPC-water and a mixture containing (per reaction):

    2.0 µl 5x reverse transcriptase buffer (Bethesda Research Laboratories, Inc., Bethesda, MD)

    0.25 µl BSA (4 mg/ml, International Biotechnologies, Inc., New Haven, CT)

1.0 μl dNTPs (10 mM each, Pharmacia Fine Chemicals, Uppsala, Sweden)

0.4 μl oligo(dT)$_{12\text{-}18}$ (0.5 mg/ml, Pharmacia Fine Chemicals)

0.25 μl RNasin (40 U/ml, Promega Corp., Madison, WI)

0.5 μl MMuLV reverse transcriptase (200 U/μl, Bethesda Research Laboratories)

The mixture (total volume 10 μl) is incubated for 1 hour at 37°C, and can then be used directly in a PCR experiment.

DESIGN OF PRIMERS FOR THE POLYMERASE CHAIN REACTION

The main approach to amplify variable region encoding DNA has been to use oligonucleotides hybridizing to sequences in the signal peptide encoding part of the immunoglobulin mRNA, together with oligonucleotides annealing with sequences encoding the constant region.[1, 2] Alternatively, FR1 encoding sequences have been used as annealing sites for the "upstream primer."[4,5] FR1 sequences can be used as upstream priming sites for PCR in cases when the N-terminal protein sequences of the antibody chains are known.[9] However, for the subsequent expression of the variable regions, it is desirable to use amplified DNA containing the native FR1 sequence. Thus, the use of an upstream primer, annealing to the signal peptide encoding region, would generally be preferred.[10]

The following general guidelines are used to design primers for the amplification of Ig variable regions:

- The GC content should be around 50%.
- If the primers are too short, the probability that they will hybridize to undesired target sequences increases, and amplified DNA fragments of the wrong size will appear. Even the most commonly used size of 20–24 nucleotides often gives rise to one or several extra bands. The best results have been obtained with primers about 28 nucleotides long.
- The primers are equipped with recognition sites for restriction enzymes in their 5' ends, for easy subcloning. A few extra bases should be added outside the recognition sites to improve the efficiency of endonuclease cutting.
- Upstream primers for immunoglobulin variable region amplification will in the majority of cases have to be degenerate, because conserved sequences upstream from the immunoglobulin encoding part of the mRNA (that is, in the signal peptide encoding or 5'-nontranslated regions) do not exist. The most conserved part of this upstream region encodes the N-terminal part of the signal peptide, and primers hybridizing to sequences

starting at the initiator methionine codon should be synthesized. If one primer mixture, with all known sequences in this region, would be synthesized, the mixture will be too degenerate. To solve this problem, the different signal peptide sequences have been classified into three groups of known related sequences.[2,10] Degenerate primers were then synthesized, with a capacity to anneal to all sequences within one group, aiming at no more than 4000–5000 different primers in each primer mixture.

We have had good experience with degenerate primers consisting of 4096 different permutations, with a normal primer concentration of 1 µM in the PCR.[1,2] Although the concentration of perfect-match or near-perfect-match primers in the PCR mixture will be lower, when using primers with a high number of permutations, the normal high amounts of PCR product with the 4096 primer mixture are obtained. This "tolerance" of degeneracy can be explained by a serial annealing of the primers to the target sequence, where initially, primers with no or only a few mismatches will anneal in the first cycles. In the following cycles, the newly synthesized fragments, containing mismatches with respect to the original sequence, serve as targets for annealing of primers with additional mismatches, compared with the original sequence, and so on.

- No degeneracy in the 3' end. Although the DNA polymerase can tolerate primers that are not absolutely complementary to the template, it is crucial that the 3' end of the primers match the template, because it is the starting point for the DNA synthesis.[11,12]

  To illustrate this, PCR was performed on the same cDNA, encoding the heavy chain variable region of a mouse monoclonal antibody, using four different upstream primers (29–30 nucleotides), containing different 3' ends (Figure 4-2). One primer (#2) had a degeneracy two nucleotides from the 3' end, that is, ...GTC(AT)GG. Figure 4-2 clearly shows that this primer gave a good PCR product. Two primers were designed on the basis of primer #2, by simply removing the two 3' GG:s and synthesizing one primer (#1) with a ...GTCT and the other (#3) with a ...GTCA 3' end. Primer #1 gave a good amplification, but primer #3, with one nucleotide mismatch in the 3' end, gave no amplification at all. Normally, the *in vivo* proofreading capability of the DNA polymerase would have removed the 3' terminal A and continued the synthesis, but this mechanism does not work *in vitro* and the DNA polymerase cannot start with a 3' end mismatch. Finally, when the A at the 3' end of primer #3 was removed, that is, ...GTC, the PCR again gave a good product (data not shown).

- Oligonucleotide sequences yielding secondary structures shall be avoided, and computer programs that identify such structures are now commercially available. However, when amplifying immunoglobulin variable regions from mRNA, there is only limited space for the upstream primer.

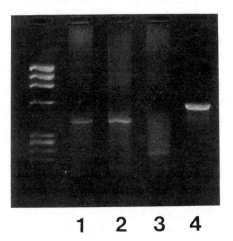

1.	5'–GGGAATTC (GC) AGG T(CG)(AC) A(AG)C TGC AG(CG) AGT C$\underline{T}$-3'	(29)
2.	5'–GGGAATTC AGG T(CG)(AC) A(AG)C TGC AG(CG) AGT C$\underline{(AT)}$G $\underline{G}$-3'	(30)
3.	5'–GGGAATTC (GC) AGG T(CG)(AC) A(AG)C TGC AG(CG) AGT C$\underline{A}$-3'	(29)

Figure 4-2. Agarose gel electrophoresis of PCR products, obtained using different upstream primers. The PCR was performed on the same cDNA, encoding the heavy chain variable regions of a mouse monoclonal antibody, using three different upstream primers (#1, #2, and #3 consisting of 29, 30, and 29 nucleotides, respectively) and a constant region (C_H1) downstream primer. Lane 1, primer #1; lane 2, primer #2; lane 3, primer #3; lane 4, PCR control. The PCR cycle was performed at 72°C (3 minutes), with a 94°C melting (1 minute) and a 58°C annealing (1 minute) temperature, with 1 minute ramp times.

The primers successfully used for amplification of the gene segments encoding the variable regions of human and mouse antibodies are presented below.

Downstream Primers

For amplification of variable regions from antibodies of different subclasses, a set of downstream primers corresponding to sequences encoding parts of the first constant region domain of heavy (C_H1) and light (C_L1) chains was used (Table 4-1).

Upstream Primers

The upstream primers used for PCR, together with a downstream primer selected for the type of antibody chain under study, are degenerate but should correspond to sequences encoding parts of the signal peptide or FR1 regions (Table 4-2).

Table 4-1. Examples of Downstream Primers

Human μ heavy chain (aa 120–125):
5'-CC<u>AAGCTT</u>AGACGAGGGGGAAAAGGGTT-3'   (1)

Human γ2 heavy chain (aa 122–127):
5'-CC<u>AAGCTT</u>GGAGCAGGGCGCCAGGGGG-3'   (2)

Human heavy chain (aa 212–219):
5'-CCC<u>ACTAGT</u>CACCTTGGTGTTGCTGGGCTTGTG-3'

Human κ light chain (aa 117–122):
5'-CC<u>AAGCTT</u>CATCAGATGGCGGGAAGAT-3'   (1)

Human κ *light chain* (aa 208–214):
5'-CCCCCC<u>TCTAGA</u>GACACTCTCCCCTGTTGAAGCT-3'

Human λ light chain (aa 120–125):
5'-CC<u>AAGCTT</u>GAAGCTCCTCAGAGGAGGG-3'   (2)

Note: Restriction enzyme sites are underlined.

Table 4-2. Examples of Upstream Primers

Human heavy chain signal peptide (aa –20 – –12):   (1)
Group HS1:
   5'-GGG<u>GAATTC</u>ATGGACTGGACCTGGAGG(AG)TC(CT)TCT(GT)C-3'

Group HS2:
   5'-GGG<u>GAATTC</u>ATGGAG(CT)TTGGGCTGA(CG)CTGG(CG)TTT(CT)T-3'

Group HS3:
   5'-<u>GAATTC</u>ATG(AG)A(AC)(AC)(AT)ACT(GT)TG(GT)
   (AT)(CGT)C(AT)(CT)(CG)CT(CT)CTG-3'

Human heavy chain FR1 (aa 1–9):
   5'-(CG)AG(GA)TGCA(GA)CTG(GC)(TA)
   <u>GCTCGAG</u>GG(GC)(GC)(GC)AG-3'

Human κ light chain signal peptide (aa –22 – –14):
   5'-GGG<u>GAATTC</u>ATGGACATG(AG)(AG)(AG)(AGT)(CT)CC
   (ACT)(ACG)G(CT)(GT)CA(CG)CTT-3'

Human λ light chain signal peptide (aa –20 – –12):
   5'-GGG<u>GAATTC</u>ATG(AG)CCTG(CG)(AT)C(CT)CCTCTC
   (CT)T(CT)CT(CG)(AT)(CT)C-3'   (2)

Human κ light chain FR1 (aa 1–8):
   5'-CCCCG(AC)(CT)<u>GAGCTC</u>(ATC)TGACCCAG(TA)CTCCA-3'

Note: Restriction enzyme sites are underlined.

CONDITIONS FOR PCR AMPLIFICATION

The following PCR protocol[2] was used for the amplification of immunoglobulin variable regions with degenerate primers: A 100 µl reaction mixture containing 2.5 U *Taq* polymerase (AmpliTaq, Perkin-Elmer-Cetus, Norwalk, CT) and 100 pmol of each primer, in a 10 Tris-HCl buffer, pH 8.3, with a final concentration of 50 mM KCl, 1.5 mM $MgCl_2$, and 0.01% gelatin.

Because of the primer degeneracy, it is hard to calculate what the optimal annealing temperature would be. When setting up a reaction for a new antibody with unknown sequence, it is therefore necessary to start a series of PCR with differing annealing temperatures to determine optimal reaction conditions. With the primer lengths normally used (see above), 50°C is a good starting point for the annealing temperature, although the primers normally work well between 42° and 60°C. In some cases, the interval of annealing temperatures for a successful PCR is very narrow. Therefore, it can be necessary to change the annealing temperature in steps of only 2°C.

The standard cycle that we use on the Perkin-Elmer Thermal Cycler is shown in Figure 4-3. It is also possible to use the auto segment extension mode to shorten the DNA synthesis phase and to save time, especially when running many cycles. For example, over one hour is saved when 60 cycles are used (Figure 4-4). This will also cause less exhaustion of the enzyme.

The reaction conditions given above are also valid when using cDNA from a single cell as a template for the reaction. The only difference from the standard protocol is that the number of cycles has to be increased. The number of cycles to be used is dependent on the productivity of the cell, that is, the number of mRNA copies present. When amplifying from a hybridoma cell, 40 cycles are often enough, as can be seen in Figure 4-5, but for one B-lymphocyte 60 cycles are routinely used.

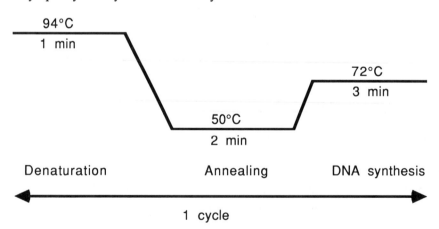

Figure 4-3. A standard PCR cycle. The ramp times are 1 minute.

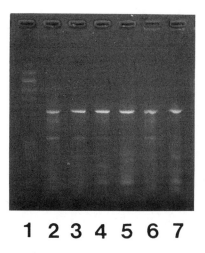

1 2 3 4 5 6 7

Figure 4-4. Comparison between use of the standard (lanes 2–4) and autosegment extension (lanes 5–7) PCR cycles for heavy chain variable region DNA amplification from small amounts of cDNA. In the autosegment extension mode, the synthesis segment was 1 minute in the initial cycle and then prolonged with 2 seconds for every new cycle. Forty PCR cycles were performed. Lane 1, *Phi* X174/*Hae* III molecular weight marker; lane 2, 100 cells; lane 3, 10 cells, lane 4, 1 cell; lane 5, 1 cell; lane 6, 10 cells; lane 7, 100 cells. 1/10 of the reaction volume was run on a 2% agarose gel and stained with ethidium bromide.

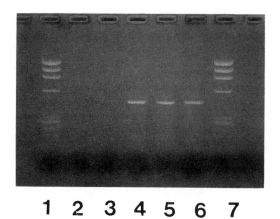

1 2 3 4 5 6 7

Figure 4-5. Heavy chain variable region amplified from cDNA of one hybridoma cell (MO6), using different numbers of PCR cycles. Lane 1, *Phi* X174/*Hae* III molecular weight marker; lane 2, 20 cycles; lane 3, 30 cycles; lane 4, 40 cycles; lane 5, 50 cycles; lane 6, 60 cycles; lane 7, *Phi* X174/*Hae* III molecular weight marker. 1/10 of the reaction volume was run on a 2% agarose gel and stained with ethidium bromide.

SEQUENCE DETERMINATION OF AMPLIFIED DNA

In the standard protocol, the chosen method for sequence determination was subcloning in M13 vectors, even though it is a rather time-consuming procedure. There are three reasons for this: (1) The short PCR-amplified fragments allow sequencing through the whole fragment using an M13 primer; that is, no additional sequencing primer needs to be synthesized; (2) The standard of M13 sequencing reactions are always very high, with readable sequences throughout; and (3) Subsequent mutagenesis work will be facilitated by having the sequence of interest in single-stranded form. Alternatively, direct sequencing of a single-stranded fragment, obtained with asymmetric PCR,[13] can be used if the only goal is to determine the nucleotide sequence of that fragment. However, direct sequencing is sometimes more troublesome, as especially seen for heavy chain variable region fragments. The same holds true for the direct sequencing protocols based on amplified double-stranded DNA.[14] If direct sequencing methods are to be employed, it is critical to use pure PCR products as starting material for the sequencing reactions.

The PCR-amplified products are purified from 2% agarose gels, either by electroelution[7] or by cutting out the band of interest and using the GeneClean procedure (BIO 101, La Jolla, CA) with glassmilk beads.

For sequencing reactions, the modified phage T7 DNA polymerase (Sequenase) supplied by United States Biochemicals Inc., Cleveland, OH, was routinely used. The protocol supplied by the manufacturer generally works well in most applications. However, it is always advisable to perform sequencing reactions with dITP substituted for dGTP (reagents supplied in the Sequenase kit) to verify sequences obtained by the standard protocol.

SUBCLONING OF AMPLIFIED DNA IN EXPRESSION VECTORS

To allow subcloning of PCR fragments into any vector, 5'-primer extensions containing recognition sequences for restriction endonucleases are used (see cDNA Synthesis section). In the case of expression vectors, it is essential to assure that the primers are designed to give the correct reading frame of the PCR fragment to be expressed.

The vector pJLA605[15] has been used for expression of human light chain variable regions in *E coli*. This vector contains the strong phage λ promoters p_L and p_R in tandem, to give a high level of transcription and also an upstream part of the *E coli* atpE gene, as the ribosome binding site for efficient translation. The upstream primer has to be equipped with an extra ATG codon, giving an initiator methionine required for the start of translation, if the primer does not include the methionine codon in the human signal peptide.

The pSW1 vector, constructed by Ward and coworkers,[16] has also been used. pSW1 contains the mouse pelB signal sequence, which directs the expressed antibody fragment into the secretory pathway of *E coli*. The level of expression in this system has varied between 1 and 10 μg/ml.

REFERENCES

1. Larrick, J.W., Danielsson, L., Brenner, C.A., Abrahamson, M., Fry, K.E., and Borrebaeck, C.A.K. 1989. Rapid cloning of rearranged immunoglobulin genes from human hybridoma cells using mixed primers and polymerase chain reaction. *Biochem. Biophys. Res. Commun.* 160:1250.

2. Larrick, J.W., Danielsson, L., Brenner, C.A., Wallace, E.F., Abrahamson, M., Fry, K.E., and Borrebaeck, C.A.K. 1989. Polymerase chain reaction using mixed primers: Cloning of human monoclonal antibody variable region genes from single hybridoma cells. *Bio/Technology* 7:934.

3. Carlsson, R., Martensson, C., Kalliomaki, S., Ohlin, M., and Borrebaeck, C.A.K. 1991. The SCID mouse. Human peripheral blood lymphocytes constitute a normal humoral immune system when transferred into SCID mice. Submitted for publication.

4. Orlandi, R., Gussow, D.H., Jones, P.T., and Winter, G. 1989. Cloning immunoglobulin variable domains for expression by the polymerase chain reaction. *Proc. Natl. Acad. Sci. USA* 86:3833.

5. Huse, W.D., Sastry, L., Iverson, S.A., Kang, A.S., Alting-Mees, M., Burton, D.R., Benkovic, S.J., and Lerner, R.A. 1989. Generation of a large combinatorial library of the immunoglobulin repertoire in phage lambda. *Science* 246:1275.

6. Chomczynski, P. and Sacchi, N. 1987. Single-step method of RNA isolation by acid guanidium thiocyanate-phenol-chloroform extraction. *Anal. Biochem.* 162:156.

7. Rappolee, D.A., Brenner, C.A., Schultz, R., Mark, D., and Werb, Z. 1988. Developmental expression of PDGF, TGF-alpha, and TGF-β genes in pre-implantation mouse embryo. *Science* 241:1823.

8. Sambrok, J., Fritsch, E.F., and Maniatis, T. 1989. *Molecular Cloning: A Laboratory Manual.* 2nd ed. Cold Spring Harbor, NY: Cold Spring Harbor Laboratory Press.

9. Larrick, J.W., Chiang, Y.L., Sheng-Dong, R., Senyk, G., and Casali, P. 1988. Generation of specific human monoclonal antibodies by *in vitro* expansion of

Acknowledgments: We thank Javier Vasquez for providing data for Figure 4-2 and to Dr. Sally Ward for providing the expression vector pSW1 as well as the *E coli* strain BMH71-18. The results presented in this chapter are derived from investigations supported by grants from the Swedish National Board for Technical Development.

human B cells: A novel recombinant DNA approach. In: *Progress in Biotechnology,* vol.5. *In Vitro Immunization in Hybridoma Technology* Borrebaeck, C.A.K. Amsterdam, The Netherlands: Elsevier Science Publishers B.V.23.

10. Kabat, E.A., Wu, T.T., Reid-Miller, M., Perry, H.M. and Gottesman, K.S. 1987. *Sequences of Protein of Immunological Interest,* 4th ed. Washington, DC: Public Health Service, NIH.

11. Sommer, R. and Tautz, D. 1989. Minimal homology requirements for PCR primers. *Nucl. Acids Res.* 17:6749.

12. Kwok, S., Kellogg, D.E., McKinney, N., Spasic, D., Goda, L., Levenson, C., and Sninsky, J.J. 1990. Effects of primer-template mismatches on the polymerase chain reaction: Human immunodeficiency virus type 1 model studies. *Nucl. Acids Res.* 18:999.

13. Gyllensten, U. 1989. Direct sequencing of *in vitro* amplified DNA. In: Erlich, H.A., ed. *PCR Technology. Principles and Applications for DNA Amplification.* New York: Stockton Press; 45.

14. Kusukawa, N., Uemori, T., Asada, K., and Kato, I. 1990. Rapid and reliable protocol for direct sequencing of material amplified by the polymerase chain reaction. *BioTechniques* 9:66.

15. Schauder, B., Blöcker, H., Frank, R., and McCarthy, J.E.G. 1987. Inducible expression vectors incorporating the *Escherichia coli atpE* translational initiation region. *Gene* 52:279.

16. Ward, E.S., Güssow, D., Griffiths, A.D., Jones, P.T., and Winter, G. 1989. Binding activities of a repertoire of single immunoglobulin variable domains secreted from *Escherichia coli. Nature* 341:544.

CHAPTER 5

Combinatorial Antibody Expression Libraries in Filamentous Phage

William Huse

The selective binding characteristics of antibodies make them well suited for use in a variety of techniques including basic research, diagnostics, and therapeutic applications. Methods are available for producing polyclonal serum or monoclonal antibodies specific for essentially any available antigen. Monoclonal antibodies are especially useful because they can be generated with homogeneous binding specificity. Methods for producing monoclonal antibodies are, however, laborious, time-consuming, and require extensive cell-culturing techniques. Generally, the production of monoclonal antibodies has been limited to murine antibodies because immunizations are required to enrich the B-cell population for antibodies with a desired specificity. Immunization also selects related B-cell clones that have undergone affinity maturation by somatic mutation. This can generate essentially an unlimited number of unique antibodies. In contrast, due to the relative inefficiency of the *in vitro* fusion and screening process, the production of monoclonal antibodies generally results in only a few hundred different antibodies. In addition, because of limitations of immunization protocols, human antibodies are not easily constructed with hybridoma methods.

Because hybridoma methods of generating monoclonal antibodies have limitations, recent attention has focused on mimicking an animal's immune system by reproducing the antibody diversity in easily manipulatable microorganisms. Initial attempts to express antibodies in a prokaryotic organism such as *Escherichia coli* were largely unsuccessful because proper folding, disulfide bond formation, and heteromeric association of heavy and light antibody chains are all required to obtain functional molecules. This was true for early attempts to express whole antibody molecules in both bacteria[1, 2] and yeast.[3] However, these initial results were overcome in *E coli* by expressing smaller antibody fragments such as Fab and F_v fragments. Successful expression of antibody molecules was first accomplished for a single antibody species composed of one unique heavy chain and one unique light chain.[4, 5] These expression methods have been subsequently expanded to the expression of heavy chain fragment libraries[6, 7] and to libraries expressing random populations of both heavy and light chain fragments.[8]

While it is difficult and time-consuming to manipulate monoclonal antibodies identified as a hybridoma, the ease with which *E coli* can be manipulated greatly reduces the time necessary for antibody production and facilitates recombinant engineering for the study and optimization of antibody-antigen binding interactions. For example, the fast growth and easy fermentation of *E coli* allows rapid and efficient large-scale production of antibody fragments. Efficient methods for transformation and manipulation of the cloned antibody fragments permit site-directed mutagenesis for the optimization of binding or specificity. Bacterial expression of diverse antibody fragment libraries allows reverse immunoscreening of larger populations of antibody fragments than could previously be obtained by conventional methods.[8] Additionally, prokaryotic systems afford the possibility of using metabolic selection techniques for the isolation of a desired antibody species. Positive selection methods are conceivable for antigen binding and catalytic function of mutant antibodies. Selection methods can be devised for the possible replacement of both constant regions through genetic markers,[9] toxins,[10] or antibody regions from a different class[11] or a different species.[12]

A great advantage of bacterially-produced antibody fragments is that protein hetergeneity resulting from nonspecific cleavages and differential protease susceptibility will be obviated because homogeneous preparations can be consistently produced. Further, Fab cDNAs can be modified before expression in a bacterial system to incorporate desired features additional to antigen binding. For example, modifications of the primary structure can be performed for subsequent conjugation of imaging or therapeutic agents. Modification by site-directed mutagenesis can also be performed for fusion to marker peptides or other sequences of useful function. Recombinant expression, therefore, combines the advantages of hybridoma expression in the native state with the advantages of *E coli* as the host.

CRITERIA FOR BACTERIAL EXPRESSION OF SINGLE ANTIBODY SPECIES

Antibody fragments may be produced in *E coli* if the folding and assembly pathway of antibodies in eukaryotic cells are faithfully reproduced. In eukaryotic cells, each of the heavy and light chains are vectorially translated into the lumen of the endoplasmic reticulum (ER). This transport mechanism requires an amino-terminal signal sequence, which is concisely cleaved off during the translocation event by signal peptidase, to produce the mature protein. In the lumen of the ER, several events must take place for the proper formation of functional antibodies. These events are protein folding, formation of disulfide bonds, and the association of individual heavy and light chains into heteromeric molecules. In addition to these critical steps, which must be mimicked in the bacterial cell, antibodies are glycosylated in the lumen of the ER and Golgi apparatus as they transit to the cell surface. Glycosylation is essential to the Fc portion of the antibody but does not, however, play a role in antigen binding.

Protein transport to the periplasm of *E coli* has been found to be functionally equivalent to eukaryotic transport of proteins.[4, 5] These prokaryotic systems also satisfy all the criteria necessary for assembly of functional antibody fragments. First, synthesis of approximately stoichiometric amounts of both chains can be accomplished by expressing both chains under the control of a single prometer. Second, transport of both precursor proteins to the periplasmic space has been found to occur efficiently and accurately with correct processing of signal sequences. Third, the antibody fragments are correctly folded into functional domains with proper disulfide bond formation. Fourth, the heavy and light chain antibody fragments are self-assembled into functional heterodimers.

RECOMBINANT ANTIBODY FRAGMENTS

Successful expression in *E coli* of functionally-equivalent antibodies was obtained when smaller portions corresponding to Fab and F_v fragments were expressed instead of entire heavy and light polypeptides. The coexpression of smaller fragments was found to increase the number of molecules in the properly folded state compared to expression of whole antibody molecules. The overall result was the accumulation of Fab or F_v fragments.

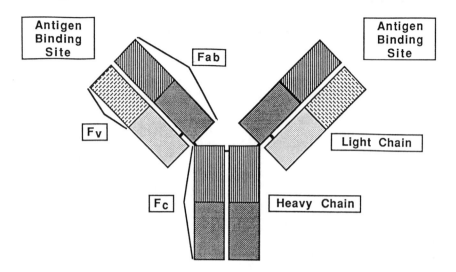

Figure 5-1. Fragments of antibody light and heavy chains expressed and secreted from *E coli* assemble to form functional Fab or F_v fragments. These fragments contain the antigen-binding domain of antibodies. Whole antibodies are not efficiently expressed in bacteria.

Fab fragments are about one third the size of an antibody molecule (Figure 5-1) and exhibit monovalent antigen binding (compared to F(ab')2 fragments, which retain both antigen-binding pockets and therefore exhibit divalent binding activity). Fab fragments can be biochemically prepared from whole antibodies by proteolytic cleavage. These fragments are well characterized as having the same binding specificities as intact antibodies. As shown independently by Skerra and Pluckthun[4] and also by Better and colleagues,[5] the same binding characteristics of biochemically prepared Fab now applies for recombinant Fab fragments. Fab fragments are stable and associate well because the constant region contributes additionally binding energy for stability. However, the yield of functional Fab fragment is significantly lower than that of the F_v fragment in *E coli*. The problem appears to be improper folding or assembly *in vivo*.[13]

The F_v fragment is the smallest fragment that still contains a complete antigen-binding pocket (see Figure 5-1). The fragment consists of only the variable regions of the heavy (V_H) and light (V_L) chains and contains identical binding properties as Fab fragment or intact antibody. A disadvantage, however, is that the smaller variable region polypeptides tend to disassociate into separate chains upon dilution. Because the disassociation constants depend on amino acid interactions at the contact sites, the actual equilibrium between V_H and V_L chains will vary between antibodies due to differences in the complementarity-determining region sequences (CDR).

Expression of isolated variable region domains has also been performed in *E coli*.[6,7] Libraries have been constructed that produce diverse populations of only V_H polypeptides.[6, 7] The rationale in doing so stems from x-ray crystallographic structures of whole antibodies that predict that a significant amount of the antigen-binding energy comes from the heavy chain alone. This loss of affinity can be somewhat restored by combining heavy chains with nonspecific light chains.[14-18] The antigen-binding affinity of isolated heavy chains for use as substitutes of whole antibody is, however, one to two orders of magnitude lower than heterodimers composed of V_H and V_L. Additionally, isolated V_H chains exhibit low solubility at temperatures above 4°C and are relatively sticky, making it likely that antibody V_H fragments, identified from expression libraries, will not retain affinity for an antigen when coexpressed with a light chain. These characteristics are probably due to the exposed hydrophobic residues, which are normally in association with a V_L chain.[7, 19]

Recombinant Antibody Fragment Libraries

The expression of antibody fragment libraries is an important extension of the recombinant expression of unique antibody species. Polymerase chain reaction (PCR) technology has allowed access to the diverse family of antibody genes as they contain conserved sequences in the 5′ and 3′ portion of the variable, framework, and whole constant region sequences. Specific amplification of antibody fragments using primers directed to these conserved sequences allows the construction of libraries containing diverse populations of heavy and light chain antibody fragments.[20, 21]

Coexpression libraries for heavy and light chain sequences have now been accomplished by first producing separate heavy and light chain libraries and then randomly combining the two libraries into a single vector population.[8] Each antibody fragment coexpressed from a single vector of randomly combined populations of heavy and light chain sequences retains all the characteristics exhibited by expression of a single antibody fragment species. The libraries produced from both heavy and light chain fragments also solve the low antigen-binding affinities associated with heavy chain libraries alone. Moreover, random combination of both chains serves as a source of diversity and, therefore, increases the total number of sequences that can be obtained.

A bacteriophage M13-based vector system is now available for construction of antibody libraries. As with bacteriophage lambda, two populations of heavy and light chain sequences are synthesized by PCR and are cloned into separate expression vectors. The heavy chain vector contains an M13 coat protein sequence so that translation of the heavy chain produces a gVIII-V_H fusion protein. Heavy and light chain vector populations are randomly combined such that only the vector portions containing the V_H and V_L

sequences are joined into a single circular vector. The combined vector directs the coexpression of V_H and V_L sequences for assembly of the polypeptides on the surface of M13. A mechanism also exists to control the expression of gVIII-V_H fusion proteins during library construction and screening. Panning high titer phage populations for antigen-binding activity also provides direct isolation of the cDNAs encoding the antibody of interest.

The M13 surface expression library compares favorably with the *in vivo* antibody repertoire in terms of size and diversity and provides the advantage of quickly obtaining functional molecules compared to standard immunologic methods. The possibility now exists that functional molecules may be obtained, if a large enough library is screened, without necessarily using standard immunization procedures. Presently, functional antibody fragments specific to a desired antigen have only been obtained from libraries constructed from cDNAs obtained from animals immunized with the antigen of interest.

The size of the mammalian repertoire is typically estimated to be on the order of 10^6 to 10^8 different antigen specificities. Surface expression libraries of this size can be obtained using standard recombinant methods and the vector system now available for this purpose (Figure 5-2). If larger diversity is needed, heavy and light chains within the initial library or from the original single chain libraries can be systematically shuffled to obtain libraries of exceptionally large numbers. Once an antibody is obtained with a desired specificity, the antigen-binding affinity can be subsequently optimized using recombinant mutagenesis procedures. The ease in which mutagenesis can be performed alleviates potential problems associated with reimmunization and rescreening of hybridomas if an antibody with an acceptable binding affinity is not obtained in the first production.

In regard to the diversity of the *in vivo* repertoire compared to the M13 system, the diversity characteristics of an unimmunized repertoire is expected to be similar to recombinant libraries in that both involve random combinations of heavy and light chains. The factors leading to this expectation, however, are different between the two systems. For example, diversity may be restricted *in vivo* due to physiologic mechanisms such as immunologic tolerance, which does not affect the diversity of a recombinant library. In contrast, restriction of diversity within the recombinant system may be inherently affected by the cloning process itself. The fortuitous presence of restriction sites in the variable region used for cloning and combination will cause those species containing such restriction sites to be eliminated within the library. More abundant mRNA species derived from stimulated cells will predominate over those species derived from unstimulated cells, because the representation of sequences within the library will mirror that found in the natural mRNA source. Likewise, the resting repertoire might over-represent less specific antibody species originating from spontaneously activated B

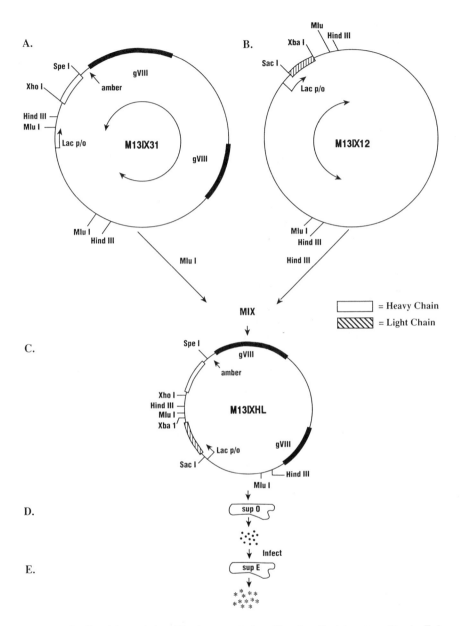

Figure 5-2. Combinatorial antibody expression libraries that have antibody Fab fragments attached to the surface of bacteria phage M13 can be constructed in two steps. First, a heavy chain and a light chain library are constructed. These libraries are combined to form a combinatorial library that coexpresses randomly paired heavy and light chains. The heavy and light chain expression is regulated by the Lac repressor, and the heavy chain is expressed as a fusion protein with pVIII of M13 when expressed in an amber suppressor strain.

cells. Another difference between the *in vivo* repertoire and a recombinant antibody library is that physiologic mechai. ns, such as somatic mutation, exist to increase the binding affini. of an antibody for a particular antigen. High-affinity antibodies resulting om these physiologic mechanisms should not be expected in recombinant libraries. Despite these apparent difficulties, minor modifications can be made to current procedures to circumvent these inherent drawbacks. These modifications include the use of different tissue sources for mRNA isolation and of different PCR primers to alleviate sequence bias. The use of optimization strategies as described above can be employed to increase antigen-binding affinities of the generated antibodies.

Screening of the recombinant libraries to obtain a functional antibody fragment provides an extreme advantage over conventional immunologic techniques. The power of recombinant methods allows easier access to a large number of different molecules in a relatively short period of time. Gene products of at least 10^6 can be readily screened in a day using reverse immunoscreening methods with labeled antigen. Equivalent protocols, employing secondary affinity reagents can also be applied. Prokaryotic systems have the additional advantage of well-characterized selection schemes. These schemes can be modified to more efficiently select for the proper combination of heavy and light chains into a single functional library with a larger diversity. For example, selection methods may also be utilized in the case of catalytic antibodies to screen antibodies based on function instead of binding affinity. In this way, the limitations imposed by assaying only for binding to a specific transition state analogue are eliminated. Once an antibody fragment is obtained with the desired binding characteristics, the applications are not limited to uses requiring only the binding properties of the antibody molecule. For applications requiring Fc effector functions, the technology already exists for grafting variable region domains into heteroglobus antibody genes to produce functional chimeric molecules. Modified antibodies of th´ ₂ nature would be of great use as therapeutics in a variety of clinical applications.

METHODS

Surface expression libraries are constructed in modified filamentous bacteriophage cloning vectors. The modifications include all the elements necessary for library construction and surface expression as gVIII fusion proteins of Fab and F_v fragments (see Figure 5-2). Two vectors are used for producing the surface expression library. Each vector is used for generating separate cDNA libraries for heavy and light chain populations. Populations of V_H or F_v sequences are cloned into the M13 heavy chain vector (Figure 5-2A) whereas V_L sequences are cloned into the M13 light chain vector (Figure 5-2B).

The vector used for cloning heavy chain PCR products (Figure 5-2A) contains, in addition to expression elements, a sequence encoding a pseudo-wild type gVIII product downstream and in frame with the cloning sites. This gene encodes the wild type M13 gVIII amino acid sequence but has been changed at the nucleotide level to reduce homologous recombination with the wild type gVIII contained on the same vector. The wild type gVIII is present to ensure that at least some functional, non-fusion coat protein will be produced. Inclusion of a wild type gVIII therefore reduces the possibility of nonviable phage production and biologic selection against certain peptide fusion proteins. Differential regulation of the two genes can also be used to control the relative ratio of the pseudo and wild type proteins.

Also contained downstream and in frame with the cloning sites is an amber stop codon. The stop codon is located between the inserted V_H sequences and the gVIII sequence. As is the function of the wild type gVIII, the amber also reduces biologic selection when combining vector portions to produce functional surface expression vectors. This is accomplished by using a non-suppressor (sup O) host strain to terminate translation after the V_H sequences.

The vector used for light chain populations (Figure 5-2B), contains the necessary expression elements and cloning sites for V_L PCR products. As with the heavy chain sector, upstream and in frame with the cloning sites is a leader sequence for sorting to the phage surface. Additionally, a ribosome binding site and Lac Z promoter/operator elements are also present for transcription and translation of the DNA sequences.

Both vectors contain two pairs of Mlu I-Hind III restriction enzyme sites (Figures 5-2A and 5-2B) for joining together the V_H and V_L encoding sequences and their associated vector sequences. Mlu I and Hind III are noncompatible restriction sites. The two pairs are symmetrically orientated about the cloning site so that only the vector portions containing the sequences to be expressed are exactly combined into a single vector. The two pairs of sites are oriented identically with respect to one another on both vectors and the DNA between the two sites must be homologous enough between both vectors to allow annealing. This orientation allows cleavage of each circular vector with opposite restriction enzymes, exonuclease digestion of 3' single strands and annealing of essential components within each vector into a single coexpression vector.

Isolation of mRNA and PCR Amplification of Antibody Fragments

Total RNA is isolated from the spleen of a single immunized mouse. The procedure is described by Chomczynski and Sacchi:[22]

1. Homogenize the spleen from a single immunized mouse in a glass homogenizer in 10 ml of denaturing solution (4.0 M guanine isothiocyanate, 0.25 M sodium citrate, pH 7.0, 0.1 M 2-mercaptoethanol).
2. Add 1.0 ml of 2 M sodium acetate, pH 4.0 and mix thoroughly.
3. Add 1.0 ml of saturated phenol and mix.
4. Add 2.0 ml of chloroform:isoamyl alcohol (24:1).
5. Vigorously mix the homogenate for 10 seconds and place on ice for 15 minutes.
6. Transfer the homogenate to a thick-walled 50-ml polypropylene centrifuge and centrifuge at 10,000 × g for 20 minutes at 4°C.
7. Transfer the upper RNA-containing aqueous layer to a new polypropylene tube and mix with an equal volume of isopropyl alcohol.
8. Incubate the mixture at –20°C for at least 1 hour to precipitate the RNA.
9. Centrifuge the precipitate at 10,000 × g for 20 minutes at 4°C.
10. Decant the supernatant and resuspend the pellet in 3 ml of denaturing solution.
11. Add 3.0 ml of isopropyl alcohol and mix vigorously.
12. Reprecipitate the RNA at –20°C for 1 hour and centrifuge as described in step 9 to collect the precipitate.
13. Wash the pellet once in 70% ethanol and dry under vacuum for 15 minutes.
14. Resuspend the RNA in an appropriate amount of diethyl pyrocarbonate (DEPC) treated dH_2O (DEPC-dH_2O; typically about 1–2 ml).

Poly A+ RNA is prepared from the total RNA for use in first strand cDNA synthesis as described by Aviv and Leder.[23] Following first round cDNA, the DNA-RNA heteroduplexes are used as templates for PCR amplification:

1. One half of the total RNA isolated from the spleen of a single mouse is adjusted to a final volume of 1 ml in DEPC-dH_2O and heated at 65°C for 5 minutes.
2. One ml of 2x high salt loading buffer is added, mixed, and allowed to cool slowly to room temperature (100 mM Tris-HCl, pH 7.5, 1 M $NaCl_2$, 2 mM disodium EDTA, pH 8.0, 2% SDS).
3. The solution is applied to an oligo-dT cellulose previously prepared by washing in 0.1 M NaOH, 5 mM EDTA and then equilibrating the column in DEPC-dH_2O.

4. Collect the initial eluate, heat for 5 minutes at 65°C, and then reapply to the column.
5. Wash the column with 2 ml of 1× high salt loading buffer (50 mM Tris-HCl, pH 7.5, 500 mM NaCl$_2$, 1 mM disodium EDTA, pH 8.0, 1% SDS).
6. Wash a second time with 2 ml of 1× medium salt buffer (50 mM Tris-HCl, pH 7.5, 100 mM NaCl$_2$, 1 mM disodium EDTA, pH 8.0, 1% SDS).
7. Elute the poly A+ mRNA with 1 ml of elution buffer (10 mM Tris-HCl, pH 7.5, 1 mM disodium EDTA, pH 8.0, 0.05% SDS).
8. Purify the mRNA by extraction with an equal volume of phenol/chloroform (1:1) followed by extraction with an equal volume of chloroform and then ethanol precipitation.
9. Wash in 70% ethanol, dry, and resuspend in DEPC-dH$_2$O.
10. First strand cDNA synthesis is performed in a 250 µl reaction volume containing 5-10 µg of poly A+ mRNA.
11. The RNA is mixed with 0.5 pmol of either the 3' V$_H$ primer for heavy chain library construction (primer 12, Table 5-1) or the 3' Vl primer for light chain library construction (primer 9, Table 5-2) and heated at 65° C for 5 minutes.
12. The mixture is allowed to cool to room temperature and is adjusted with 5× reverse transcription buffer and DEPC-H$_2$O to obtain a final concentration of 0.8 mM dNTP, 100 mM Tris-HCL, pH 8.6, 10mM MgCl$_2$, 40 mM KCl, 20 mM 2-mercaptoethanol.
13. Moloney-Murine Leukemia virus reverse transcriptase, 26 units, is added and the solution is incubated at 40°C for 1 hour.
14. The resultant cDNA is purified by extraction and precipitation as described above and used for PCR amplification.

Primers used for amplification of heavy chain sequences (Fd) are shown in Table 5-1. PCR amplification is performed, as described by Saiki and coworkers[24] in eight separate reactions as described by Sastry and colleagues.[6] Each reaction contains one of the 5' primers (primers 2–9, Table 5-1) and one of the 3' primers (primer 12, Table 5-1). Other primers that can be used for amplification in a single reaction mixture are also shown in Table 5-1. Primer 1 is a 5' degenerate primer and primer 10, also a 5' primer, incorporates inosine at four degenerate positions. The remaining 3' (primer 11) is used to construct F$_v$ fragments. The underlined region of the 5' primers incorporates an Xho I site in the PCR products. For the 3' primers a Spe I restriction site is incorporated. These restriction sites are used for cloning amplified products into the heavy chain vector in a predetermined reading frame for expression.

Table 5-1. Heavy Chain Primers

1.	5'- AGGT(C,G)(C,A)A(G,A)CT(G,T)<u>CTCGAGT</u>C(T,A)GG -3'
2.	5'- AGGTCCAGCTG<u>CTCGAGT</u>CTGG -3'
3.	5'- AGGTCCAGCTG<u>CTCGAGT</u>CAGG -3'
4.	5'- AGGTCCAGCTT<u>CTCGAGT</u>CAGG -3'
5.	5'- AGGTCCAGCTT<u>CTCGAG</u>TCAGG -3'
6.	5'- AGGTCCAACTG<u>CTCGAGT</u>CTGG -3'
7.	5'- AGGTCCAACTG<u>CTCGAGT</u>CAGG -3'
8.	5'- AGGTCCAACTT<u>CTCGAGT</u>CTGG -3'
9.	5'- AGGTCCAACTT<u>CTCGAGT</u>CAGG -3'
10.	5'- AGGTIIAICTIC<u>TCGAGT</u>C(T,A)GG -3'
11.	5'-CTATTA<u>ACTAGT</u>AACGGTAACAGTGGTGCCTTGCCCCA -3'
12.	5'- AGGCTT<u>ACTAGT</u>ACAATCCCTGGGCACAAT -3'

Primers used for amplification of mouse kappa light chain sequences are shown in Table 5-2. The PCR products are subsequently cloned into the M13 light chain vector for V_L library construction. The primers are designed to contain restriction sites that are compatible with the proper orientation and reading frame of the vector and not present in conserved sequences of the mouse light chain mRNA. As with the heavy chain sequences, PCR is performed in independent reactions using five separate sets of primers to insure unbiased amplification of mRNA sequences. Each reaction contains one of the 5' primers (primers 3 to 7; Table 5-2) and one of the 3' primers (primer 9; Table 5-2). The remaining 3' (primer 8; Table 5-2) can be used for construction of F_v fragments. The remaining 5' primers (primers 1 and 2; Table 5-2) can be used for single tube amplifications. The underlined portion of the 5' primers depicts a Sac I restriction site and an Xba I site for the 3' primers.

PCR amplification is performed for both the heavy and light chain sequences as described below.

1. PCR amplification is performed in 100 μl reaction volume containing ~5.0 μg of the above cDNA-RNA heteroduplexes from the reverse transcription reaction, 300 nmol each of the 3' and 5' primers for heavy or light chain amplification, 200 mM dNTP, 50 mM KCl, 10 mM Tris-HCl, pH 8.3, 15 mM MgCl₂, 0.1% gelatin, and 2 units of Thermus aquaticus DNA polymerase.
2. Overlay the reaction mixture with mineral oil.
3. Perform 40 cycles of amplification using the following regime: (1) denature at 92°C for 1 minute, (2) anneal at 52°C for 2 minutes, (3) polymerize at 72°C for 1.5 minutes.

Table 5-2. Light Chain Primers

1.	5'- CCAGTTCC<u>GAGCTC</u>GTTGTGACTCAGGAATCT -3'
2.	5'- CCAGTTCC<u>GAGCTC</u>GTGTTGACGCAGCCGCCC -3'
3.	5'- CCAGTTCC<u>GAGCTC</u>GTGCTCACCCAGTCTCCA -3'
4.	5'- CCAGTTCC<u>GAGCTC</u>CAGATGACCCAGTCTCCA -3'
5.	5'- CCAGATGT<u>GAGCTC</u>GTGATGACCCAGACTCCA -3'
6.	5'- CCAGATGT<u>GAGCTC</u>GTCATGACCCAGTCTCCA -3'
7.	5'- CCAGTTCC<u>GAGCTC</u>GTGATGACACAGTCTCCA -3'
8.	5'- GCAGCATT<u>CTAGA</u>TGGGCAGCTCCAGCTTGCC -3'
9.	5'- GCGCCG<u>TCTAGA</u>ATTAACACTCATTCCTGTTGAA -3'

4. Extract the amplified samples twice with an equal volume of phenol/chloroform (1:1), once with an equal volume of chloroform and ethanol precipitate.

5. Resuspend the products in a small volume of TE (10 mM Tris-HCl, pH 7.5, 0.5 mM EDTA). Combine the heavy chain products and adjust the concentration to 1 µg/µl with TE. Do the same with the light chain products.

6. To prepare the PCR products for library construction, double digest each mixture to completion with the appropriate restriction enzymes. Heavy chain products: digest with Xho I (125 units) and Spe I (10 units) at 2.5 µg/30µl of buffer containing 150 mM NaCl, 8 mM Tris-HCl, pH 7.5, 6 mM $MgSO_4$, 1 mM DTT, 200 µg/ml BSA. Light chain products: digest with Sac I (200 units) and Xba I (200 units) at 2.5 µg/500 µl of buffer containing 33 mM Tris acetate, pH 7.85, 66 mM K acetate, 10 mM Mg acetate, 0.5 mM DTT.

7. Purify the products on a 1% agarose gel by electroelution of the 700 bp species and ethanol precipitation. Resuspend at 10 ng/µl.

Library Construction

Surface expression libraries are constructed in two steps. In the first step, separate heavy and light chain libraries are constructed in different M13-based vectors (Figures 5-2A and 5-2B). In the second step, the two resultant libraries are combined at the Mlu I-Hind III sites present in each vector (Figure 5-2C). Heavy and light chain PCR products can be cloned using the cloning sites provided in the vectors and PCR primers; however, to ensure that sequences are not destroyed by restriction, PCR products can be inserted into single-strand vectors using exonuclease digestion and hybridization of the single-stranded regions as described below. For this protocol, disregard the restriction digests of PCR products described above.

1. In separate tubes, combine at 5 μg all heavy chain PCR products and light chain PCR products, ethanol precipitate, and resuspend each mixture in 20 μl of NaOAc buffer (33 mM Tris acetate, pH 7.9, 10 mM Mg-acetate, 66 mM K-acetate, 0.5 mM DTT).
2. Add 5 units of T4 DNA polymerase and incubate the reactions at 30°C for 5 minutes to remove 3′ termini by exonuclease digestion.
3. Stop the reactions by heating at 70° C for 5 minutes.
4. Prepare the heavy chain vector by restriction with Stu I and the light chain vector by restriction with Eco RV, followed by exonuclease digestion as described in steps 2 and 3 above.
5. Anneal in NaOAc buffer the PCR products with their respective vectors at 1:1 molar ratio using a final concentration of 10 ng/ml.
6. Electroporate the DNA from each annealing into *E coli* MK30-3.

Surface Expression Library Construction. Construction of a surface expression is performed by restricting each population of heavy and light chain containing vectors with Mlu I and Hind III, respectively. The 3′ termini of each restricted population is digested with a 3′ to 5′ exonuclease as described above for inserting sequences into the cloning sites. Vector populations are mixed, allowed to anneal, and introduced into an appropriate host. A nonsuppressor strain should be used during initial construction of the library to ensure that sequences are not selected against due to lethal expression of fusion proteins. Phage isolated from a nonsuppressor library can be used to infect a suppressor strain for surface expression antibody fragments.

1. Isolate double strand V_H and V_L sector populations.
2. Digest 5 μg of the V_L sector population with an excess of Hind III and 5 μg of the V_H population with an excess of Mlu I.
3. Stop each reaction by phenol/chloroform extraction, followed by ethanol precipitation.
4. Resuspend each pellet in 20 μl of NaOAc buffer and add 5 units of T4 DNA polymerase. Incubate at 30°C for 5 minutes.
5. Stop the reactions by heating at 70°C for 5 minutes.
6. Mix the vector populations at a final concentration of 10 ng of each vector|μl and allow to anneal at room temperature overnight.
7. Electroporate into MK30-3 cells.

Panning of Surface Expression Libraries. Surface expression phage are affinity-isolated by panning on antigen.[25]

1. Infect at a multiplicity of infection of 10 an amber suppressor strain (XL1 Blue)TM from phage stocks prepared from MK30-3.
2. Induce the cultures with 2 mM IPTG and purify the phage particles PEG precipitation and cesium chloride equilibrium centrifugation.

3. Coat polystyrene petri plates with 1 ml of 1 mg/ml streptavidin in 0.1 m NaHCO$_3$, pH 8.6, 0.02% NaN3 overnight at 4°C. Remove and block for 1 hour using 29 mg/ml BSA, 3 µg/ml streptavidin, 0.1 M NAHCO$_3$, pH 8.6, 0.02% NaN3. Wash the plates 3 times with TBS containing 0.5% Tween 20.

4. Biotinylate the antigen and incubate 5 µl (2–3 µg) with a 50 µl portion of the library overnight at 4°C.

5. Dilute the phage with 1 ml of TBS–0.5% Tween 20 and transfer to the streptavidin coated plates.

6. Incubate for 10 minutes at room temperature with rocking and remove the unbound phage.

7. Wash the plates 10 times with TBS–0.5% Tween 20 over a period of 30–90 minutes.

8. Elute the bound phage with 800 µl of sterile elution buffer (1 mg/ml BSA, 0.1 M HCl, pH adjusted to 2.2 with glycerol) for 15 minutes.

9. Neutralize the eluates with 48 µl of 2 M Tris base.

10. Titer a 20-µl portion of each eluate on MK30-3 with dilutions of input phage.

Reverse Immunoscreening for Antigen Binding.   Reverse immunoscreening is performed similarly to standard plaque screening methods, except that antigen is used for the detection instead of antibody. Usually the antigen is labeled, but it can be modified with a reagent such as biotin to be capable of being labeled.

1. Plate as follows a volume of the titered combinatorial Fab phage at a density that yields ~30,000 phage per 150 mm plate:
   - Add to the phage stock 600 µl of exponentially-growing *E coli*
   - Absorb for 15 minutes at 37°C
   - Add 7.5 ml of top agar, mix, and distribute evenly across the surface of a prewarmed agar plate

2. Incubate the plates at 37°C for 5 hours.

3. Overlay the plates with nitrocellulose filters that had been pretreated with a solution of 10 mM isopropyl-beta-D-thiogalactopyranoside (IPTG).

4. Incubate for an additional 4 hours at 37°C.

5. Mark the orientation of the filters with a needle dipped in waterproof ink by punching at least 3 asymmetric holes around the circumference of the plates.

6. Remove the filters and was once in TBST solution for 5 to 15 minutes (20 mM Tris-HCl, pH 7.5, 150 mM NaCl, 0.05% polyoxyethylene soriban monolaurate (Tween-20).

7. Perform a duplicate lift by placing a second nitrocellulose filter pre-soaked in IPTG, mark the orientation, remove the filters, and wash in TBST solution as described in step 6 above.
8. Wash all filters in a fresh solution of TBST for an additional 15 minutes.
9. Place the filters in blocking solution for 1 hour at room temperature (20 mM Tris-HCl, pH 7.5, 150 mM NaCl, 1% BSA).
10. Transfer to a fresh blocking solution containing 125^I-labeled or biotinylated antigen at a concentration of ~ 0.1 μM.
11. Agitate the filters for 1 hour at room temperature.
12. Wash the filters 3–5 times in TBST for 5 minutes each wash to remove any unbound antigen.
13. Visualize the lifts by autoradiography for 125^I-labeled antigen or by streptavidin conjugated enzyme label. Note: For streptavidin enzyme labeling, the incubation and washes performed with primary antigen should be repeated with the secondary streptavidin conjugate.

Antigen-binding Specificity. To obtain a quick determination of Fab binding specificity, competition experiments with unlabeled antigen can be performed on nitrocellulose lifts of positive phage. In this analysis, filter lifts of plaques are incubated with labeled antigen in the presence of increasing concentrations of unlabeled inhibitor.

1. Spot in duplicate about 100 phage particles per spot directly onto a bacterial lawn.
2. Overlay the filter with an IPTG-soaked filter and incubate at 25°C for 19 hours.
3. Wash the filters with TBST and block in blocking solution as described above for filter screening.
4. Incubate in 125^I-labeled or biotinylated antigen (~ 0.1 μM) in the presence of varying concentrations of unlabeled antigen using the conditions described above for screening.
5. Visualize by autoradiography or enzyme-conjugated streptavidin.

CONCLUSION

A filamentous phage vector system designed for the construction and screening of antibody expression libraries has been described. When infected into bacteria, the phage directs the expression of antibody Fab fragments attached to the phage coat. This facilitates the screening of large numbers of antibody constructs. Once an antibody has been identified it can be sequenced and altered by site-directed mutagenesis to enhance the affinity and specificity of the antibody.

REFERENCES

1. Cabilly, S., Riggs, A.D., Pande, H., Shively, J.E., Holmes, W.E., Rey, M., Perry, L.J., Wetzel, R., and Heyneker, H.L., 1984. Generation of antibody activity from immunoglobulin polypeptide chains produced in *Escherichia coli. Proc. Natl. Acad. Sci. USA* 81:3273.

2. Boss, A., Kenten, J.H., Wood, C.R., and Emtage, J.S. 1984. Assembly of functional antibodies from immunoglobulin heavy and light chains synthesized in *E. coli. Nucleic Acids Res.* 12:3791.

3. Wood, C.R., Boss, M.A., Kenten, J.H., Calvert, J.E., Roberts, N.A., and Emtage, J.S. 1985. The synthesis and *in vivo* assembly of functional antibodies in yeast. *Nature* 314:446.

4. Skerra, A. and Pluckthun, A. 1988. Assembly of a functional immunoglobulin Fv fragment in *E. coli. Science* 240:1038.

5. Better, M., Chang, C.P., Robinson, R.R., and Horwitz, A.H. 1988. *Escherichia coli* secretion of an active chimeric antibody fragment. *Science* 240:1041.

6. Sastry, L., Alting-Mees, M., Huse, W.D., Short, J.M., Sorge, J.A., Hay, B.N., Janda, K.D., Benkovic, S.J., and Lerner, R.A. 1989. Cloning of the immunological repertoire in *Escherichia coli* for generation of monoclonal catylytic antibodies: Construction of a heavy chain variable region-specific cDNA library. *Proc. Natl. Acad. Sci. USA* 86:5728.

7. Ward, S.E., Gussow, D., Griffiths, A.D., Jones, P.T., and Winter, G. 1989. Binding activities of a repertoire of single immunoglobulin variable domains secreted from *Escherichia coli. Nature* 341:544.

8. Huse, W.D., Sastry, L., Iverson, S.A., and Kang, A.S. 1989. Generation of a large combinatorial library of the immunoglobulin repertoire in phage lambda. *Science* 246:1275.

9. Neurberger, M.S., Williams, G.T., and Fox, R.O. 1984. Recombinant antibodies possessing novel effector functions. *Nature* 312:604.

10. Moller, G. 1982. Antibody carriers of drugs and toxins in tumor therapy. *Immunol. Rev.* 62.

11. Neurberger, M.S., Williams, G.T., Mitchell, E.B., Jouhal, S.S., Flanagan, J.G., and Rabbitts, T.H. 1985. A hapten-specific chimaeric IgE antibody with human physiological effector function. *Nature* 314:268.

12. Jones, P.T., Dear, P.H., Foote, J., Neurberger, M.S., and Winter, G. Replacing the complementarity-determining regions in a human antibody with those from a mouse. *Nature* 321:522.

13. Pluckthun, A. 1990. Antibodies from *Escherichia coli. Nature* 347:497.

14. Roholt, O.A., Radzimski, G., and Pressman, D. 1965. Preferential recombination of antibody chains to form effective binding sites. *J. Exp. Med.* 122:785.

15. Hong, R. and Nissomoff, A. 1966. Heterogeneity in the complementation of polypeptide subunits of a purified antibody isolated from an individual rabbit. *J. Immunol.* 96:622.

16. Porter, R.R. and Weir, R.C. 1966. Relationship to antibody specificity. *J. Cell. Comp. Physiol.* 67, Suppl. 1: 51.

17. Fougereau, M., Olins, D.E., and Edelman, G.M. 1964. Reconstitution of anti-phage antibodies from L and H polypeptide chains and the formation of interspecies molecular hybrids. *J. Exp. Med.* 120:349.

18. Klinman, N.R. 1971. Regain of homogeneous binding activity after recombination of chains of "monofocal" antibody. *J. Immunol.* 106:1330.

19. Orlandi, R., Gussow, D.H., Jones, P.T., and Winter, G. 1989. Cloning immunoglobulin variable domains for expression by the polymerase chain reaction. *Proc. Natl. Acad. Sci. USA* 86:3833.

20. Chiang, Y.L., Sheng-Dong, R., Brow, M.A., and Larrick, J.W. 1989. Direct complementary DNA cloning of the rearranged immunoglobulin variable region. *Biotechniques* 7:360.

21. Larrick, J.W., Danielsson, L., Brenner, C.A., Abrahamson, M., Fry, K.E., and Borrebaeck, C.A.K. 1989. Rapid cloning of rearranged immunoglobulin genes from human hybridoma cells using mixed primers and the polymerase chain reaction. *Biochem. Biophys. Res. Commun.* 160:1250.

22. Chomczynski, P. and Sacchi, N. 1987. Single-step method of RNA isolation by acid guanidinium thiocyanate-phenol-chloroform extraction. *Analytical Biochemistry* 162:156.

23. Aviv, H. and Leder, P. 1972. Purification of biologically active messenger RNA by chromatography on oligothymicylic acid-cellulose. *Proc. Natl. Acad. Sci. USA* 69:1408.

24. Saiki, R.K., Gelfand, D.H., Stoffel, S., Scharf, S.J., Higuchi, R., Horn, G.T., Mullis, K.B., and Erlich, H.A. 1988. Primer-directed enzymatic amplification of DNA with a thermostable DNA polymerase. *Science* 239:487.

25. Parmley, S.F. and Smith, G.P. 1988. Antibody-selectable filamentous fd phage vectors: affinity purification of target genes. *Gene* 73:305.

CHAPTER 6

Expression and Purification of Antibody Fragments Using *Escherichia coli* as a Host

E. Sally Ward

Escherichia coli is an attractive host for the expression of recombinant proteins. This host has many advantages, such as rapid growth and the availability of many different types of cloning vectors. The expression of antibody fragments in *E coli* has been revolutionized by two reports in 1988 of vectors for the secretion of these proteins into the periplasmic space.[1,2] A major advantage of the use of these secretion systems over the production of immunoglobulin fragments as intracellular inclusion bodies[3-5] in *E coli* is that the secretion of recombinant protein in soluble form avoids the need for protein solubilization from the isolated inclusions after cell lysis and inclusion purification. Such solubilization procedures generally result in some loss of activity, and moreover, they are more tedious than isolation from either periplasmic fractions or culture supernatant. Thus, the development of se-cretion systems for the production of antibody fragments in *E coli* has opened up new avenues for the genetic manipulation of these biologically important proteins. For example, repertoires of genes encoding immunoglobulin frag-ments can be isolated by the polymerase chain reaction (PCR) cloned in *E coli* for expression, and clones producing Fab, F_v fragments, and single heavy chain variable (V_H) domains with antigen-binding activities can be identified.[6-12]

In this chapter, the methodology for the production of soluble, secreted antibody fragments using *E coli* as a host will be described. This will include the expression of F_v, Fab fragments, and single V_H domains, and also the screening of repertoires of V_H domains for antigen-binding activities. The recently developed system for the expression of antibody fragments on the surface of bacteriophage fd[13] will also be discussed. The use of the PCR[14] to generate combinatorial repertoires will not be covered, however, as these techniques have been described elsewhere in this volume (see Chapters 4 and 5).

EXPRESSION VECTORS FOR THE PRODUCTION OF FRAGMENTS

The expression vectors originally described for the secretion of antibody F_v and Fab fragments in *E coli* have been used as the basis for the design of the vectors shown in Figure 6-1. The vectors are derived from pUC19.[15] The incorporation of restriction sites into conserved regions at the 5' and 3' ends of the immunoglobulin genes[6] allows forced cloning of genes encoding antibody heavy and light chain variable domains (V_H and V_L domains, respectively). Several other expression/secretion vectors have been developed over the last few years,[1,2,9] but the methodology in this chapter is relevant for the vectors shown in Figure 6-1. The restriction sites shown for the cloning of the fragments are also incorporated at analogous positions in the oligonucleotide primers used to isolate the genes from antibody producing cells[6, 7] (see Figure 6-2), and this allows the direct cloning of the PCR products for expression. Thus, the genes cloned into these vectors all have the same 5' and 3' codons, upstream and downstream of the cloning sites, respectively (see Figure 6-2). This is generally not a concern for the cloning and expression of immunoglobulin fragments with antigen-binding activities, as the residues in these regions of the antibody genes are highly conserved.[16] However, if the presence of the native 5' and 3' ends of the genes are required, for example, for structural work, it may be desirable to incorporate the true 5' and 3' termini using oligonucleotide directed mutagenesis.

CLONING OF ANTIBODY GENES FOR EXPRESSION

The most convenient and rapid way to isolate the genes encoding from antibody-producing cells is to use the PCR and designed oligonucleotide primers. Many different primer sequences have now been published, and these are designed by comparative analyses of the existing sequences of

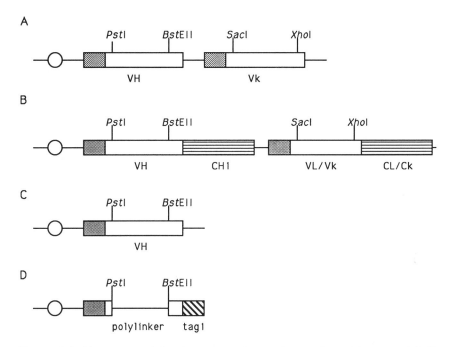

Figure 6-1. Vectors used for the expression and secretion of immunoglobulin fragments in *E coli* for the production of: A, F_v fragments; B, Fab fragments; C, single V_H domains; and D, repertoires of single V_H domains, with carboxy terminal c-myc peptides.[7] Restriction sites used for the cloning of the genes are shown, and these sites are also incorporated into PCR primers. Open circle = lacz promoter and stippled box = pelB leader sequence.[2] The vector backbone for all the constructs is pUC19.[15]

immunoglobulin genes (for example, those published in the Kabat data base[16]). Species-specific primers can be made[6,9,10,12,17-19] and the isolated genes can be randomly combined to generate either Fab fragments or single chain F_v fragments, using either splicing by overlap extension (SOE)[20, 21] or ligation at unique restriction sites.[9] Thus, there are now a number of techniques available that can be used to isolate repertoires of V_H and V_L genes from antibody-producing cells derived from a number of different species. Moreover, genetic manipulation can be used to recombine V_H and V_L genes in a random fashion. The challenges now lie in the development of suitable expression and selection systems to facilitate the identification of recombinant clones that produce antigen-binding activities of the desired specificities and affinities.

As the V(D) and J elements encoding immunoglobulin V_H and V_L domains form a single exon during recombination, it is possible to isolate, by PCR, the genes for these domains directly from genomic DNA.[7] For repertoire cloning from antibody-producing cells, there are questions concerning

Light chain variable (V_K) domains

```
D    I    E    L                        L    E    I    K    R
GAC ATC GAG CTC........cloning site..............CTC GAG ATC AAA CGG
        SacI                            XhoI
```

$V_K$back 5' GAC ATT GAG CTC ACC CAG TCT CCA 3'

V_K for 5' CCG TTT CAG CTC GAG CTT GGT CCC 3'

Heavy chain variable (V_H) domains

```
Q    V    Q    L    Q                    V    T    V    S    S
CAG GTG CAG CTG CAG........cloning site........G GTC ACC GTC TCC TCA
          PstI                           BstEII
```

$V_H$back 5' AG GT(C/G) (A/C)A(A/G) CTG CAG (C/G)AG TC(A/T)GG 3'

$V_H$for 5' TGA GGA GAC GGT GAC CGT GGT CCC TTG GCC CC 3'

Figure 6-2. Cloning strategy for murine V_H and V_L genes using the PCR. The designed PCR primers for the V_κ ($V_\kappa$for and $V_\kappa$back) and V_H ($V_H$for and $V_H$back) genes are shown, and the restriction sites for cloning are indicated by underlining. The conserved 5' and 3' sequences for the V_H and V_L genes, which are present in the vectors, are also shown. The pelB leader sequences are in translational frame with the 5' ends of the V_H and V_κ genes.

whether the use of genomic DNA or cDNA in the PCR is preferable. If the ultimate aim is to isolate antigen-binding activities from immunized mice, then it is preferable to use cDNA, despite the fact that this takes slightly longer than the use of genomic DNA. The reasons for this are as follows: (1) When genomic DNA is used, both productively and nonproductively rearranged genes are amplified. For example, in the repertoire cloning of V_H domain genes from mouse spleen DNA, it was found that a significant number of nonproductively rearranged genes were isolated.[7, 22] (2) As antigen-specific B cells are stimulated *in vivo*, the antigen-specific mRNA levels increase. Thus, cDNA synthesis should result in the enrichment of genes encoding antigen-specific variable domains.

EXPRESSION OF F_V AND FAB FRAGMENTS IN *E COLI*

Using the plasmids shown in Figure 6-1 and the methods for expression and affinity purification shown in Protocols 6-1 through 6-3, yields of up to 10

Protocol 6-1. Growth and Induction of *E coli* Recombinants for Expression
(Large Scale)

1. Grow recombinant bacteria up in 1 liter 2 × TY* + 100 μg/ml ampicillin + 1% w/v
    glucose to early stationary phase (overnight incubation for about 16–20 hours) at
    37°C with shaking at 250 rpm.
2. Centrifuge cultures at 6000 rpm for 10 minutes at 20°C and resuspend the cell
    pellets in 50 mM NaCl or 2 × TY.
3. Centrifuge cells at 6,000 rpm for 10 minutes at 20°C, and resuspend in 1 liter 2 ×
    TY + 100 μg/ml ampicillin +1mM isopropyl-thiogalactopyranoside (IPTG). The
    media should be prewarmed to 37°C.
4. Induce the culture for expression by growth at 37°C with shaking at 250 rpm for
    24–28 hours.
5. Stand the culture on ice for 1–2 hours.
6. Centrifuge the culture at 10,000 rpm at 4°C for 30 minutes.
7. Filter the culture supernatant through Nalgene 0.45 μm filters.
8. Pass the culture supernatant through an antigen affinity column (for lysozyme
    sepharose, for example, see Protocol 6-3).

*2 × TY comprises, per liter: 10 g bactotryptone, 10 g yeast extract, and 5 g NaCl.

Protocol 6-2. Coupling of Lysozyme to CNBr-activated Sepharose

1. Add 200 ml 2M Na_2CO_3 (dissolved at room temperature) to beads,* on ice.
2. Add acetonitrile/CNBr† solution; some of the CNBr may precipitate. Stir with a
    glass rod for 2 minutes and then pour into a sintered glass filtration funnel.
    Filter through immediately, and wash with 2 liters ice-cold H_2O.
3. Transfer drained beads to a 1l Erlenmeyer and add lysozyme** and 200 ml
    coupling buffer (0.1 M $NaHCO_3$, pH 8.5/0.5 M NaCl).
4. Leave at room temperature and stir every 10 minutes for about 2 hours, then
    leave for another 2 hours.
5. Filter and was with blocking buffer (0.1M $NaHCO_3$, pH 10.9; the high pH
    hydrolyzes imido-carbonate structures formed in CNBr reaction).
6. Take OD_{280} of filtrate to calculate the amount of lysozyme not coupled. The
    coupling should be at least 98% efficient.
7. Suspend resin in 300 ml blocking buffer, and leave overnight at room temperature.
8. Collect lysozyme-sepharose by filtration, and wash alternately with 4 × 400 ml
    0.1 M HOAc/0.5 M NaCl pH 4 or coupling buffer.
9. Wash with PBS plus 0.02% of NaN_3, and resuspend 50/50 w/v in this solution.
    Store at 4°C. The lysozyme-sepharose should be stable for many months.

*110 ml Sepharose CL-4B (Pharmacia) washed with 2 liters 0.1 M NaCl, and resuspended in
200 ml 0.1 m NaCl, chilled on ice (ice/water)
†Use fresh CNBr, dissolve 20 g in 20 ml CH3CN.
**500 mg lysozyme (Sigma) dissolved in 50 ml 10 mM Na acetate, pH 4.8/40 mM NaCl.
Lysozyme does not dissolve well in coupling buffer.

Protocol 6-3. Purification of Anti-lysozyme Immunoglobulin Fragments Using Lysozyme Sepharose

---

1. Pack column (about 10 ml bed volume for 1–2 liters culture, but this depends on the coupling density of the lysozyme to the sepharose). Set the column up at 4°C.
2. Wash the column through with 3 column volumes of 50 mM diethylamine* (260 μl diethylamine in 50 ml of water).
3. Wash the column with about 5 column volumes of phosphate buffered saline (PBS).
4. Pass supernatant (prepared as in Protocol 6-1) through column, either under gravity or by pumping.
5. Wash column with 10 column volumes of PBS.
6. Wash column with 3–5 column volumes of 500 mM NaCl/50 mM Tris-Cl pH 8.5.
7. Elute antibody fragments with 50 mM diethylamine, collecting fractions in tubes containing 0.1 × fraction volume of 1M Tris-Cl pH 7.4. It is important to neutralize the fractions as soon as they elute from the column.

---

*This is a suitable eluant for purification of anti-lysozyme D1.3 fragments. For other immunoglobulin fragments, alternative eluants may be preferable.

mg/liter F_v fragment[7] and 5 mg/liter Fab fragment (unpublished observations) can be obtained for the anti-lysozyme D1.3 antibody. Protocols 6-1 through 6-3 are for the purification of anti-lysozyme immunoglobulin fragments. With modifications, such as variation of elution conditions and use the appropriate antigen, these methods are generally applicable to immunoglobulin fragments of other specificities. As an alternative to the procedure for CNBr activation of sepharose in Protocol 6-2, CNBr-activated sepharose is commercially available.

The fragments can be purified directly from the culture supernatant if the cells are induced for expression for prolonged periods, because the pelB leader[2] sequence directs the secretion of the fragments into the periplasmic space, and the recombinant protein then leaks into the supernatant.[7] This leakage is presumably due to high periplasmic concentrations of antibody fragment in addition to a decrease in the viability of the cells after the initiation of induction. Culture supernatants of relatively large numbers of recombinants can, therefore, be easily screened by growing up cells as small scale (1.5 ml or less) cultures and then inducing for expression, as described in Protocol 6-4. The culture supernatants can be analyzed for expression levels of recombinant fragments by Western blotting, following the procedure in Protocol 6-5. We routinely find that the antibody fragments (F_vs, Fabs, and V_H domains) can be detected without concentration of the culture supernatant, and this procedure offers a rapid way to analyze expression levels.

Lower levels of expression than about 10 mg/liter may be obtained for some F_vs, and a possible reason for this is that the V_H and V_L are not stably

Protocol 6-4. Growth and Induction of *E coli* Recombinants for Expression
(Small Scale for Screening for Expression Analyses)

---

1. Grow up recombinants as 1.5 ml cultures in 2 ö TY (see Protocol 6-1 for composition) + 100 μg/ml ampicillin + 1% w/v glucose for 8–10 hours at 37°C with shaking at 250 rpm.
2. Harvest cells by centrifugation in a microfuge at full speed, for 30 seconds at room temperature.
3. Wash pellets in either 1 ml 50 mM NaCl or 1 ml 2 × TY at room temperature.
4. Harvest cells by centrifugation as in step 2. Resuspend pellets in 2 ö TY plus 100 μg/ml ampicillin + 1 mM IPTG.
5. Transfer cultures to suitable tubes and grow at 37°C with shaking at 250 rpm for 16–20 hours.
6. Stand cultures on ice for 1 hour.
7. Centrifuge cultures for 3 minutes in a microfuge at full speed, at room temperature or 4°C.
8. The supernatant can be analyzed by Western blotting (see Protocol 6-5) or ELISA (see Protocol 6-6).

---

associated after leakage into the culture supernatant. There are several ways of overcoming this:

1. The expressed F_v fragments can be isolated from the periplasmic space, where the higher local concentration of the heterodimer may favor association. For example, associated V_H/V_L heterodimers of the anti-phosphorylcholine antibody McPC603 can be isolated by osmotically shocking recombinant cells, whereas this F_v dissociates if diluted into the culture supernatant[1] (Skerra, personal communication).
2. The F_v can be expressed as a single chain F_v fragment (scF_v) in which the V_H is linked by a synthetic linker to the V_L domain.[23-25] This drives the association, but there may be two problems associated with this approach, as follows: (a) the affinity of the scF_v may be lowered by the presence of the linker. This is probably due to the linker peptide, which may sterically hinder the association of F_v with antigen, or may change the overall folding of the V_H and V_L domains; and (b) the yield of secreted scF_v fragment may be lower than that of the F_v fragment. Yields are still in the milligram per liter range[25] (unpublished observations), and hence this may not be a significant problem.
    As an alternative to secretion, high yields of recombinant scF_v have been obtained by intracellular expression, followed by cell lysis, solubilization (using 6M guanidinium hydrochloride) and renaturation.[25]
3. Intrachain disulfide bridges can be engineered into the V_H and V_L domain genes, to stabilize the V_H-V_L association.[26] This may overcome the problems associated with possible effects of the scF_v linker on the antigen-binding site. This approach is not generally applicable to

Protocol 6-5. Analysis of the Expression Levels of Immunoglobulin Fragments by Western Blotting

---

1. Grow the cells as indicated in Protocol 6-4. The culture supernatants can be mixed with an equal volume of SDS polyacrylamide gel running buffer, boiled for three minutes and loaded onto an SDS polyacrylamide gel. Despite the high concentration of salt in the sample, this does not appear to affect the running of the gel.
2. Transfer the electrophoresed proteins onto nitrocellulose (NC, Schleicher and Schuell BA85 generally gives satisfactory results, although many other brands of NC are available). Use of a semi-dri transblot apparatus is convenient as transfer is complete in 0.5–1 hour.
3. After electrophoretic transfer, incubate the NC in about 10–20 ml of phosphate buffered saline (PBS) plus 3% w/v bovine serum albumin, fraction V (PBSB), to block free sites on the NC. Incubate at room temperature for twenty minutes with agitation.
4. Incubate the NC in 10–20 ml PBSB containing 1:1–2000 dilution of primary sera. For purified monoclonal antibodies, use at a concentration of 10–50 μg/ml. The optimal concentration of sero/monoclonal used should be determined by titration, and will clearly depend on the titer of the antibody/sera. Incubate for 1–2 hours at room temperature with gentle agitation.
5. Wash the NC in 100 ml of PBS for ten minutes at room temperature with gentle agitation, and repeat wash once.
6. Incubate the NC in a 1:1–2000 dilution of horseradish peroxidase conjugated to secondary antibody (for example, if the primary sera is derived from rabbit, use anti-rabbit horseradish peroxidase conjugate). The optimal concentration used should be determined by titration. Incubate at room temperature for one hour with gentle agitation.
7. Wash NC three times in about 100 ml of PBS plus 0.1% v/v Triton X-100, for ten minutes for each wash, at room temperature with gentle agitation.
8. Incubate NC in one of the following horseradish peroxidase substrates: (a) chloro-1-napthol (CN), dissolved at 3 mg/ml in 10 ml methanol, then mixed with 40 ml PBS plus 50 μl H_2O_2; (b) diaminobenzidine (DAB), dissolved at 0.5 mg/ml in PBS and then mixed with 400 μl of 0.5 w/v % $CoCl_2$ plus 20 μl H_2O_2. Note: DAB is a more sensitive substrate than CN, and is therefore suitable if the signals are low. The background with DAB is much higher than that with CN, however. CN can be used prior to DAB, and if the signals with CN are weak or undetectable, it is advisable to use DAB, which can be added subsequently to CN after rinsing the filter with distilled H_2O.
9. For both substrates, stop the reaction by washing the NC with excess H_2O.

---

repertoire cloning, however, as one of the engineered cysteine residues is located at position 55 or 56 of the V_L domain.[26] Thus, this residue cannot be readily incorporated during PCR isolation of full length V_L domain genes.

4. V_H and V_L domain genes can be cloned into vectors designed for the expression of Fab fragments, which contain C_H1 and C_κ domain genes[9]

(see Figure 6-1). In this respect, experiments have been carried out to analyze the association of the VHD1.3 domain with 8 different V_Ls, in F_v and Fab constructions (see Figure 6-1) using chemical crosslinking with Lomant's reagent (unpublished observations). In the crosslinking experiments, crude dialysed supernatant of recombinants can be analyzed by Western blotting after treatment with the chemical crosslinker. Co-expression of the VHD1.3 domain with these heterologous V_Ls from F_v-like constructions, followed by analysis of heterodimer formation by crosslinking, indicated that only 1/8 of the heterologous V_Ls paired stably with the VHD1.3 domain to constitute an F_v fragment. In contrast, in all of the Fab constructions the expressed protein was heterodimeric, suggesting that in these Fabs, the interaction of the C_H1 and C_κ domain both drives and stabilizes the association of the VHD1.3 domain with "heterologous" V_Ls.

5. It has recently been demonstrated that the expression yield of recombinant proteins in *E coli* can be increased dramatically by growing and inducing the cells to express protein at lower temperatures[27, 28] (for example, 23°C). The lower rate of protein synthesis under these conditions facilitates the folding of the polypeptide into a native conformation. In addition, a low concentration of inducer (0.005 mM IPTG) was found to increase the expression yields for secreted subtilisin.[28] Thus, to optimize the secretion levels of immunoglobulin fragments, it is advisable to alter both growth/induction temperature and inducer concentration.

X-RAY CRYSTALLOGRAPHY OF BACTERIALLY PRODUCED F_v FRAGMENTS

For the anti-lysozyme D1.3 F_v fragment, the bacterially expressed protein has been crystallized and the high resolution structure solved to 1.9 Å resolution.[29, 30] One of the important implications of this structural study is that it demonstrates that the bacterially expressed F_v fragment folds in the same way as the V_H and V_L domains of the parent immunoglobulin that is produced by mammalian cells.[31] This suggests by extension that, in general, bacterially expressed antibody fragments will fold in a similar way to antibodies produced in mammalian cells. However, there may be exceptions to this rule—for example, if an antibody is glycosylated on the variable domains. In this case it may be more desirable to use mammalian cell expression systems,[32-35] particularly if the glycosylation sites are located close to the site of antibody-antigen interaction.

EXPRESSION OF SINGLE V$_H$ DOMAINS

The initial reports of the secretion of F$_v$ and Fab fragments have now been extended to the secretion of heavy chain variable domains (V$_H$ domains or "dAbs"). The observation that the anti-lysozyme VHD1.3 domain binds antigen with high affinity in the absence of a paired V$_L$ domain led to the generation of repertoires of V$_H$ domain genes from the spleen of immunized mice and to the identification of clones producing V$_H$ domains with antigen-binding activities.[7]

To screen the clones for production of antigen-binding activities, the procedure in Protocol 6-6 is routinely used. It is important to use milk powder as a blocking agent, as this minimizes the nonspecific binding. Other blocking agents, such as 3% weight by volume (w/v) bovine serum albumin or fetal calf serum, have been found to be not nearly as effective. The blocking agent used is particularly important when screening V$_H$ domains, as they tend to be relatively "sticky." In addition, V$_H$ domains that are nonspecific have been isolated; these tend to bind to any protein antigen with high affinity. Thus, it is essential to screen V$_H$ domains that appear to have binding affinity for the immunogen against a variety of other protein antigens to ensure that they are specific.

The anti-lysozyme V$_H$ domains isolated from pools of five recombinants, using the method in Protocol 6-6, were cloned out and the nucleotide sequences were determined. The respective V$_H$ domain proteins (designated V$_H$3 and V$_H$8) were purified, using the growth conditions in Protocols 6-1 through 6-3, and the affinities for lysozyme binding in solution were characterized by stopped flow and fluorescence quench and found to be of the order of 20 nM.[7] Thus, the anti-lysozyme V$_H$ domains appear to have high affinities for antigen binding and furthermore, appear to be specific, as enzyme-linked immunoassays (ELISA) using four different protein antigens and two mixed protein antigens showed no evidence of nonspecific binding.

The yields of the V$_H$ domains are routinely lower than those of antibody F$_v$ or Fab fragments, and using the growth conditions shown in Protocol 6-1, are about 0.5 mg/liter culture. The rather low yields are probably due, in part at least, to the hydrophobic nature of V$_H$ domains, caused by the exposure of residues that are normally "capped off" by a paired V$_L$ domain.[36] This may cause some of the expressed, secreted V$_H$ domain to aggregate in the periplasmic space, rather than leak out into the culture supernatant in soluble form. In support of this, yields of up to 4 mg/liter of a secreted V$_H$ domain have been obtained by isolation from the periplasm by osmotically shocking the recombinant cells. The released protein is solubilized with urea and then refolded (P. Hudson, personal communication).

Protocol 6-6. Analysis of Culture Supernatants by ELISA and Detection of Antigen-binding Activities

1. Grow the cells as indicated in Protocol 6-1 or 6-4, or, alternatively, for screening large numbers of colonies, grow as described in steps 2–8 below.
2. Toothpick recombinant colonies into wells of 96 well microtiter plates, either singly or in pools of up to five colonies. The wells should contain 200 µl of 2 × TY + 100 µg/ml ampicillin + 1% w/v glucose.
3. Incubate at 37°C for 16–20 hours, standing (although the plates can be shaken and incubated for a shorter period of time, for example 10 hours).
4. Pellet the cells by centrifugation of the plates at 3 K at room temperature for 10 minutes to pellet the cells, in a centrifuge with a microtiter plate head fitting.
5. Remove and discard the supernatant with a multichannel pipettor.
6. Wash the cells once with either 200 µl 50 mM NaCl or 200 µl 2 × TY per well. Pellet the cells by centrifugation as in step 4.
7. Discard the supernatants and resuspend the pellets in a 2 × TY + 100 µg/ml ampicillin + 1 mM IPTG. Incubate at 37°C for 15–20 hours.
8. Stand the plates on ice for 1 hour, centrifuge the plates as in step 4, and transfer the supernatants into microtiter plates that have been coated with antigen and blocked (see below).
9. For the ELISA, coat microtiter plates for either 2 hours at 37°C or overnight at room temperature, with antigen at a concentration of 50 µg/ml–3mg/ml in either PBS or 50 mM NaHCO$_3$ pH 9.6.
10. Discard the antigen solution and rinse the plates with PBS, two times.
11. Pipette 200 µl of blocking solution (2% w/v milk powder in PBS) into each well. Incubate at 37°C for 2 hours.
12. Discard the blocking solution and rinse the wells two times with PBS.
13. Transfer the recombinant culture supernatants into the wells and incubate at 37°C for 1 hour.
14. Discard the supernatants and wash the wells three times with PBS.
15. Pipette 200 µl of primary antibody at a 1:1–2000 dilution in milk powder/PBS for sera, or 10–50 µg/ml for purified monoclonal antibody (the concentration used should be determined by titration, and clearly will depend on the titer of the antibody/sera). Incubate for 1 hour at 37°C.
16. Wash the wells three times with PBS.
17. Pipette 200 µl of secondary antibody (horseradish peroxidase conjugate) at a 1:1–2000 dilution in 2% milk powder/PBS. The optimal dilution of the antibody conjugate should again be determined by titration. Incubate at 37°C for 1 hour.
18. Wash the plates 3–6 times with PBS. The number of washes depends on the sera used in these assays, and should be optimized to maximize the signal-to-noise ratio in pilot studies. If high background appears to be a problem, washing with PBS plus 0.1% v/v Tween-20 three times, followed by three times with PBS alone, is recommended.
19. Pipette 180 µl of substrate solution* into each well and incubate for up to 30 minutes at room temperature.
20. Stop the reaction by addition of 20 µl 0.05% sodium azide in 50 mM citric acid to each well.

*0.55 mg/ml 2é2é-azinobis(3-ethylbenthiazoline sulphonic acid) dissolved in 25 mM sodiumcitrate/25 mM citric acid.

The generality of V_H domains with different antigen-binding specificities has been shown by the following studies:

1. A V_H domain derived from an anti-neuraminidase monoclonal antibody has been expressed and purified from the *E coli* periplasm and shown to retain binding affinity for neuraminidase (P. Hudson, personal communication).

2. V_H domain genes derived from anti-hapten monoclonals have been used to replace $V\alpha$ and $V\beta$ domains of T cell receptors. Functional TCR-CD3 complexes in which the V_H-Cα or V_H-Cβ chimeras pair with either native TCR α or β chains were expressed in T cell transfectomas. These surface-bound, chimeric receptors bind to the appropriate hapten,[37-39] indicating that these V_H domains have significant binding affinities for their cognate antigen.

3. Indirect support for the existence of V_H domains that have antigen-binding affinities comes from x-ray crystallographic data. For the majority of crystal structures of the antibody-antigen complexes solved to date, it is evident that the V_H domain makes a greater number of interactions than the V_L domain.[31, 40, 41] An extreme example of this is the anti-lysozyme D1.3 antibody, for which 9/12 of the hydrogen bonding interactions made during antibody-antigen interaction involve the heavy chain, and of these, six involve CDR3 residues of the heavy chain.[31]

HYDROPHOBIC NATURE OF V_H DOMAINS: POSSIBLE WAYS TO IMPROVE THEIR PROPERTIES

The V_H domains are rather hydrophobic, as the residues that normally interact with a paired V_L domain are exposed.[36] Judicious replacement of these residues with more hydrophilic ones may result in V_H domains that have higher expression yields and solubility. These V_H domains could have uses in situations where small size is an advantage, as they are about 1/12th the size of a complete immunoglobulin molecule. There are many unanswered questions, however, concerning the immunogenicity, clearance rates, and specificity of dAbs if they are to be used *in vivo* in therapy. The half life of such small proteins may be extremely low *in vivo;* for a single chain F_v fragment, which is approximately twice the size, the half life of the α phase for clearance *in vivo* is 30 minutes.[42] This suggests that the V_H domains will have similarly low *in vivo* stability. Although this may render them useful in imaging studies, for example, where rapid clearance is advantageous, their utility as reagents, where half lives of the order of days is desirable, is limited.

COMBINATORIAL LIBRARIES OF V_H AND V_L GENES

One of the technical advantages of V_H domains is that fragments with antigen-binding activities can be isolated without the need to randomly combine and match V_H and V_L genes. When gene repertoires are isolated using the PCR from murine splenocytes, for example, the V_H/V_L matching that originally existed within a given cell is lost. Thus, to isolate F_v or Fab fragments with antigen-binding activities, ways of randomly combining the genes and screening, or preferably selecting, the expressed heterodimers for antigen-binding activities must be developed. In this respect, several major steps towards suitable screening/selection systems have recently been reported.[9, 13]

The cloning of combinatorial repertoires of V_H and V_L genes into a phage lambda expression system[9] has been described. The lambda vector was designed to express Fab fragments. Recombinant clones that produced Fabs with antigen-binding activities towards the hapten NPN were identified at a frequency of about 1 in 10,000 from the phage libraries.[9] This expression system has subsequently been used to isolate Fabs with binding activities towards polypeptide antigens, from both human[10,12] and mouse[11] immunoglobulin repertoires.

The observation that no Fd (V_H-C_H1) expressing clones with antigen-binding activities were identified in the study by Huse and colleagues[9] is not surprising in view of our observations with the anti-lysozyme FdD1.3 fragment; although the VHD1.3 binds lysozyme with high affinity, the corresponding Fd fragment has no apparent affinity for binding to lysozyme coated surfaces (either lysozyme sepharose or in ELISAs) when expressed in the absence for the D1.3 light chain (unpublished observations). This suggests that the Fd expressed alone folds aberrantly, possibly interfering with binding antigen by folding back on itself. This observation for the D1.3 fragment may be a general feature for Fd fragments expressed in bacteria.

SURFACE EXPRESSION OF IMMUNOGLOBULIN FRAGMENTS

Recently, a system for the expression of single chain F_v fragments on the surface of bacteriophage fd has been reported.[13] This system allows the selection of phage expressing antigen-binding activities from repertoires of V_H and V_L genes. The V_H and V_L genes can be randomly combined by PCR and then expressed as scFvs on the phage surface.[43] As the recombinants can be selected on antigen-coated surfaces prior to screening, such a selection system has a major advantage over the existing screening systems. This system allows almost unlimited numbers of recombinants to be screened, by selection, for the expression of antigen-binding activities, and this greatly reduces the number of recombinants that need to be screened. Using such systems, it should be possible to isolate antigen-binding activities, by selection, from *in vitro* repertoires that are close in size to the *in vivo* immune repertoire (estimated to be 10^8 in humans). In addition, this type of surface expression system, coupled to *in vitro* mutagenesis, will allow higher affinity variants of antibody fragments to be readily isolated, and could therefore have considerable use in antibody engineering. Improved immunoglobulin variants obtained using such surface expression systems can subsequently be cloned into secretion vectors, to allow purification of the recombinant antibody fragments as either F_v, Fab fragments, or scFvs.

CONCLUSIONS

It is now relatively straightforward to use the PCR to isolate genes encoding immunoglobulin fragments. The expression of the fragments in *E coli* as secreted protein facilitates purification. Moreover, secretion in this prokaryotic host offers several advantages over mammalian cell expression systems, particularly with respect to rapidity of growth and economics. Immunoglobulin fragments can be obtained in yields of milligrams per liter of bacterial culture, and the protein can be harvested either directly from the culture supernatant or the periplasm.

Single V_H domains, scFvs, or Fabs with antigen-binding activities can be isolated from repertoires of immunoglobulin fragments by screening, or more recently, by selecting. Thus, repertoire cloning, in which the genes of antibody-producing cells are obtained by the PCR, followed by expression in this prokaryotic host, is an attractive route toward the isolation and expression of the desired antigen-binding activities. The technology in this area is rapidly developing to make this route for production of clonal antibodies more and more powerful. Using such techniques, it is possible to isolate and identify recombinant clones producing fragments with antigen-binding activities in a matter of days. It will probably be a long time, however, before such systems are able to circumvent the need to immunize animals for the generation of high affinity antibodies.[44]

Acknowledgments: I would like to thank Greg Winter, Detlef Güssow, Jefferson Foote, Andrew Griffiths, Peter Jones, and Tim Clackson for their valuable contributions to the work described above. While this work was carried out, I was a Senior Medical Research Fellow at Sidney Sussex College, Cambridge.

REFERENCES

1. Skerra, A. and Plückthun, A. 1988. Assembly of a functional immunoglobulin F$_v$ fragment in *Escherichia coli. Science* 240:1038.
2. Better, M., Chang, C.P., Robinson, R.R., and Horwitz, A.H. 1988. *Escherichia coli* secretion of an active chimeric antibody fragment. *Science* 240:1041.
3. Boss, M.A., Kenten, J.H., Wood, C.R., and Emtage, J.S. 1984. Assembly of functional antibodies from immunoglobulin heavy and light chains synthesised in *E. coli. Nucl. Acids Res* 12:3791.
4. Cabilly, S., Riggs, A.D., Pande, H., Shively, J.E., Holmes, W.E., Rey, M., Perry, L.J., Wetzel, R., and Heyneker, H.L. 1984. Generation of antibody activity from immunoglobulin polypeptide chains produced in *Escherichia coli. Proc. Natl. Acad. Sci. USA* 81:3273.
5. Kurokawa, T., Seno, M., Sasada, R., Ono, Y., Onda, H., Igarashi, K., Kikuchi, M., Sugino, Y., and Honjo, T. 1983. Expression of human immunoglobulin E chain in *E. coli. Nucl. Acids Res* 11:3077.
6. Orlandi, R., Güssow, D.H., Jones, P.T., and Winter, G. 1989. Cloning immunoglobulin variable domains for expression by the polymerase chain reaction. *Proc. Natl. Acad. Sci. USA* 86:3833.
7. Ward, E.S., Güssow, D., Griffiths, A.D., Jones, P.T., and Winter, G. 1989. Binding activities of a repertoire of immunoglobulin variable domains secreted from *Escherichia coli. Nature* 341:544.
8. Sastry, L., Alting-Mees, M., Huse, W.D., Short, J.M., Sorge, J., Hay, B.N., Janda, K.D., Benkovic, S.J., and Lerner, R.A. 1989. Cloning of the immunological repertoire in *Escherichia coli* for generation of monoclonal catalytic antibodies: construction of a heavy chain variable region-specific cDNA library. *Proc. Natl. Acad. Sci. USA* 86:5278.
9. Huse, W.D., Sastry, L., Iverson, S.A., Kang, A.S., Alting-Mees, M., Burton, D.R., Benkovic, S.J., and Lerner, R.A. 1989. Generation of a large combinatorial library of the immunoglobulin repertoire in phage lambda. *Science* 246:1275.
10. Mullinax, R.L., Gross, E.A., Amberg, J.R., Hay, B.N., Hogrefe, H.H., Kubitz, M.M. Greener, A., Alting-Mees, M., Ardourel, D., Short, J.M., Sorge, J.A., and Shopes, B. 1990. Identification of human antibody clones specific for tetanus toxoid in a bacteriophage immunoexpression library. *Proc. Natl. Acad. Sci. USA* 87:8095.
11. Caton, A.J. and Koprowski, H. 1990. Influenza virus haemagglutinin-specific antibodies isolated from a combinatorial expression library are closely related to the immune response of the donor. *Proc. Natl. Acad. Sci. USA* 87:6450.
12. Persson, M.A.A., Caothien, R.H., and Burton, D.R. 1991. Generation of diverse high-affinity human monoclonal antibodies by repertoire cloning. *Proc. Natl. Acad. Sci. USA* 88:2432.
13. McCafferty, J., Griffiths, A.D., Winter, G., and Chiswell, D.J. 1990. Phage antibodies: filamentous phage displaying antibody variable domains. *Nature* 348:552.

14. Saiki, R.K., Gelfand, D.H., Stoffel, S., Scharf, S.J., Higuchi, R., Horn, G.T., Mullis, K.B., and Erlich, H.A. 1988. Primer-directed enzymatic amplification of DNA with a thermostable DNA polymerase. *Science* 239:487.

15. Yanisch-Perron, C., Viera, J., and Messing, J. 1985. Improved M13 phage cloning vectors and host strains: nucleotide sequences of the M13mp18 and pUC19 vectors. *Gene* 33:103.

16. Kabat, E.A., Wu, T.T., Reid-Miller, M., Perry, H.M., and Gottesman, K.S. 1987. *Sequences of Proteins of Immunological Interest.* U.S. Department of Health and Human Services, U.S. Government Printing Office.

17. Larrick, J.W., Danielson, L., Brenner, C.A., Abrahamson, M., Fry, K.E., and Borrebaeck, C.A. 1989. Rapid cloning of rearranged immunoglobulin genes from human hybridoma cells using mixed primers and the polymerase chain reaction. *Biochem. Biophys. Res. Commun.* 160:1250.

18. Larrick, J.W., Danielson, L, Brenner, C.A., Wallace, E.F., Abrahamson, M., Fry, K.E., and Borrebaeck, C.A. 1989. Polymerase chain reaction using mixed primers: cloning of human monoclonal antibody variable region genes from single hybridoma cells. *Biotechnology* 7:934.

19. Chiang, Y.L., Sheng-Dong, R., Brow, M.A., and Larrick, J.W. 1989. Direct cDNA cloning of the rearranged immunoglobulin variable region. *BioTechniques* 7:360.

20. Davis, G.T., Bedzik, W.D., Voss, E.W., and Jacobs, T.W. 1991. Single chain antibody (SCA) encoding genes: one step construction and expression in eukaryotic cells. *Biotechnology* 9:165

21. Clackson, T., Güssow, D., and Jones, P.T. 1991. General applications of PCR to gene cloning and manipulation. In: *PCR: A Practical Approach.* Oxford, U.K.: Oxford University Press. In press.

22. Güssow, D., Ward, E.S., Griffiths, A.D., Jones, P.T., and Winter, G. 1989. Generating binding activities from *Escherichia coli* by expression of a repertoire of immunoglobulin variable domains. In: *Cold Spring Harbor Symposia on Quantitative Biology*, vol. LIV: 265.

23. Bird, R.E., Hardman, K.D., Jacobson, J.W., Johnson, S., Kaufmann, B.M., Lee, S.L., Pope, S.H., Riordan, G.S., and Whitlow, M. 1988. Single-chain antigen binding proteins. *Science* 242:423.

24. Huston, J.S., Levinson, D., Mudgett-Hunter, M., Tai, M-S., Novotny, J., Margolies, M.N., Ridge, R.J., Bruccoleri, R.E., Haber, E., Crea, R., and Opperman, H. 1988. Protein engineering of antibody binding sites: recovery of specific activity in an anti-digoxin single-chain F_V analogue produced in *Escherichia coli. Proc. Natl. Acad. Sci. USA* 85:5879.

25. Whitlow, M. and Fipula, D. 1991. Single-chain F_V proteins and their fusion proteins. In: *A Companion to Methods in Enzymology.* San Diego: Academic Press. In press.

26. Glockshuber, R., Malia, M., Pfitzinger, I., and Plückthun, A. 1990. A comparison of strategies to stabilize immunoglobulin F_V fragments. *Biochemistry* 29:1362.

27. Cabilly, S. 1989. Growth at sub-optimal temperatures allows the production of functional, antigen-binding Fab fragments in *Escherichia coli. Gene* 85:553.

28. Takagi, H., Morinaga, Y., Tsuchiya, M., Ikemura, H., and Inouye, M. 1988. Control of folding proteins secreted by a high expression secretion vector,

pIN-III-ompA: 16 fold increase in production of active subtilisin E in *Escherichia coli. Biotechnology* 6:948.

29. Boulot, G, Eisele, J.L., Bentley, G.A., Bhat, T.N., Ward, E.S., Winter, G., and Poljak, R. 1990. Crystallization and preliminary x-ray diffraction study of the bacterially expressed F_v from the monoclonal anti-lysozyme antibody D1.3 and of its complex with the antigen, lysozyme. *J. Mol. Biol.* 212:617.

30. Bhat, T.N., Bentley, G.A., Fischmann, T.O., Boulot, G., and Poljak, R.J. 1990. Small rearrangements in structures of F_v and Fab fragments of antibody D1.3 on antigen binding. *Nature* 347:483.

31. Amit, A.G., Mariuzza, R.A., Phillips, S.E.V., and Poljak, R.J. 1986. Three-dimensional structure of an antigen-antibody complex at 2.8 Å resolution. *Science* 233:747.

32. Neuberger, M.S. 1983. Expression and regulation of immunoglobulin heavy chain gene transfected into lymphoid cells. *EMBO J.* 2:1373.

33. Oi, V.T., Morrison, S.L., Herzenberg, L.A., and Berg, P. 1983. Immunoglobulin gene expression in transformed lymphoid cells. *Proc. Natl. Acad. Sci. USA* 80:825.

34. Whittle, N., Adair, J., Lloyd, C., Jenkins, L., Devine, J., Schlom, J., Raubistchek, A., Colcher, D. and Bodmer, M. 1987. Expression in COS cells of a mouse-human chimeric B72.3 antibody. *Protein Engineering* 1:499.

35. Riechmann, L, Foote, J., and Winter, G. 1988. Expression of an antibody F_v fragment in myeloma cells. *J. Mol. Biol.* 203:825.

36. Chothia, C., Novotny, J., Bruccoleri, R., and Karplus, M. 1985. Domain association in immunoglobulin molecules: the packing of variable domains. *J. Mol. Biol.* 186:651.

37. Gross, G., Waks, T., and Eshhar, Z. 1989. Expression of human-T-cell receptor chimeric molecules as functional receptors with antibody type specificity. *Proc. Natl. Acad. Sci. USA* 86:10024.

38. Goverman, J., Gomez, S.M. Segesman, K.D., Hunkapiller, T., Laug, W.E., and Hood, L. 1990. Chimeric immunoglobulin-T cell receptor proteins form functional receptors: implications for T cell receptor complex formation and activation. *Cell* 60:929.

39. Becker, M.L.B., Near, R., Mudgett-Hunter, M., Margolies, M.N., Kubo, R.T., Kaye, J., and Hedrick, S.M. 1989. Expression of a hybrid immunoglobulin-T cell receptor protein in transgenic mice. *Cell* 58:911.

40. Stanfield, R.L., Fieser, T.M., Lerner, R.A., and Wilson, I.A. 1990. Crystal structures of an antibody to peptide and its complex with peptide antigen at 2.8 Å. *Science* 248:712.

41. Padlan, E.A., Silverton, E.W., Sheriff, S., Cohen, G.H., Smith-Gill, S.J., and Davies, D.R. 1989. Structure of an antibody-antigen complex: crystal structure of the HyHel-10 Fab-lysozyme complex. *Proc. Natl. Acad. Sci. USA* 86:5938.

42. Whitlow, M. 1991. In: *Keystone Symposia on Molecular and Cellular Biology.* Abst. N116, Supplement 15 E, March 16–26, 1991, and personal communication.

43. Clackson, T., Griffiths, A.D., Hoogenboom, H., and Winter, G. 1991. Presented at Keystone Symposia on Molecular and Cellular Biology, March 16-26, 1991.

44. Winter, G., and Milstein, C. 1991. Man-made antibodies. *Nature* 349:293.

CHAPTER 7

Design of Expression Vectors and Mammalian Cell Systems Suitable for Engineered Antibodies

Stephen D. Gillies

The earliest reports of the successful expression of recombinant antibody genes in transfected mammalian cells focused on the genetic elements regulating immunoglobulin gene expression.[1-4] The use of cloned genomic DNA fragments of functionally rearranged light (L) and heavy (H) chain genes made it possible to identify those genetic elements, (for example, enhancers and promoters) that interact with specific DNA binding proteins and instruct the cell to express the gene at a very high rate. While these first studies involved the use of cultured lymphoid cell lines, more recent work has explored the use of heterologous systems, from yeast[5] and insect cells[6] to monkey (COS) cells[7] and Chinese Hamster Ovary (CHO) cells.[8, 9] Unlike the results obtained by bacterial expression,[10,11] all of the systems that allow the antibody to be secreted out of the cell appear to assemble functional antibody molecules. Thus, the information necessary for H and L chain association, as well as inter-H chain association and disulfide bond formation, is encoded in the primary sequence of the H and L chains.

The choice of one expression system over another is dictated by the ultimate purpose of a given undertaking. For example, if the goal is to create a therapeutic product that will be needed in large (kilogram) quantities, then the issue of scale-up and manufacturing becomes of paramount importance. Nonetheless, the efficacy of the antibody product may be dependent on post-translational modifications (for example, glycosylation) that are only performed properly by mammalian cell systems. While yeasts have been shown to secrete fully assembled antibodies with antigen-binding acitvity, the ability of such antibodies to fix complement is severely impaired by the high mannose-type oligosaccharide attached to the sole N-linked glycosylation site in the second C_H2 heavy chain domain.[5]

More recently it has been shown that recombinant antibodies can also be expressed in an insect (*Spodoptera*) cell system. Like yeast cell expression, it is unclear whether insect cell glycosylation will affect biologic activity. The other concerns with the antibody produced in either yeast or insect cells include both the issues of increased immunogenicity and more rapid clearance by asialo-oligosaccharide and mannose receptor-binding cells (hepatocytes and macrophages). It is likely, therefore, that there are no economic advantages of these systems (with reported yields of from 2 to 5 mg per liter of culture media) over the use of cultured, engineered mammalian cells, especially now that high-level expression (greater than 100 mg/l) in serum-free media is possible with both permanently established, transfected mouse and hamster cell lines.[12, 13]

Transient expression of antibodies in COS cells has also been described[7] and has the advantage of allowing for a more rapid characterization of antibody function. In this case, engineered expression constructs (plasmids) containing SV40 origins of replication and the antibody H and L-chain genes are introduced into COS (CV-1-origin-SV40) cells that constitutively express the SV40 T antigen. The circular plasmids replicate (as would the SV40 genome) to very high numbers as autosomal DNA, and in this way express and secrete relatively high levels of antibody for two to three days, after which the cells die. This system is most useful for testing antibody variants such as those in which the antigen-binding sites (of a murine monoclonal antibody, for example) have been transplanted into the framework of another species. Such "humanization" procedures[14] may involve multiple attempts before an appropriate antibody affinity is obtained.[15] The ability to rapidly assess the expressed antibodies for binding activity would benefit from the transient expression format. Once the desired antibody is obtained, however, the large-scale manufacturing is only feasible, from economic and regulatory perspectives, through the use of permanently established cell lines. This chapter will focus on vectors suitable for the establishment of cell lines expressing recombinant antibodies.

The approach taken in constructing antibody expression vectors depends on several factors: (1) the cloning method used in generating the antibody-encoding DNA sequences (for example, genomic DNA versus cDNA), (2) the choice of separate vectors for each antibody chain or the combination of both on a single plasmid, and (3) the choice and number of selectable marker genes. Antibodies have been expressed using most of the combinations of these choices, but those that have resulted in the highest levels of expression will be described. These include two different approaches in lymphoid (hybridoma) cells: one using stepwise expression of an engineered light chain gene (genomic DNA) followed by the subsequent expression of an engineered heavy chain gene in the same cell; and a second using cDNA cassettes together with constant region gene fragments that encode both chains on a single plasmid vector. A third system using direct expression of cDNAs and two marker genes (one for the original selection of transformants and a second for gene amplification) in CHO cells has also been described[13] but will not be detailed here because similar gene amplification methodologies have already been discussed for the expression of other proteins.[16, 17]

All three systems have been described in the literature and have resulted in expression levels in excess of 50 mg/l in spent culture media. The expression levels that have been reported are likely to be best-case examples with a single set of antibody variable (V) regions. Thus, the general utility of each method will only be known after further examples are tested. It should also be pointed out that the levels of expression reported in the literature are often determined in different ways and, as a result, are often difficult to compare. This is particularly problematic when anchorage-dependent cells (for example, CHO) are compared with cells grown in suspension (for example, hybridomas) and the specific productivities (μg protein/10^6 cells/24 hours) are measured.

When the merits of these systems are compared, an additional consideration must be made—by what method and to what extent will the transfected cell line be scaled up for production in the future? The levels of expression of attached CHO transfectant cell lines most often greatly exceed those of their suspension-adapted counterparts. These differences are seen at the level of mRNA accumulation[18] and likely reflect differences in RNA metabolism between the two modes of growth. The implication is that one must decide whether to commit to a scale-up method designed for attached cells, which most likely will involve much higher capital costs, or settle for lower specific productivity in suspension-adapted cells, which can be grown in much simpler bioreactors (stirred tank or air-lift fermenters). Transfected hybridoma/myeloma cells, on the other hand, do not change their productivity upon scaling up because they are initially isolated as suspension culture clones.

EXPRESSION VECTORS BASED ON THE USE OF GENOMIC DNA FRAGMENTS

The use of genomic DNA has the advantage of regulatory signals contained on the fragments that are essentially the same as those of the endogenously expressed antibody genes. These include promoter elements, transcriptional enhancers, RNA splice signals, and polyadenylation sites. The one exception is the constant region of the κ chain, which contains a relatively weak enhancer upstream (relative to transcription) of the $C_κ$ coding sequence.[19] Because H and L chains are equally expressed *in vivo*, a second enhancer (or other type of transcriptional activator) is likely to be positioned far downstream and has indeed been located several thousand base pairs downstream of the mouse gene segment.[20] Nonetheless, early reports demonstrated that cloned, functionally rearranged antibody genes could be introduced into myeloma and hybridoma cells and result in the expression of small amounts of antibody (generally 1–5 mg/l of spent culture media).[21] It was also shown that the active V region fragments of one species (generally mouse) could be combined with the C regions of another (generally human), resulting in chimeric antibodies.[22] Because this method is currently the most widely used application of recombinant antibody technology, the following discussions will use the construction of chimeric mouse/human antibodies as an example.

The major disadvantage of the genomic DNA approach is that the cloning of the desired genomic V regions is often laborious and time-consuming, because many hybridomas contain multiple rearranged genes. Once the V regions have been cloned, the insertion into an expression vector is relatively straightforward. Because all V regions are rearranged to the same set of joining (J) sequences, upstream of the C regions,[23] the same restriction sites are found in the VC introns of the rearranged genes (on the 3' side of the V region exon). These include a unique EcoRI site on the 3' side of V_H exons and a unique Hind III site on the 3' side of the $V_κ$ exons in the mouse system. It is then necessary to identify a unique restriction site on the 5' side of the V region exon that is sufficiently upstream so that the transcriptional promoter sequence is included in the resulting fragment. The best way to ensure that all the appropriate information is included is to sequence the entire fragment. When a site is identified, the ligation of synthetic linkers can be used to adapt the fragment so that all V_H 5' sites are BamHI (for example) and all $V_κ$ 5' sites are XbaI (for example). Vectors can then be constructed that will be useful for any newly cloned V regions where V_H exons are introduced as BamHI-EcoRI fragments and $V_κ$ exons are introduced as KbaI-HindIII fragments. Alternatively, the upstream site can be the same as the downstream site so that V_H fragments are inserted as EcoRI fragments and $V_κ$ fragments are inserted as HindIII fragments, as in the example in Figure 7-1 (described in the following section).

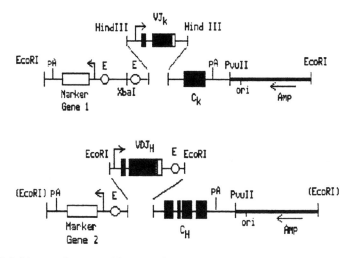

Figure 7-1. Vectors for recombinant antibody expression.

Stepwise Expression of L and H Chains

The combined size of the V and C region fragments can be rather large, making it more practical to assemble the chimeric H and L recombinant genes in separate plasmid vectors. These vectors must also contain marker genes for selection of those cells that have taken up the transfected DNA. Figure 7-1 shows an example of how the V_H and V_κ gene fragments from a mouse hybridoma can be assembled into expression vectors designed for the stepwise expression of the recombinant antibody. The position of the various regulatory elements (for example, enhancers and promoters) for each transcription unit are indicated. Each vector has its own marker gene, used for selection of successfully transfected cells, and these are generally based on the use of SV40 control regions. The pSV2gpt and pSV2neo plasmids[24, 25] have been widely used, wherein the SV40 early enhancer/promoter drives the coding sequences of either guanosine phosphoribosyl transferase or an enzyme conferring resistance to the neomycin analog G418, respectively. A polyadenylation signal from SV40 is positioned after the translational termination site in both cases.

For the present constructions it was necessary to mutate the unique HindIII in the pSV2-derived vectors, because it will be used as an insertion site for V_κ fragments. This is done by cutting with HindIII, blunting the ends by filling the "sticky ends" with deoxyribonucleotide triphosphates (dNTPs) and the Klenow fragment of DNA polymerase, and religating the plasmid. It is also necessary to add restriction sites upstream of the marker gene transcription units for subsequent ligation steps. In the present example, an

XbaI site was added to what was originally a PvuII site (using synthetic linkers) for use in the L chain vector. A EcoRI site was added to the analogous PvuII site in the H chain vector. In both cases, EcoRI linkers were added to what was originally a BamHI site in the pSV2 vectors, just downstream of the marker gene polyadeylation sites.

The middle of the linearized plasmid maps in Figure 7-1 shows the insertion sites for the cloned V region fragments. Note that in the L chain vector, an enhancer has been placed upstream of the insertion site. This is because the enhancer located in the intron of the κ gene, as noted above, is not sufficiently strong enough to result in high level expression in transfected cells. The placement of the more powerful H chain enhancer in this position is strongly recommended. The mouse H chain enhancer can be isolated as a XbaI to EcoRI fragment and the EcoRI site can then be changed to a HindIII site with synthetic linkers. In the case of the V_H gene fragment, the use of EcoRI site as the 3' end (in the mouse system) ensures that the H chain enhancer will be contained in the recombined transcription unit. Thus, the enhancer is not present in the vector as well.

Representative constant regions are shown downstream of the V region insertion sites. The C regions of the human $\gamma 1$ and κ chains can be obtained as HindIII-PvuII and EcoRI-XbaI fragments, respectively, and can be modified with synthetic linkers so that they can be assembled into the vectors in Figure 7-1. A specific example follows. The HindIII to PvuII fragment of the human $C\gamma 1$ gene is subcloned in pBR322 digested with the same enzymes. The resulting plasmid is digested with HindIII and the ends are blunted by incubation with the Klenow fragment of DNA polymerase I in the presence of dNTPs. The blunt DNA is then ligated overnight at 4°C to a molar excess of phosphorylated EcoRI linkers (5'PO$_4$-gGAATTCc-3') using T4 DNA ligase (about 0.5 μg of plasmid DNA and 1 μg of linkers in a volume of 20 μl). The ligation mixture is extracted with phenol:CHCl$_3$, ethanol precipitated, and transformed into competent bacteria. Restriction analyses of transformants should identify clones that are missing the original HindIII site but now have an EcoRI site on the 5' side of the C$\gamma 1$ gene.

A similar process can then be carried out to change the restriction sites flanking the Cκ gene from EcoRI to HindIII (5' side) and from XbaI to PvuII (on the 3' side). The C$_\kappa$ gene is subcloned in pBR322 as a HindIII to PvuII fragment. The steps needed to construct the vectors in Figure 7-1 (using pSV2neo as marker gene 1 and pSV2gpt as marker gene 2) are detailed below.

Light Chain Vector Assembly.
1. Digest pSV2neo with PvuII and add XbaI linkers. Transform the ligated DNA, identify correct clones, and isolate modified plasmid

DNA. Digest the new plasmid with HindIII, fill the ends (Klenow + dNTPs) and religate to remove the HindIII site. Finally, digest with BamHI, fill the ends (Klenow + dNTPs), and ligate with EcoRI linkers. Transform bacteria and screen by restriction analyses for a clone with the new site. Prepare DNA, digest with EcoRI and XbaI, and gel-purify the fragment.

2. Isolate the mouse immunoglobulin H chain enhancer fragment and subclone in a plasmid vector as an XbaI-EcoRI fragment. Many commercially available vectors contain polylinkers with the necessary cloning sites. Digest with EcoRI, fill the ends, and ligate to HindIII linkers. Transform the DNA and identify the correct clone. Prepare the 680 bp XbaI-HindIII fragment and purify by gel electrophoresis. Alternatively, the entire fragment can be cloned and modified to contain the HindIII in one step using the polymerase chain reaction (PCR) and the appropriate primers.

3. Subclone the human C_x gene as described above or clone with PCR using primers that place a HindIII site on the 5' side and a PvuII site on the 3' side (downstream of the polyadenlyation site) of the coding region. Subclone in pBR322 as a HindIII-PvuII fragment and then digest with HindIII and EcoRI.

4. Ligate the three fragments together in equimolar amounts and transform bacteria. Analyze the resulting clones by restriction analyses. The final vector, which will be called pLneo for convenience, contains a unique HindIII site for the insertion of any functionally rearranged V regions. As noted above, this vector design requires that the V region fragment contains its own transcriptional promoter. After insertion, the correct orientation must be verified by restriction analysis or by DNA sequencing.

Heavy Chain Vector Construction.

1. Subclone the cloned HindIII to PvuII fragment of the human Cγ1 gene fragment (or the analogous fragment for the constant region of choice) between the HindIII and PvuII sites in plasmid pBR322. This plasmid already has an EcoRI site just upstream of the HindIII site, so that no linking is necessary unless one wishes to eliminate the HindIII site.

2. Digest pSV2gpt with PvuII and BamHI and blunt the latter site using Klenow polymerase, as before. Ligate overnight with EcoRI linkers and then heat-inactivate the ligase at 65°C. Digest with EcoRI to remove excess linkers and generate fragment monomers. Gel purify the linked fragment.

3. Digest the pBR322 vector containing the Cγ1 gene fragment with EcoRI, extract with phenol:CHCl$_3$, and treat with alkaline phospha-

tase to remove the 5' phosphate groups. Re-extract with phenol:CHCl₃ and gel purify. Ligate approximately 50 ng of the dephosphorylated plasmid DNA with 100 ng of the EcoRI-linked fragment from step 2 and transform competent bacteria. Screen transformants for the presence of the EcoRI fragment containing the gpt marker gene.

4. It is necessary to inactivate the EcoRI site between the pBR322 and gpt gene sequences so that the site upstream of the C_H region (where V regions are to be inserted) will be unique. This can be done by performing a partial digestion with limiting amounts of EcoRI that can be optimized to produce the greatest amount of plasmid molecules that have been cut only one time. Using these conditions, partially digest 5–10 µg of DNA. Extract with phenol:CHCl₃ to stop the digestion, ethanol precipitate, and fill the sticky ends (Klenow + dNTPs). Gel purify full-length linear plasmid DNA, using a small amount of DNA cut with PvuII (which cuts only once) as a size marker. The purified DNA is then circularized by ligation and transformed into competent bacteria. Transformants are then screened by EcoRI digestion for those containing only one site. Multiple enzyme digests can be used to test which site has been inactivated. The final vector, which we will call pHgpt, now contains a unique site upstream of the C_H region for insertion of functionally rearranged V_H regions. As noted above for the L chain, the V_H region fragment must contain a functional transcriptional promoter because none is provided by the vector.

Transfection of Myeloma or Hybridoma Cells. The lymphoid cell lines that are most often used for transfection experiments are the myeloma line P3X63.Ag8.653[26] and the hybridoma line Sp2/0Ag14.[27] Both lines are nonimmunoglobulin producers and have used extensively as fusion partners for the generation of hybridomas. Neither cell line is easily transformed by the calcium phosphate precipitation method[28] but both can easily be transfored using either protoplast fusion[3, 29] or electroporation techniques.[30]

For stepwise selection it is probably best to use the neo gene together with the L-chain vector, as in the example above. This is because L chain can be excreted by cells when it is expressed without the H chain, but the converse it not true. It is also possible to get multiple gene copies of neo vectors into these cells, allowing for higher expression levels. In contrast, only very small numbers of gpt vectors are found in transformants (unpublished observations), suggesting that high levels of gpt are toxic to the cell. The first transfection step serves as an opportunity to maximize the expression of L chain, which then pairs with newly synthesized H chain (which cannot be secreted in the absence of L chains) in the second step. Thus, high levels of H chain will be tolerated by the cell because it will associate with the available

L chain to form whole antibody. In this way it should be possible to select highly productive lines.

A recommended procedure is to: (1) Transfect Sp2/0Ag14 cells with the pLneo vector by protoplast fusion as described[3] and select for transformants in growth medium containing the neomycin analog G418 at 1 mg/ml; (2) isolate surviving clones and test for the expression of chimeric L chain by enzyme-linked immunosorbent assay (ELISA) of culture supernatants; (3) test the specific productivities of the positive clones and freeze down the five best L chain producers; and (4) culture the candidate L chain producers without G418 for two passages and transfect with the pHgpt vector as above. Plate cells in 96-well dishes containing xanthine at a final concentration 50 µg/ml (Hepes buffer) should be used at 10 mM to buffer the medium to pH 7.3 and allow cells to recover from the transfection process for 24 to 48 hours. Feed wells with a 50% exchange of volume with the selection medium containing xanthine, Hepes buffer, and mycophenolic acid (1 µg/ml). G418 can be added back to the medium if desired. Test surviving clones for the secretion of whole chimeric antibody. An ELISA based on an anti-human Fc capture antibody and detection with an anti-human κ antibody is useful to discriminate between the expression of individual chains and intact antibody.

Points to Consider. The construction that has been described can be modified in many ways, including the use of directional cloning for the insertion of V regions. In this case a stuffer fragment would be used to bridge the 5' and 3' sites, and the linker used on the 5' side of each V region would match the site in the vector. It is important to choose those sites that rarely, if ever, appear in antibody coding regions, such as SalI, XhoI, BamHI, and XbaI.

During the stepwise transfection process it is advisable to select several L chain producers as potential recipient lines for the second transfection step. This is because individual clones can have highly variable transformation frequencies, thus making it necessary to try more than one in the H-chain transfection step. It may also be necessary to grow the cells in the absence of the drug used in the first selection step in order to increase the transformation frequency. The drug can be added back after the cells have recovered from the transfection process, if desired, but generally the second drug selection (in this case mycophenolic acid) is sufficient to select for clones producing both H and L chains.

Simultaneous Expression of L and H Chains

There are several different approaches to the simultaneous expression of both antibody chains that utilize a single transfection step. One such method involves combining all of the necessary genetic information on a single vector. Because this approach is easier with the use of cDNA rather than with genomic DNA, it will be discussed in the cDNA expression section below. The other methods involve the cotransfection of two separate plasmids, such as those described above, and the subsequent drug selection for either or both of the marker genes. It is possible to select for resistance to two drugs simultaneously, but the frequency is usually quite low, perhaps due to the overall reduction in cloning efficiency imposed by the drugs themselves. If only one marker is going to be selected, it is best if it is the marker that is physically linked to the H chain gene. This is because cells that express H chain in the absence of L chain tend to grow less well than those that express both chains or only L chain. If the drug selection favors expression of the linked H chain in the transformants, those cells that are selected are more likely to express the unselected (cotransfected) L chain as well. In either case, the chance that a cell is going to take up and express the genes encoded by two separate plasmids is generally going to be much less than the expression of genes from one contiguous stretch of DNA.

The method used for transfection is an important factor in choosing the approach for the simultaneous expression of antibody chains. Methods that utilize purified DNA, such as calcium phosphate precipitation and electroporation, are better for cotransfection of two separate plasmid DNAs, especially when the plasmids are first linearized by restriction enzyme digestion. This is likely to be due to the ligation of the mixture of DNAs in the cell to form a high molecular weight structure that is subsequently integrated into chromosomal DNA. Methods such as protoplast fusion, in which supercoiled plasmid is introduced into the recipient cell, have not generally been used for the cotransfection of two separate plasmids, with one notable exception. Oi and Morrison[31] have described an approach that involves the use of two separate vectors that are maintained in the same bacterial host. This is accomplished by using two marker genes for drug selection as well as two separate replication origins that can coexist and replicate in the same bacterium. These authors have reported reasonably high cotransfection frequencies with this protocol and double selection for the gpt and neo markers.

The methods for constructing the vectors necessary to simultaneously express both the L and H chain are the same as those just described for stepwise expression. The only modification that would be required for the use of two separate vectors harbored in a single bacterium would be to replace the pBR322 sequences (replication origin and ampicillin resistance gene) in one of the vectors in Figure 7-1 with a segment derived from the compatible plasmid pACYC184 and the gene for chloramphenicol resistance.[31] The three most commonly used approaches to single-step expression and some of the considerations for each variation follow.

Single Plasmid Encoding Both Chains

Benefits	1.	Highly efficient at producing both chains.
	2.	A single plasmid is used, with one selectable marker gene.
	3.	Works well with either electroporation or protoplast fusion.
Problem	1.	Difficult to fit all genomic DNA fragments on a single plasmid—more useful for expression of cDNA.

Separate Plasmids/Selection for One Marker

Benefits	1.	Construction of plasmids is easier and is adaptable to stepwise approach.
	2.	The use of only one selecting drug avoids problems in lowered cloning efficiency.
Problem	1.	Selection of single-chain producers, but this can be reduced if the selected drug marker is on the H chain vector.
	2.	Requires electroporation method for efficient co-transfection of unselected plasmid.

Separate Plasmids/Selection for Two Markers

Benefits	1.	Frequency of antibody secretors is high among double transformants.
	2.	Can be used with electroporation or protoplast fusion (in special case of compatible plasmids).
Problem	1.	Lower overall number of clones obtained due to lowered cloning efficiency.

EXPRESSION VECTORS BASED ON THE USE OF cDNA

The cloning of genetic information as cDNA, either by standard reverse transcription of mRNA or by PCR methodologies,[32, 33] is much simpler and more rapid than the cloning of genomic fragments. While cloning is simpler, expression of the information is not. Because cDNA represents only the coding sequence of a gene and lacks regulatory signals for transcription, additional information has to be included in the vector. Both promoter and enhancer sequences, as well as polyadenylation signals, need to be positioned properly so that, upon insertion, the cDNA is flanked by the promoter at the 5' end and polyadenylation site at the 3' end.

An additional complication arises when one wishes to recombine variable and constant regions, as in the construction of mouse/human chimeric antibodies, using cloned cDNA sequences. The cDNA represents a fusion of the V and C region sequences through RNA splicing and, unlike genomic fragments, the V regions can not be easily separated from the C region and re-expressed with that of another species. Two approaches have been used to overcome this problem. The first involves the mutagenesis of sites in the V and C regions that create a common restriction sequence that can be used to recombine them, as in the case of chimeric antibodies.[34] The second approach involves the reconstruction of the original splice donor site of the V region so that it can be combined with C region gene fragments in their genomic configuration.[35] The latter method has the advantages that no changes in the original protein sequences are necessary and that the modified V region can be used together with any exon that has a splice acceptor site maintaining the same reading frame. This approach will be detailed below as an example of how traditional cDNAs or PCR products encoding a murine monoclonal antibody can be modified and expressed in a cDNA expression vector.

Adapting H and L Chain cDNAs for Recombinant Antibody Expression

As discussed above, cDNAs encoding the H and L chains of an antibody provide only the instructions for the translation into protein of what was originally mRNA. During the cloning process other sequences are either added to or omitted from the final DNA product, depending on how the cloning step was performed. For example, if cDNA cloning was performed using reverse transcriptase and oligo dT priming (off of the polyA tail of the mRNA), the DNA sequence would contain a short stretch of polyA at the 3′ end (Figure7-2B). This is only a problem if the cDNA is going to be expressed without further modification (for example, changing the C region), in which case it is best to remove these sequences by restriction enzyme digestion (if a convenient site is available) or partial exonuclease digestion. In either case, a new restriction stie that is compatible with the expression vector should be added with synthetic linkers. Synthetic linkers can also be used during the cloning process to provide unique 5′ end restriction sites (Figure 7-2B) and provide the sticky ends needed to ligate the cDNA to the vector in the cloning step.[35]

Another way of avoiding the polyA stretch is to directly link the cloned cDNA to a genomic fragment containing the same C region (because they would have restriction sites in common). This scheme, shown in Figure 7-2C, would also provide the polyadenylation signal for subsequent expression. Vectors have been designed to accomodate this approach with a human γ3κ

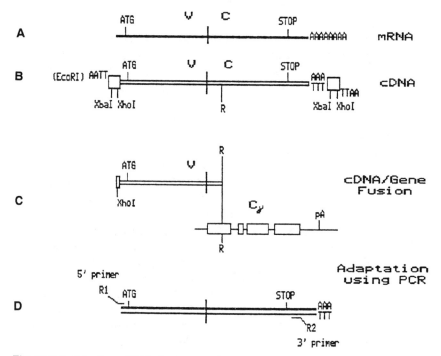

Figure 7-2. Adapting cDNAs for expression.

antibody.[12] When PCR is used for the cloning step it is possible to use 3′ end primers that lie just after the end of the coding sequence, but upstream of the polyA stretch (Figure 7-2D). The PCR primer can also include a convenient restriction site for subsequent ligation to the expression vector. PCR can also be used on cDNAs that have been cloned by traditional methods in order to place convenient restriction sites (R1 and R2) at both the 5′ and 3′ ends. The 5′ end primer should be located upstream of the initiating ATG codon unless the vector has been designed to provide it.

Construction of cDNA Cassettes

A convenient system that is useful for the direct expression of cDNAs and for constructing chimeric antibodies from cloned cDNAs or PCR products representing only V regions involves the use of V region cassettes.[35] The construction begins during the cloning process itself through the use of synthetic linkers containing restriction enzyme cleavage sites. These sites will match those in the expression vector that has been specifically designed to accomodate such cassettes. The other modification that is required is the reconstruction of a splice donor site at the end of each V region, so that it may be joined to any constant region containing a functional splice acceptor site. The construction of a chimeric antibody using standard cDNA cloning methods will be used as an example of how this system can be set up.

The vector that will be used for expression of the chimeric antibody is shown in Figure 7-3. It contains directional cloning sites for the separate insertions of a V_κ and a V_H cassette. In this particular design, the V_κ cloning site is downstream of the promoter and contains a unique XbaI. The 3' site is a unique BamHI site. The V_κ cassette will have to have a 5' XbaI site, upstream of the ATG translation initiation site (because the vector does not provide this element), and a BamHI site will have to be located at the 3' end, after the reconstructed splice donor site. The V_H cloning site is flanked by unique XhoI and HindIII sites and so these sites will need to be placed at the 5' and 3' ends of the V_H cassette, respectively.

The 5' restriction sites are added to the cDNA during the construction of the library. Separate libraries can be made for the H and L chains using the appropriate linkers; however, we have found it simple to make one polylinker containing both the XbaI and XhoI sites, preceded by the four base 5' overhang, AATT, that provides an EcoRI "sticky" end for cloning into the EcoRI site of the phage vector lgt10.36 The final synthetic linker is 5'-AATTCTCGAGTCTAGA-3', which is annealed to the partial complementary strand 3'-GAGCTCAGATCT-PO4-5', leaving a nonphosphory-

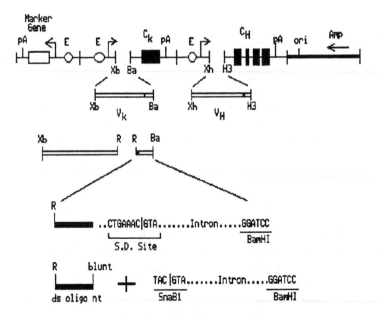

Figure 7-3. A modular vector for H and L chain expression.

lated 5' AATT overhang (for subsequent ligation to the phosphorylated EcoRI site in the phage DNA) and a phosphorylated blunt end for ligation to blunt double-stranded cDNA. The cDNA is prepared by reverse transcription of mRNA, followed by "nick-translated" DNA repair synthesis of the second strand as described by Gubler and Hoffman.[36] Because the end that ligates to the cDNA is the only one phosphorylated, there is no polymerization of linkers that require removal by EcoRI digestion. After ligation of linker and cDNA, the library can be fractionated by acrylamide gel electrophoresis and only the cDNAs that are long enough to encode the complete cDNA can be cut from the gel and eluted (approximately 0.9–1.0 kb for the L chain and 1.4–1.6 kb for the H chain). These are then ligated to EcoRI-cut λgt10 DNA and packaged into phage. Full-length cDNAs are then identified for both the H and L chains and each now has an EcoRI, XhoI, and XbaI site at its 5' end.

The next step is to recreate a splice donor site for each V region cassette. The V regions from each cDNA are sequenced to verify their intact coding regions and to identify unique restriction (R) sites close to the junctions with the C regions (see Figure 7-3). Synthetic linker fragments are then synthesized, spanning the sequence from the restriction site to the exact V/C junction. In the example shown, a synthetic linker fragment is blunt-end ligated to a synthetic intron fragment. This intron fragment, based on the intron between the leader and V exons of the MOPC141 H chain,[37] was synthesized and cloned as either a SnaBI to BamHI fragment (for the L chain cassette) or a SnaBI to HindIII fragment (for the H chain cassette). The exact sequence of this intron is not important, and many other sequences can be used in its place; however, the sequence should be long enough to ensure that the final intron is at least 80–90 base pairs long to ensure sufficient splicing. Digestion with SnaBI generates a blunt end that is suitable for ligation to the blunt end of the linker and generates a functional splice donor site.

The ligation product should be sequenced by subcloning the combined linker/intron into a sequencing vector with multiple cloning sites and priming sites for dideoxy sequencing. Often it is necessary to include another restriction site upstream of the unique (R) site in the V region for this purpose. After sequencing, the linker/intron fragment can be excised from the vector and joined to the remaining portion of the V region. In the vector design shown in Figure 7-3, it is necessary to insert the final XbaI to BamHI V_κ fragment into the expression vector before inserting the XhoI to HindIII V_H fragment. This is because of the positioning of the XhoI and XbaI sites in the synthetic linker. If the V_H fragment was inserted first, there would be two XbaI sites in the resulting plasmid, whereas insertion of the V_κ fragment eliminates the upstream XhoI site. The V_κ-containing plasmid can be cut with XhoI and HindIII and ligated to the V_H fragment, constructed in the same manner as the V_κ fragment, to give the final antibody expression vector.

When this vector is introduced into myeloma or hybridoma cells, transcription from the promoters would result in fusion mRNAs consisting of the 5′ untranslated region of that promoter, the coding sequence of the V region cassettes precisely spliced to the desired constant region and the 3′ untranslated region of that genomic fragment. Polyadenylation would also be dictated by the natural signals contained in the genomic fragment. For all of the human Cγ gene fragments, the information necessary for expression of the secreted forms is contained within HindIII-PvuII fragments.

Simultaneous Expression of H and L Chains Using cDNAs

The expression vector shown in Figure 7-3, including the three transcription units and bacterial plasmid sequences, is not too large for efficient replication, partly because of the reduced size of the V region cassettes. This makes it amenable to all the various transfection methodologies involving either purified DNA or protoplast fusion. It has been show that the latter method is much preferred due to its simplicity and due to the fact that it results in transfectants with much higher productivity.

Several different versions of this basic vector can be constructed using different promoter, enhancer, and marker gene combinations. We have found[35] that the most reliable and efficient vector utilizes the mouse immunoglobulin H chain enhancer, mouse metallothionein I promoters, and the mutant dhfr gene[38] as selectable marker. When this vector is combined with the protoplast fusion method of transfection (using hybridoma Sp2/0 as recipient cell), we consistently select cells that are highly productive. These cells can then be incubated in progressively higher concentrations of methotrexate, which results in still higher levels of production. Once cells are adapted to a moderately high concentration of methotrexate (5 μM), they should be subcloned twice and the highest producers at each step should be selected. This approach has been used to express several chimeric and human antibodies and results in cell lines capable of producing from a minimum of 50 mg/l to as much as 200 mg/l of spent culture supernatant.

The cassette approach can be a very useful and flexible way to express recombinant antibodies. The major problem arises when the cDNAs contain one of the unique sites (XhoI, XbaI, BamHI, or HindIII) used for the construction. This makes it necessary to use partially digested fragments for certain steps or mutagenesis to remove the unwanted restriction site.

A potential limitation to the use of dhfr selection, as described above, is that the only lymphoid cell that is efficiently transformed by this method is Sp2/0 Ag14. This is somewhat limiting but future work may result in additional cell lines that are amenable to this approach. Another alternative is the use of double selection techniques, whereby the dhfr vector is cotransfected with another selectable marker (for example, neomycin resistance) to establish clones containing both plasmids. Culturing cells in increased concentrations of methotrexate might then be used to increase expression.

CONCLUSIONS

Several approaches to the expression of recombinant antibodies have been described utilizing DNA sequences obtained by either genomic, traditional cDNA, or PCR methodologies. Those methods that utilize rapid cloning techniques and that are amenable to strategies for the further modification of the protein will likely be the most widely used. The use of V region cassettes, together with modular vectors (where independent functional units are flanked by unique restriction sites), should allow for the independent assortment of antibody V regions or modified C regions (for example, truncated H chains, fusion proteins).

The most widely used cell system will probably be the transfected myeloma/hybridoma cell, although improvements in the expression of antibodies in CHO cells make this a viable alternative. In both cases, the most productive systems are those that allow for the initial selection for transfectants, followed by adaptation to increased drug concentration (systems using dhfr selection for methotrexate resistance). Both cell types have also been successfully grown in serum-free or protein-free media, which make protein purification and the related regulatory issues less problematic. The cost of manufacturing with mammalian cell culture is also greatly reduced when productivity is high, and purification is relatively simple.

REFERENCES

1. Rice, D. and Baltimore, D. 1982. Regulated expression of an immunoglobulin kappa gene introduced into a mouse lymphoid cell line. *Proc. Natl. Acad. Sci. USA* 79:7862.
2. Oi, V.T., Morrison, S.L., Herzenberg, L.A., and Berg, P. 1983. Immunoglobulin gene expression in transformed lymphoid cells. *Proc. Natl. Acad. Sci. USA* 80:825.
3. Gillies, S.D., Morrison, S.L., Oi, V.T., and Tonegawa, S. 1983. A tissue-specific transcription enhancer element is located in the major intron of a rearranged immunoglobulin heavy chain gene. *Cell* 33:717.
4. Neuberger, M.S. 1983. Expression and regulation of immunoglobulin heavy chain gene transfected into lymphoid cells. *EMBO J.* 2:1373.
5. Horwitz, A.H., Chang, C.P., Better, M., Hellstrom, K.E., and Robinson, R.R. 1988. Secretion of functional antibodies and Fab fragment from yeast cells. *Proc. Natl. Acad. Sci. USA* 85:8678.

6. Haseman, C.A. and Capra, J.D. 1990. High-level production of a functional immunoglobulin heterodimer in a baculovirus expression system. *Proc. Natl. Acad. Sci. USA* 87:3942.

7. Whittle, N., Adair, J., Lloyd, C., Jenkins, L., Devine, J., Schlom, J., Raubitschek, A., Colcher, D., and Bodmer, M. 1987. Expression in COS cells of a mouse-human chimeric B72.3 antibody. *Prot. Engin.* 1:499.

8. Cattaneo, A. and Neuberger, M.S. 1987. Polymeric immunoglobulin M is secreted by transfectants of non-lymphoid cells in the absence of immunoglobulin J chain. *EMBO J.* 6:2753.

9. Colcher, D., Milenic, D., Roselli, M., Raubitscheck, A., Yarranton, G., King, D., Adair, J., Whittle, N., Bodmer, M., and Schlom, J. 1989. Characterization and biodistribution of recombinant and recombinant/chimeric constructs of monoclonal antibody B72.3. *Cancer Res.* 49:1738.

10. Boss, M.A., Kenton, J.H., Wood, C.R., and Emtage, J.S. 1984. Assembly of functional antibodies from immunoglobulin heavy and light chains synthesized in *E. coli. Nucleic Acids Res.* 12:3791.

11. Cabilly, S., Riggs, A.D., Pande, H., Shively, J.E., Holmes, W.E., Rey, M., Pery, L.J., Wetzel, R., and Heyneker, H.L. 1984. Generation of an antibody activity from immunoglobulin polypeptide chains produced in *Escherichia coli. Proc. Natl. Acad. Sci. USA* 81:3273.

12. Gillies, S.D., Dorai, H., Wesolowski, J., Majeau, G., Young, D., Boyd, J., Gardner, J., and James, K. 1989. Expression of human anti-tetanus toxoid antibody in transfected murine myeloma cells. *Bio/technology* 7:799.

13. Page, M.J. and Sydenham, M.A. 1991. High-level expression of the humanized monoclonal antibody Compath-1H in Chinese hamster ovary cells. *Bio/technology:* 9:64.

14. Riechmann, L., Clark, M., Waldmann, H., and Winter, G. 1988. Reshaping human antibodies for therapy. *Nature* 332:323.

15. Queen, C., Schneider, W.P., Selick, H.E., Payne, P.W., Landolfi, N.F., Duncan, J.F., Avdalovic, N.M., Levitt, M., Junghans, R.P., and Waldmann, T.A. 1989. A humanized antibody that binds to the interleukin 2 receptor. *Proc. Natl. Acad. Sci. USA* 86:10029.

16. Kaufman, R.J. 1990. Selection and coamplification of heterologous genes in mammalian cells. *Methods Enzymol.* 185:537.

17. Okamoto, M., Nakayama, C., Nakai, M., and Yanagi, H. 1990. Amplification and high-level expression of a cDNA for human granulocyte-macrophage colony-stimulating factor in human lymphoblastoid Namalwa cells. *Bio/technology* 8:550.

18. Cockett, M.I., Bennington, C.R., and Yarranton, G.T. 1990. High level expression of tissue inhibitor of metalloproteinases in Chinese hamster ovary cells using glutamine synthetase gene amplification. *Bio/technology* 8:662.

19. Picard, D. and Schaffner, W. 1984. A lymphocyte-specific enhancer in the mouse immunoglobulin gene. *Nature* 307:80.

20. Meyer, K.B. and Neuberger, M.S. 1989. The immunoglobulin κ locus contains a second, stronger B-cell-specific enhancer which is located downstream of the constant region. *EMBO J.* 8:1959.

21. Ochi, A., Hawley, R.G., Hawley, T., Shulman, M.J., Traunecker, A., Kohler, G.,

and Hozumi, N. 1983. Functional immunoglobulin M production after transfection of cloned immunoglobulin heavy and light chain genes into lymphoid cells. *Proc. Natl. Acad. Sci. USA* 80:6351.

22. Morrison, S.L. and Oi, V.T. 1984. Transfer and expression of immunoglobulin genes. *Ann. Rev. Immunol.* 2:239.

23. Tonegawa, S. 1983. Somatic generation of antibody diversity. *Nature* 302:575.

24. Mulligan, R.C. and Berg, P. 1981. Selection for animal cells that express the *Escherichia coli* gene coding for xanthine-guanine phosphoribosyl transferase. *Proc. Natl. Acad. Sci. USA* 78:2072.

25. Southern, P.J. and Berg, P. 1982. Transformation of mammalian cells to antibiotic resistance with a bacterial gene under the control of the SV40 early region promoter. *J. Molec. Appl. Genet.* 1:327.

26. Kearney, J., Radbruch, A., Liesegang, B., and Rajewsky, K. 1979. New mouse myeloma cell line that has lost immunoglobulin expression but permits the construction of antibody-secreting hybrid cell lines. *J. Immunol.* 123:1548.

27. Shulman, M., Wilde, C., and Kohler, G. 1978. A better cell line for making hybridomas secreting specific antibodies. *Nature* 276:269.

28. Graham, F.L. and van der Eb, A.J. 1973. Transformation of rat cells by DNA of human adenovirus 5. *Virology* 52:456.

29. Sandri-Goldin, R.M., Goldin, A.L., Levine, M., and Glorioso, A.J. 1981. High frequency transfer of cloned herpes simplex virus type I sequences to mammalian cells by protoplast fusion. *Molec. Cell Biol.* 1:743.

30. Potter, H., Weir, L., and Leder, P. 1984. Enhancer-dependent expression of human κ immunoglobulin genes introduced into mouse pre-B lymphocytes by electroporation. *Proc. Natl. Acad. Sci. USA* 81:7161.

31. Oi, V.T. and Morrison, S.L. 1986. Chimeric antibodies. *Biotechniques* 4:214.

32. Orlandi, R., Gussow, D.H., Jones, P.T., and Winter, G. 1989. Cloning immunoglobulin variable domains for expression by the polymerase chain reaction. *Proc. Natl. Acad. Sci. USA* 86:3833.

33. Larrick, J.W., Danielsson, L., Brenner, C.A., Abrahamson, M., Fry, K.E., and Borrebaeck, C.A.K. 1989. Polymerase chain reaction using mixed primers: Cloning of human monoclonal antibody variable region genes from single hybridoma cells. *Bio/technology* 7:934.

34. Liu, A.X., Mack, P.W., Champion, C.I., and Robinson, R.R. 1987. Expression of mouse:human immunoglobulin heavy-chain cDNA in lymphoid cells. *Gene* 54:33.

35. Gillies, S.D., Lo, K.-M., and Wesolowski, J. 1989. High-level expression of chimeric antibodies using adapted cDNA variable region cassettes. *J. Immunol. Methods* 125:191.

36. Gubler, U. and Hoffman, B.J. 1983. A simple and very efficient method for generating cDNA libraries. *Gene* 25:263.

37. Sakano, H., Maki, R., Kurosawa, Y., Roeder, W., and Tonegawa, S. 1980. Two types of somatic recombination are necessary for the generation of complete immunoglobuline heavy-chain genes. *Nature* 286:676.

38. Simonsen, C.C. and Levinson, A.D. 1983. Isolation and expression of an altered mouse dihydrofolate reductase cDNA. *Proc. Natl. Acad. Sci. USA* 80:2495.

CHAPTER 8

"Plantibodies": Expression of Monoclonal Antibodies in Plants

Andrew Hiatt, Ruth Pinney

PLANT CELL CULTURE AND TRANSFORMATION

Two characteristics of plant cells make them valuable tools for the synthesis and analysis of antibodies. First, many plant cells can be propagated either as clumps of cells on agar plates (callus), as liquid suspension cultures, or as protoplasts from which the cell walls have been removed.[1-3] Protoplasts in particular are useful as a system for the rapid evaluation of engineered antibodies (see method 4). Second, whole plants can be regenerated from callus cultures or protoplasts.[1, 4] Regenerated plants can express antibodies at levels greater than 1% of total extractable protein.[5] In addition, genetic recombination as a result of sexual crossing of regenerated plants is a novel method for assembling heavy and light chain pairs as well as more complex immunoglobulin structures.

DNA-mediated transformation of plant cells can be accomplished in a variety of ways.[6-13] The most commonly used method is to employ *Agrobacterium tumefaciens* as the delivery vehicle for introduction of re-combinant vectors to the plant cell nucleus.[11-13] Although the process of regeneration required to obtain antibody-producing plants can take as long as four months, the basic manipulations and reagents required to induce regeneration are very simple. Because plant development is controlled by small, heat-stable, organic molecules, preparation of media for either regeneration or de-differentiated growth is straightforward. Antibody production from protoplasts also requires only relatively simple procedures. Expression and evaluation of antibodies from small-scale protoplast preparations can be accomplished within three days. Protoplasts may be an appropriate system for the screening of large numbers of antibody constructs resulting from mutagenesis strategies or from polymerase chain reactions (PCR).

A key component in the transformation of plants is *Agrobacterium*. This method of plant cell transformation is accomplished simply by co-cultivation of leaf segments with the bacterium containing the Ti plasmid, which is the causal agent in neoplastic transformation of many types of plant cells.[11-13] In nature, infection of stems with soil-borne *Agrobacterium* results in de-differentiation and proliferation of cells above the crown (termed a *crown gall*). A common characteristic of these transformed cells is the production of the opine class of amino acids. Genes encoding enzymes responsible for opine production (for example, nopaline synthase) are derived from the Ti plasmid. These genes, as well as others responsible for neoplastic transformation and nuclear integration, are contained in a 20 kb section of the Ti plasmid called *T-DNA*. Transfer of the T-DNA from *Agrobacterium* into the plant cell nucleus is followed by heritable genomic integration of the T-DNA. The *Agrobacterium* never enters the plant cell but responds to chemical signals (for example, acetosyringone) released by wounded cell walls to elicit the transfer and integration of genetic material.[14] Integration of T-DNA is not sequence-specific and requires only a region of DNA adjacent to the border of the T-DNA/Ti plasmid junction.[15] In practice, this means that any plasmid DNA containing a border region can be stably integrated into a plant cell nucleus. Removal of genes involved in neoplastic transformation (for example, those directing opine production) does not prevent integration. Constructs containing promoters that are active in plant cells can be used to direct the expression of selectable markers (for example, neomycin phosphotransferase for kanamycin resistance). Heterologous cDNAs or genes can be inserted into the T-DNA. The T-DNA/Ti border will direct integration of plasmid DNA, resulting in transformed plant cells devoid of neoplastic characteristics. These cells can be fully regenerated into mature, fertile plants.[16]

Vectors have been developed that contain plant-selectable markers, promoters upstream from polylinkers, and *Escherichia coli* and *Agrobacterium* origins of replication.[17] In practice, these vectors are propagated in *E coli*;

introduction into *Agrobacterium* is accomplished by mating in the presence of a helper plasmid.[18] Because the process of transformation is mediated by a recombinant bacterium, a spectrum of transformation events is possible. The *Agrobacterium* can contain a single gene or cDNA of interest, a defined population of cDNAs, or a genomic library of DNA fragments.[19]

In conjunction with the capacity for sexual recombination, plant transformation offers a powerful approach for studying the dynamics of the synthesis and assembly of multimers. With respect to expression of antibodies in plants, an *Agrobacterium* population could contain a plasmid with an individual cDNA encoding an Ig chain or a repertoire of various plasmids with cDNAs for expression of different heavy or light chain constructs. Consequently, expression of antibodies representing novel combinations of heavy and light chains, or a repertoire of mutagenized F_v or F_c regions[20, 21] containing novel binding, effector, or catalytic capabilities, can be produced by a sexual cross. Identification of progeny containing the desired characteristics is easily accomplished by enzyme-linked immunosorbent assay (ELISA).

METHOD 1: INTRODUCTION OF PLASMIDS INTO *AGROBACTERIUM* USING THE TRIPARENTAL MATING PROCEDURE

The Variety of Available Vectors

Virtually all plant expression vectors are designed for *Agrobacterium*-mediated transformation. The discovery that *Agrobacterium* can transfer T-DNA segments into plant cells has resulted in the construction of several T-DNA-containing plasmid vectors that are useful for plant transformation.[22, 23] These constructs are termed binary vectors because they have a broad host range origin of replication and drug resistance markers for selection and maintenance in both *Agrobacterium* and *E coli* in addition to a T-DNA segment containing a selectable marker effective in plants and unique restriction sites for convenient introduction of foreign DNA. These vectors have eliminated the requirement for homologous recombination into the Ti plasmid of *Agrobacterium*. Their primary drawback is that cloning into these vectors is generally more difficult than for standard *E coli* vectors. The plant expression vectors generally have low copy numbers in *E coli*, no way of easily identifying the presence of inserted DNA, and often relatively few restriction sites. Because improved expression vectors are being reported on a regular basis,[24] many of these drawbacks may be eliminated in the near future.

Strategies of Vector Construction

A primary consideration that must be addressed prior to vector construction is whether or not secretion is the desired biosynthetic route. Most of the characterization of antibodies from plants performed to date has been on antibodies that have been targeted for secretion through the plasma membrane.[5] Techniques for the efficient production of intracellular antibodies have yet to be described.

General techniques for the isolation of RNA, PCR of immunoglobulin chains from RNA, and ligation of the PCR products into vector DNA will not be covered in detail in this chapter except to point out some general considerations of strategy. First of all, if the nucleotide sequences of the immunoglobulin chains are entirely known, then the PCR strategy will be straightforward. If these sequences are not known, then one will have to rely on degenerate populations of oligonucleotides at the 5' end of the immunoglobulin transcript. The methods described by Orlandi and colleagues[25] have been used for the cloning by PCR of nearly full length antibody transcripts. These PCR products do not contain the signal sequence but rely on the relatively limited degeneracy of codons in FR1. Because efficient antibody expression in plants is dependent on the presence of a leader sequence, vectors that contain a mouse immunoglobulin signal sequence upstream from a polylinker region were constructed. Ligation of the PCR product into the polylinker results in the introduction of a gly-thr-ser-ser sequence just prior to the first amino acid of the mature immunoglobulin. We have found that, in plants, virtually any signal sequence can be employed to initiate efficient assembly and secretion of a functional antibody. This includes mouse signal peptides as well as longer pre-pro-sequences derived from other eukaryotes.

An additional consideration is that because the plant expression vectors are generally large already and contain only one promoter and one polylinker region, it is probably wise to express only one immunoglobulin in each vector and to transform separate plants with individual heavy and light chain-expressing vectors. As described below, plants expressing functional antibodies are found in the progeny of a cross pollination between the individual heavy or light chain containing plants.

Introduction of Vectors Into *Agrobacterium*

The molecular mechanisms by which *Agrobacterium* carries out the transposition of DNA from bacterial plasmid to eukaryotic nucleus have yet to be fully elucidated.[11-13] As more research is done, our ability to manipulate *Agrobacterium* may result in improved strategies for plant transformation. In practice, techniques for the introduction of vector DNA into *Agrobacter-*

ium are simple and efficient, being no more than a conjugation of two bacterial strains in the presence of a helper bacterium. The techniques described are nearly universal for any bacterial conjugation; we will describe the techniques used with the pMON530 vector[17] and its derivatives, with *Agrobacterium* strain A208.

METHOD 1: PROTOCOLS

Overnight cultures of *E coli* carrying the plant expression vector, *E coli* carrying the pRK2013 helper plasmid[18] and the appropriate *Agrobacterium* strain (for example, strains A208, 3111, or LBA4404)[17] are prepared in LB broth. The two *E coli* strains can be grown at 37°C; the *Agrobacterium* must not be grown at temperatures higher than 30°C. *Agrobacterium* grows slowly, so the inoculation to get a stationary phase culture overnight must be somewhat higher than for *E coli*. Maintenance of *Agrobacterium* strains on agar plates for long periods of time should be discouraged. Generally, plates used to inoculate liquid cultures should not be more than two weeks old. As with most bacterial strains *Agrobacterium* can be stored in 50% glycerol at –70°C indefinitely.

Aliquots (0.1 ml) of the overnight cultures are mixed in a sterile Eppendorf tube, then spun at 5000 × g at room temperature to pellet the bacteria, which are then resuspended in 0.1 ml of LB containing no antibiotics. As a control, a mixture of bacteria containing only the *Agrobacterium* and the pRK2013 cells is prepared. Ten µl of the resuspended cells is spotted onto a fresh LB agar plate and left overnight at 28°C. A loopful of the 10 µL spot is then streaked onto the appropriate selection plates. In the case of pMON530, the selection is kanamycin, spectinomycin, and chloramphenicol to isolate *Agrobacteria* bearing the vector. Single colonies or bacterial streaks should be visible in two days.

One of the problems with using a bacterium as the means of introducing a foreign gene into a plant is the potential for recombination of the vector. Using the pMON530 vector, the majority of transforming DNA after the triparental mating is in some way rearranged. Although this does not prevent the transfer and selection of viable recombinants expressing immunoglobulins, the recombination events reduce the efficiency of transformation of the plant. Improved binary vectors for efficient plant transformation have been published[26] and should be considered. A review of the literature will reveal that many vectors have been developed, and they should each be considered on the basis of their relative merits. There are also a variety of *Agrobacterium* strains available that are efficient and disarmed.

In view of the potential for recombination, it is advisable not to pick single colonies from the *Agrobacterium* mating for use in subsequent transformations, but to use a population of *Agrobacterium* instead. *Agrobacterium* from the mating should be re-streaked onto fresh selection plates prior to infection of plant cells.

METHOD 2: TRANSFORMATION AND REGENERATION OF TOBACCO LEAF DISCS

There are two primary considerations that have to be addressed before initiating plant transformations. The first is the choice of plant to be transformed and the second is the space and equipment requirements for growth of the transformants. Not all plants can be transformed with *Agrobacterium* and, in addition, not all plants are easily regenerable. Tobacco has been used extensively as a model system due to the efficiency of infection of *Nicotiana* with *Agrobacterium* and the ease with which tobacco leaf segments can be regenerated into mature plants. Other similar plants, such as tomato, potato, and petunia, can also be easily transformed and regenerated. For any preliminary experiments that are aimed at the characterization of an antibody produced in a plant, tobacco is strongly recommended. All of the protocols presented here are intended for tobacco; other plants will have variations that have been reported in the literature.

Once regenerated, tobacco is also an easy plant to maintain and manipulate genetically. An adequate source of light is one of the most important factors in the regeneration and growth characteristics of the plant. In general, plant regeneration is performed in an incubator (Percival Manufacturing Co., Boone, IA) containing sixteen 20-watt fluorescent bulbs; after root formation the plantlets are transferred to 3-inch diameter pots containing potting soil and are grown on light racks consisting of a bank of bulbs (40-watt F40CW, Philips) attached to storage racks (Amco Corp., Chicago, IL). To avoid infection of the plants with insects, the plant room should have no unfiltered air intake from the outdoors as well as limited traffic through the room. All of the transformation procedures should be performed in a BioGard hood (Baker Company, Sanford, ME) or equivalent.

METHOD 2: PROTOCOLS

Reagents

MSO: 4.4 g of Murashige and Skoog basal salts with minimal organics (MSMO) from Sigma #M6899, 30 g of sucrose, and 800 ml distilled water to a 2.0 l flask. Stir to dissolve and adjust pH to 5.8 with 5.0 N KOH. Then add

7.0 g agar, adjust volume to 1.0 l, and autoclave for 25 minutes. MSO refers to the basal salts solution containing no plant hormones.

MS10: Same preparation as MSO, except add 1.0 ml of MS10 hormones before the pH determination step. The plant hormones can be autoclaved.

MS10 stock hormones: 10 mg of napthalene acetic acid (NAA, Sigma #N0640) and 100 mg of benzylaminopurine (BAP, Sigma #B9395) is added to 50 ml distilled H_2O. The hormones can be pre-dissolved in 5 ml of 95% ethanol before diluting to the appropriate concentration in water. The hormone solution stores well at room temperature with a shelf life of about a month. Final concentration should be 0.2 µg/ml for NAA and 2.0 µg/ml for BAP.

Antibiotics: For MS10 or MSO + kanamycin, carbenicillin or cefoxtaximum 200 mg kanamycin (Sigma #K-4000), 500 mg carbenicillin (Sigma #C-1389) or 500 mg cefotaximum (Calbiochem) are dissolved in 10 ml of distilled water. The antibiotics are then sterilized by passage through a 0.2 micron Gelman acrodisc (Gelman #4192) and dripped directly into autoclaved medium that has cooled to about 50°C.

Surface Sterilization

For the following transformations, leaves from healthy young tobacco plants are required. Tobacco plants are started by sprinkling some seeds onto moist potting soil and patting down gently. Shoots will appear in about one week; after two weeks the shoots should be transferred into individual 4-inch containers of potting soil. Plants are ready for transformation after another three weeks. The age of plant that provides the material for transformation is a matter of judgement. In general, the plants should be about six inches high and should have fully expanded leaves, although in our experience somewhat older plants are perfectly suitable for providing transformable leaf segments. Leaf sterilization is accomplished as follows:

A single leaf is placed in a dish of 20% household bleach (v/v), 0.1% SDS (w/v), where it is completely submerged and occasionally agitated for eight minutes. After bleaching, the leaves are rinsed in 95% ethanol for a minute and rinsed again in sterile double-distilled water where they are left until being cut into discs. During the sterilization, the leaf should maintain its rigidity and the sterilizing solutions should not infiltrate the leaf structure. This would be seen as a darkening of the underside of the leaf.

Leaf Dissection

Using leaves that do not show any blemishing from sterilization, leaf discs are punched with a sterile hole puncher with a 5-mm bore. Each disc is placed basal side up on an MS10 plate. As many as thirty discs can be arranged on a single plate. In planning any transformation, it is important to remember two controls. The first is the regeneration control. About twenty leaf discs are placed on a plate containing MS10 without any antibiotics. These discs are not exposed to *Agrobacterium.* Regeneration of these discs should begin within 2–3 weeks. If no regeneration is observed, then the effective hormone concentration is incorrect. The second control is for leaf cell death. About twenty leaf discs are placed on a MS10 plate containing kanamycin. Yellowing of the leaves should be observed within 2–3 weeks; otherwise, the kanamycin is not sufficiently effective. Although regeneration of leaf discs occurs rapidly in the absence of any selection, transformed cells that are regenerating from a population of dying cells will generally take up to two months to appear.

Infection With *Agrobacterium*

From a selection plate containing kanamycin, chloramphenicol, and spectinomycin, a colony is scraped off and vortexed in 2 ml of LB liquid. Alternatively, a 2 ml overnight culture of the *Agrobacterium* is used. Discs are successively immersed into culture and placed on MS10 plates in the same basal-side-up orientation. In practice, the suspension of Agrobacteria can be poured onto the plate containing the leaf discs. The discs are swirled to ensure that contact with the *Agrobacterium* is complete. The *Agrobacterium* is then removed with a sterile pipette. The whole operation should take only a couple of minutes. Sufficient *Agrobacterium* is left on the plate to ensure infection during two days of incubation. After infection each plate should be double wrapped with parafilm and placed for 24 hours in a Percival chamber set at 30°C and at a 16-hour light cycle.

Selection and Propagation

Each disc is washed in sterile water for 10 minutes and then gently agitated to remove most of the *Agrobacteria* and finally blotted dry on sterile Whatman filter paper. After blotting, the discs are placed basal side down in MS10 + cefotaximum (500 µg/ml, Calbiochem) plates, wrapped in Parafilm, and placed in a Percival chamber for six days. During this time, the *Agrobacterium* is killed and the leaf discs initiate regeneration in the absence of selection. The leaf discs are then transferred to MS10 plates containing 200 µg/ml kanamycin and 50 µg/ml of cefotaximum to select for transformed regenerants. The primary problem during the next month is contamination. In cases where the carbenicillin or cefotaximum does not effectively kill the *Agrobacterium*, that stage has to be repeated. Unfortunately, kanamycin and carbenicillin are not compatible antibiotics, so it is best to use them separately where possible.

The next stage of development is the most variable in terms of time for callus and shoot formation. Usually, callus appears after two weeks and shoots with internodes a week or two later. However, callus formation can take over a month. To facilitate faster growth of callus and quicker propagation of shoots, section the callus with a sterile No. 4 surgical scalpel handle with a Feather No. 21 blade. (Any razor will do, but this system with the long stainless steel handle and replaceable blade allows one to work easily and cleanly.) Smaller sections of callus will result in faster regeneration than do larger clumps.

After internodes develop on shoots, start to transfer the shoots to MSO and kanamycin (200 μg/ml + cefotaximum). Remove each shoot at the base as close as possible to its callus. However, try not to take any callus portion of the base. Callus tissue seems to discourage root formation in MSO selection. Roots should appear soon (in about two weeks) , and as they do, transfer them to soil. With shoots that do not form roots, cut the base of the stems once more, to remove any callus that sometimes forms, and replace them in fresh MSO selection. However, if roots still do not appear it may be an indication that the shoot is not a true transformant. Every transformation and regeneration has some of these rootless kanamycin-resistant non-transformants.

Potting soil is prepared by saturating with tap water in 3 1/2 × 4-inch pots. Remove the plantlet gently from the agar, taking care not to damage the roots, and delicately break the agar between the roots. This is done under a tap with a stream of lukewarm water running over the plant. Place the shoot in a half inch deep hole in the soil and cover with a clear plastic top (PlantCon, Flow Laboratories, McLean, VA) or loose plastic wrap. During the early stages of growth in soil, the shoots must gradually adapt to lower humidity. As a rule of thumb, the plants are kept covered until they are a sufficient size to push the cover off themselves.

As the shoots grow they will require some fertilization. A twice weekly application of 20-20-20 all purpose fertilizer at the recommended dilution is sufficient. Shoots should be about three inches high and have at least four leaves before one of the leaves is removed for screening.

Screening for Immunoglobulin Production

A whole leaf or a piece of leaf about 5 cm² is placed in a small mortar and pestle on ice. 200 μl of 1 M sodium phosphate, pH 7.5, and 50 μl of 100 mM PMSF is placed onto the leaf, which is homogenized with the pestle. This type of homogenization will provide enough material for ELISAs. The homogenized leaf is spun at 10,000 × g and the clear supernatant is applied directly to appropriately treated microtiter wells. The wells are generally coated with goat anti-mouse (GAM) kappa or gamma chain specific antibodies. The plant extract is left to incubate at 4°C overnight, then washed extensively with distilled water. The second antibody can be biotinylated GAM-kappa or gamma chain specific. Detection of biotin binding can be by glucose oxidase or HRPO conjugated to streptavidin and the appropriate color development chemistry.

For immunoglobulin production, most regenerated plants express detectable levels of heavy or light chain. Those plants expressing the highest levels should be tagged for sexual crossing. The remaining positive plants should be allowed to self fertilize, and the seeds should be stored in a refrigerator.

Sexual Cross for Progeny Production

Flowers will begin to appear (depending on the light conditions) after about one month in potting soil. Flowers on the two plants to be crossed should be about the same age. Tobacco plants will flower continuously, so flowers that are not used for crossing should be discarded prior to pollen production. Flowers to be used as females in the cross should be tagged. Just after the chosen female flower begins to turn pink but prior to petal opening (before any pollen production has occurred), the anthers are removed. This is done by making a small slit in the petal with a scalpel. The five immature anthers (which should be light green) are then removed. A flower from a pollen donor plant is then removed from its plant. This flower should be about two days older than the female flower, fully opened, and should contain yellow pollen on each anther. Pollination of the ovary on the female flower is accomplished by touching the stigma with an anther. The pollen donor flower is then discarded and the female flower is left to set seed. After about 2–3 weeks, a dried, brown seed pod is removed from the plant. The seed pod is cut in half and the seeds are collected on a filter paper. There should be about one thousand seeds. In a typical cross between kappa and gamma plants, about 10–20 progeny should be screened to identify antibody-producing plants. Because there are often multiple copies of transforming DNA in each parental plant, the segregation of heavy and light chains does not follow Mendelian ratios. In our experience, approximately 40% of the progeny produce antibody, and 10% of the progeny produce antibody at levels greater than 1% of total protein.

Because the effectiveness of sterilization of the leaf is going to determine how much work is subsequently required to isolate a transformed regenerant, this step should be given special attention. It is recommended that the sterilization protocol be optimized so that the correct amount of bleach and

SDS as well as the correct exposure be determined. Overexposure of the leaf will result in reduced regeneration efficiency and underexposure will result in fungal contamination. To optimize, perform the sterilization on different leaves under varying conditions; place leaf discs on MS10 plates with no selection. Regeneration should occur after about two weeks with no contamination.

Another important consideration is that kanamycin selection should be maintained until roots begin to appear. An absence of root formation indicates a false positive that is relatively resistant to the antibiotic but that is not a transformant. False positives routinely appear but they never form roots in the presence of kanamycin.

METHOD 3: PURIFICATION OF ANTIBODIES FROM PLANTS

Antibodies derived from tobacco are virtually identical to antibodies derived from hybridoma cells. The primary detectable difference is found in the composition of carbohydrate in the oligosaccharide. As far as purification is concerned, any affinity technique can be used to purify the antibody. Protein A-Sepharose has been used to purify antibody from clarified homogenates of tobacco leaf. There are two characteristics that distinguish purification from a plant source. First, although the antibody is secreted past the plasma membrane, it is still retained within the leaf. This means that homogenization is required to obtain a solution of antibody that is appropriate for affinity purification. Second, tobacco cells contain proteases that must either be inhibited or prevented from coming into contact with the antibody. The following conditions of homogenization are ideal for preparing milligram quantities of antibody from tobacco leaves.

METHOD 3: PROTOCOLS

A porcelain mortar and pestle sufficiently large to hold 200 ml (Coors, USA #60323 & #60322) is chilled on ice prior to addition of leaf sections. 50 g of tobacco leaf are cut into small sections (about 1 cm^2) with clean scissors. 100 ml of cold extraction buffer is then added to the leaf sections, which are ground by hand until they have the consistency of a wet paste.

Extraction Buffer: 50 mM Tris-HCl, 50 mM Na$_2$EDTA, pH 7.5, 2 mM PMSF (from a 100 mM stock in ethanol).

The homogenate is spun at 48,000 × g (Beckman JA-20 rotor or equivalent). The supernatant is used immediately for affinity isolation. The homogenate generally should not be stored longer than is absolutely necessary. If freezing or storage at 4°C can not be avoided, the homogenate must be re-centrifuged to remove phenolics that will come out of solution from tobacco extracts.

In cases such as Protein A-Sepharose purification of the IgG₁ subclass, the homogenization buffer must be compensated to contain high concentrations of salt. This can also result in precipitation of phenolics and some proteins that should be removed by centrifugation.

The yield of antibody from 1 g of leaf will obviously depend on the level of expression of that particular plant. A plant that expressed antibody at 1.3% of total extractable protein has been routinely used for purifications. This is equivalent to approximately 100–200 μg of antibody per gram of original leaf.

METHOD 4: TRANSIENT EXPRESSION OF ANTIBODIES IN TOBACCO PROTOPLASTS

Transient expression in tobacco protoplasts is a technique that can be used for the rapid evaluation of engineered antibodies. The protocols that have been employed allow one to perform an ELISA or any other binding assay within two days obtaining a purified plasmid preparation containing the antibody cDNAs of interest. The antibodies that are produced can be full length and glycosylated, or truncated constructs in which constant regions have been removed. The rapidity and ease with which plant protoplasts can produce antibodies makes this a potentially useful technique for evaluating populations of mutagenized heavy or light chain cDNAs. In addition, because in our experience PCR copies of immunoglobulin transcripts often contain errors, protoplast expression is an easy method for verifying the functionality of cloned immunoglobulin cDNAs.

The transfer of foreign genes into *Nicotiana tabacum* protoplasts can be accomplished by simple electro-manipulations of the cell membranes. The following protocols describe how to isolate the protoplasts, perform the electroporation, culture the transgenic protoplasts, and concentrate the gene product for analysis.

METHOD 4: PROTOCOLS

Reagents

Enzyme Solution: One liter of enzyme solution is prepared and aliquoted into thirty 50-ml tubes and frozen. Two tubes containg 60 ml are then defrosted for one digestion. pH to 5.4 with KOH and store at –20°C.

Reagent	Per Liter	Final
Mannitol	91.1 gm	500 mM
$CaCl_2 \cdot 2H_2O$	1.47 gm	10 mM
Mes	0.59 gm	3 mM
Cellulysin (Calbiochem 219466)	1.0 gm	0.1%
Macerase (Calbiochem 441201)	1.0 gm	0.1%
Driselase (Sigma 0-9515)	1.0 gm	0.1%

Mannitol Buffer: pH to 7.0 KOH, aliquot, and store at –20°C.

Reagent	Per Liter	Final
Mannitol	72.9 gm	0.4 M
$CaCl_2 \cdot 2H_2O$	2.90 gm	20 mM
Hepes	1.2 gm	5.0 mM
BSA	1.0 gm	0.1%

Electroporation Solution: Aliquot into 15 ml tubes and store at –20°C.

Reagent	Per Liter	Final
$CaCl_2 \cdot 2H_2O$	3.68 gm	25 mM
Mannitol	72.90 gm	0.4 M

Protoplast Culture Solution: pH to 5.7 with KOH, aliquot, and store at –20°C.

Reagent	Per Liter	Final
Sucrose	152.9 gm	0.4 m
Murashige and Skoog Basal Salts (Sigma M-6899)	4.5 gm	—
Hepes	1.2 gm	5.0 mM
2,4-Dichlorophenoxyacetic acid (Sigma D-8407)	100 µl of 10 mg/ml solution	—

Isolation of Protoplasts from *Nicotiana tabacum*

The procedures for isolating viable protoplasts for electroporation take into account the variability of plant tissue conditions, the fragility of protoplasts, and the toxicity of enzymes upon the protoplasts. The leaves for protoplast isolation were cut at the same time each day. Mid-afternoon cuttings yield protoplasts with densities that are appropriate to the following harvesting protocol. Mid-afternoon digestion with the enzymes for cell wall removal is also convenient because the protoplasts are harvested the next morning for electroporation.

Without cell walls, protoplasts would burst in an isotonic condition; therefore, isolation is carried out in an enzyme solution with added mannitol and calcium chloride to ensure optimal osmotic pressures and stabilization of the plasma membrane.

Choose four healthy young leaves from four different six-week-old tobacco plants. Rinse well in distilled water and blot dry. Cut out mid-veins and larger veins from leaves, slice into 1 × 10-mm pieces. Slicing the leaves into cross-sections gives enzymes access to the inner cells. Cuttings are transferred into 100 × 25 mM plastic petri dishes (no more than 1.5 g of cuttings per plate, to produce a large surface-to-depth ratio). Twenty milliliters of enzyme solution is added to each plate. The protoplasts are incubated with the enzyme solution in the dark for 15–18 hours. Gentle shaking of the petri dishes just before harvesting causes release of more protoplasts. The protoplast mixture is checked after 15 hours every thirty minutes to determine optimal time for protoplast release. Our optimal protoplast release time was found to be 17 hours. Most of the cells should be perfectly spherical and transparent; numerous chloroplasts should be visible near the plasma membrane.

Harvesting the Protoplasts

Gentle and thorough washings of the protoplast preparations in buffer must be performed to remove any residual enzyme solution that would be deleterious to cell viability. After washings, cell viability is determined after incubation with fluorescein diacetate. A viable protoplast will produce an active esterase that cleaves the acetate from the fluorescein, causing the cell to fluoresce.

All transfers of the fragile protoplasts are carried out gently by using wide base pipets (plastic pipettes are ideal because the tips can be easily cut off).

Filter protoplasts to remove debris by pouring incubation mixture of each petri dish onto a 75 mm screen. Pass the protoplasts through the screen into a 50 ml conical tube, centrifuge at 200 × g for four minutes, and then aspirate the supernatant. Resuspend pellets in 30 ml of Mannitol Buffer and centrifuge at 100 × g for two minutes. The protoplast pellet is gently resuspended in 5 ml of Mannitol Buffer and transferred to another 50-ml conical tube. Repeat the Mannitol Buffer wash. Resuspend the protoplast pellet in 5 ml of Electroporation Solution and count the cell in a hemocytometer. The concentration of protoplasts is adjusted with electroporation solution to yield approximately 10^6 cells/ml. Cell viability is determined after incubating 0.2 ml of protoplasts with one drop of fluorescein diacetate (10 mg/ml) and observing fluorescence under a Zeiss Axiophot Photomicroscope.

Electroporation

Exposure of protoplasts to a brief electric field creates micropores in their membranes. During this period, plasmid DNA can be directly introduced into the cell.

Field strength, pulse width, and number of pulses all affect cell viability and transfection frequency. Increasing these factors obviously augments the permeability of the cells, but also causes lysis of a larger number of protoplasts. Thus, the optimal combination of these factors must be determined for each system.

To determine optimal conditions, one must take into account the following three components of the electroporation mixture:

1. Electroporation solution—ionic and osmotic concentration
2. Cells—number and type
3. DNA—quantity and configuration

We use a 0.4 molar mannitol electroporation solution to maintain the osmotic balance. Additions of 5–25 mM of $CaCl_2$ are made to the mannitol solution to improve electro-transfection yield. In our transient assays, 15–20 µg of circular DNA per 1.0 ml of electroporation mixture is used. The resultant mixture produces a solution with a measured resistivity between 8 and 11 ohms. The pulse amplitude setting is then adjusted to produce a field strength between 3.5 and 3.8 kv/cm. Cells at this field strength are lysed at the approximate rate of 10%. The instruments used are the BTXT-800 square wave Transfector and the BTX Optimizor (Biotechnologies and Experimental Research, Inc., San Diego, CA). Instrument settings for the square wave Transfector are as follows: pulse amplitude—825–975 (dependent upon resistivity measurement); pulse width—80 ms; number of automatic pulses—2–4.

Approximately 20 µg of the plasmid DNA is gently mixed with 1.0 ml of the protoplasts suspended in electroporation solution. This mixture is transferred into a 1.83-mm gap flat pack chamber (BTX). The chamber is then positioned and resistivity measurements of the mixture are taken. The voltage is set according to the resistance of the solution to produce a field strength of approximately 3.8 kv/cm. The electroporated mixture is left undisturbed for three minutes and then gently centrifuged; the pellet is resuspended in culture solution and transferred to 6-well culture plates, where it is incubated in the dark at 50–75 rpm.

Concentration of Secreted Antibody

Each culture is collected into a 3-ml culture tube and frozen to facilitate cell lysing. After the frozen tubes are thawed and spun, the supernatant is saved. The protoplasts are further lysed by aspirating them several times with a 26-gauge needle into a tuberculin syringe. The aspirated protoplasts are spun in a 1.5-ml microcentrifuge tube. The supernatant from these protoplasts is added to the corresponding supernatant from the first spin. To remove the salts and sugars from the samples, 2.5 ml of each preparation is run through a PD-10 Sephadex G-25 M column (Pharmacia). Distilled water is used as the equilibration buffer and elution buffer.

Concentration can be performed by ultrafiltering the sample through an anisotropic membrane. Centricon-30 (Amicon) is pre-rinsed to remove glycerin and azide by centrifuging 2.0 ml of the sample at 5000 rpm for two hours. Alternatively, one can concentrate protein in the culture medium by adding three volumes of cold acetone. Alter incubating at –20°C for one hour, quantitative recovery of the antibody is accomplished by centrifugation.

Because the electroporation and ELISA are relatively rapid techniques for the expression and evaluation of the antibody, the limiting step, in terms of the number of constructs that can be screened in a week, is probably the preparation of DNA. The optimum concentration of DNA for the protocols presented above is 15–20 µg/ml. Although cesium gradient purified plasmid DNA is used, a typical plasmid miniprep should yield a sufficient quantity of plasmid. Most of our experiments have been performed using the pMON530 vector, which is a low copy plasmid. To increase the yield of DNA from minipreps, a vector containing the plant promoter, polylinker, and plant 3′ polyadenylation region has been recently constructed in pBluescript. This vector is not capable of selection in plants, nor can it be introduced into *Agrobacterium;* it is used solely for the transient expression of antibodies in the protoplast system. Because minipreps using this plasmid yield considerably more DNA than the pMON530 plasmid, the number of electroporations that can be performed each week is increased. Although we have not attempted to screen large numbers of antibody constructs, one person could probably perform and evaluate up to 100 electroporations per week.

CONCLUSIONS

The synthesis of antibodies in plants is a technology that is still in its infancy. There is still much to be improved upon as different applications are considered. For plant biologists, the possibility of using antibodies that accumulate within a defined intracellular environment opens the possibility of manipulating the metabolism and development of plants. Because methods for the intracellular expression of antibodies have yet to be described, realizing this goal will require a considerable effort. For antibody engineers, expression in tobacco protoplasts could be used as a rapid method for evaluating the results of mutagenesis on the binding or catalytic properties of an antibody or for ensuring that transcripts have been amplified with fidelity by PCR. Clearly, improvements can be made in the efficiency of protoplast expression to allow for more complex evaluation of the produced antibody in addition to simple binding assays. Finally, because there is an enduring interest in using antibodies for therapeutic purposes, agricultural production offers a means of obtaining large quantities of antibodies at a relatively low cost. In order for this goal to be realized, far more information about the immunogenicity of plant-derived antibodies in a mammalian recipient is needed. It is hoped that the techniques described in this chapter will encourage research into the possibilities of plant-derived antibodies.

REFERENCES

1. Bhozwani, S.S. and Razdan, M.K. 1983. *Plant Tissue Culture: Theory and Practice.* Amsterdam: Elsevier, 43–71.
2. Harkins, K.R., Jefferson, R.A., Kavanaugh, T.A., Bevan, W., and Galbraith, D.W. 1990. Expression of photosynthesis-related gene fusions is restricted by cell type in transgenic plants and in transfected protoplasts. *Proc. Natl. Acad. Sci. USA* 87:816.
3. Potrykus, I. and Shillito, R.D. 1988. Protoplasts: Isolation, Culture, Plant Regeneration. In: Weissbach, A. and Weissbach, H., eds. *Methods for Plant Molecular Biology.* San Diego, CA: Academic Press, 355–385.
4. Skoog, F. and Miller, C.O. 1957. Chemical regulation of growth and organ formation in plant tissues cultured *in vitro. Symp. Soc. Exp. Biol.* 11:118.
5. Tiatt, A.C., Cafferkey, R., and Bowdish, K. 1989. Production of antibodies in transgenic plants. *Nature* 342:76.
6. Saunders, J. 1989. Plant gene transfer using electrofusion and electroporation. In: Neumann, E., Sowers, A.E., and Jordan, C.A., eds. *Electroporation and Electrofusion in Cell Biology.* New York: Plenum Publishing Co., 343–354.
7. Saunders, J. 1986. Behavior and viability of tobaccor protoplasts in response to electrofusion parameters. *Plant Physiol.* 80:177.
8. Knight, D.E. 1981. Rendering cells permeable by exposure to electric fields. *Tech. Cell. Physiol.* 113:1.
9. Weaver, J.C. and Powell, K.T. 1989. Theory of Electroporation. In: Neumann, E., Sowers, A.E., and Jordan, C.A., eds. *Electroporation and Electrofusion in Cell Biology.* New York: Plenum Publishing Co., 111–126.
10. Boynton, J.E., Gilham, N., Harris, E., Hosler, J., Johnson, A., Jones, A., Randolp, B., Robertson, D., Klein, T., Shark, K., and Sanford, J. 1988. Chloroplast transformation in *Chlamydomonas* with high velocity microprojectiles. *Science* 240:1534.

11. Nester, E.W. and Kosuge, T. 1981. Plasmids specifying plant hyperplasias. *Ann. Rev. Microbiol.* 35:531.

12. Bevan, M.W. and Chilton, M.D. 1982. T-DNA of the *Agrobacterium* T1 and R1 plasmids. *Ann. Rev. Genet.* 16:357.

13. Zambryski, P., Goodman, H., Van Montagu, M., Schell, J. 1983. In: Shapiro, J. ed. *Mobile Genetic Elements.* New York: Academic Press. 505.

14. Melchers, L., Regensburg-Tunik, T., Bourret, R., Sedee, N., Schilperoort, R., and Hooykas, P. 1989. Membrane topology and functional analysis of the sensory protein Vir A of *Agrobacterium tumefaciens. EMBO J.* 8:1919.

15. Rogers, S.G., Horsch, R., and Fraley, R. 1988. Gene Transfer in Plants: Production of Transformed Plants Using Ti Plasmid Vectors. In: Weissbach, A. and Weissbach, H., eds. *Methods for Plant Molecular Biology.* San Diego, CA: Academic Press, 423–436.

16. Zambryski, P., Joos, H., Genetello, C., Leemans, J., Van Montagu, M., and Schell, J. 1983. Ti plasmid vector for the introduction of DNA into plant cells without alteration of their normal regeneration capacity. *EMBO J.* 2:2143.

17. Rogers, S.G., Klee, H.J., Horsch, R.B., and Fraley, R.T. 1987. Improved vectors for plant transformation: Expression cassette vectors and new selectable markers. *Methods Enzymol.* 153:253.

18. Ditta, M., Stanfield, S., Corbin, D., and Helinski, D. 1980. Broad host range DNA cloning system for gram-negative bacteria: Construction of a gene bank of *Rhizobium meliloti. Proc. Natl. Acad. Sci.* 77:7347.

19. Klee, H., Hayford, M., and Rogers, S. 1987. Gene rescue in plants: A model system for "Shotgun" cloning by retransformation. *Mol. Gen. Genet.* 210:282.

20. Clarke, N., Lien, D., and Schimmel, P. 1988. Evidence from cassette mutagenesis for a structure–function motif in a protein of unknown structure. *Science* 240:521.

21. Baldwin, E. and Schultz, P. 1989. Generation of a catalytic antibody by site-directed mutagenesis. *Science* 245:1104.

22. Hoekema, A., Hirsch, P.R., Hooykaas, P.J.J. and Schilperoort, R.A., 1983. A binary vector strategy based on separation of vir and T-region of the *Agrobacterium tumefaciens* Ti plasmid. *Nature* 303:179.

23. Holsters, M., deWarle, D., Depicker, A., Messens, E., Van Montague, M., and Schell, J. 1979. Transfection and transformation of *Agrobacterium tumefaciens. Mol. Gen. Genet.* 63:181.

24. An, G., Watson, B.D., Stachel, S., Gordon, M.P., and Nester, E.W. 1985. New cloning vehicles for transformation of higher plants. *EMBO J.* 4:277.

25. Orlandi, R., Gussow, D.H., Jones, P.T., and Winter, G. 1989. Cloning immunoglobulin variable domains for expression by the polymerase chain reaction. *Proc. Natl. Acad. Sci. USA* 86:3833.

26. McBride, K.E. and Summerfelt, K.R. 1990. Improved binary vectors for *Agrobacterium*-mediated plant transformation. *Plant Molecular Biology* 14:269.

Index

Page numbers in *italics* indicate illustrations.